New Horizons in Collecting

JOHN MEBANE
New Horizons
Cinderella Antiques

in Collecting

SOUTH BRUNSWICK

NEW YORK: A. S. BARNES AND CO., INC.

LONDON: THOMAS YOSELOFF LTD

For my mother — with love

Contents

	Preface	9
1.	The Magic Wand	15
2.	Early Ballyhoo: Advertising Cards	21
3.	Broadsides, Posters and Handbills	29
4.	Sugar and Spice . . .	38
5.	"Hello, Central" . . .	45
6.	That Great Game of Politics	53
7.	Statuary for the Masses: John Rogers	62
8.	American Art Pottery: Weller Ware	69
9.	Up and Coming: Roseville Pottery	76
10.	Dedham Pottery: Rediscovered	82
11.	Household Necessities: Boxes	86
12.	"Knock, Knock . . . Who's There?"	93
13.	Doorstops — Collect and Use Them	100
14.	Guideposts to the Past: Old Maps	104
15.	Signs of the Times	109
16.	Don't Kick the Can — Save It	120
17.	The Fireplace Makes a Comeback	129
18.	Saving Grandpa's Whiskers: The Mustache Cup	139
19.	Wars to End Wars: Military Mementoes	144
20.	Magazine Collecting Can Pay Off	148
21.	"Go West, Young Man" — and Save Those Western Books	157
22.	Carder's Steuben Glass	164
23.	Mary Gregory Glass: It's Easy to be Fooled	171
24.	Satin Glass May Be for You	176
25.	Heisey Glass — Now's the Time to Buy It	183
26.	They Smell Good Too: Perfume Bottles	189
27.	For the "Iniquitous" Weed: Tobacco Jars	195
28.	To Cleanse Oneself: The Washbowl and Pitcher	203
29.	The Fascinating World of Miniaturia	207

30. Strike up the Band: Collecting Sheet Music 213
31. Mechanical Musical Instruments: What Ingenious Men! 222
32. Victorian Furniture — No? Yes? Maybe? 232
33. Primitive Collectibles of Rural America 240
34. How to Buy and Sell Antiques by Mail 248
35. You Owe It to Yourself to Visit a Museum 256
Selected Bibliography 267
Index 276

Preface

One of the compensations for the anguish involved in putting together a book of this sort lies in the acquisition of new friends while in the pursuit of information.

Long ago we came to the conclusion that folk who collect antiques are nicer than anybody, unless it be the folk who sell them. Contrary to the practices of so many business and professional persons who hold the secrets of their success close to their vests, those who concern themselves, one way or another, with collectors' items not only are willing but often are anxious to share their knowledge with others.

With few exceptions, antique dealers will give freely of their time to impart knowledge to the new collector or even to the casual customer. Collectors almost invariably are willing to share their knowledge about antiques with fellow collectors.

In the course of writing this book, the author called upon many knowledgeable persons for information and assistance. The response to his requests was more than gratifying. In some cases these contacts have led to a continuing exchange of correspondence and to new friendships.

To all who have helped so generously, the author expresses his deep appreciation.

For special editorial assistance he is indebted to the following: Mr. Bly Corning, Flint, Michigan; Mr. Eric E. Ericson, Denver, Colorado; Mr. Carl Gustkey, President, Imperial Glass Corporation, Bellaire, Ohio; Mr. Robert G. Hayman, R.F.D. 1, Carey, Ohio; Mr. Clarence H. Hogue, Covina, California; Mr. A. G. Lyon, Sr., Hartford, Connecticut; Mr. Robert Miller, Oak Ridge, Tennessee; Mr. Wayne M. Nelson, Concord, North Carolina; Mr. and Mrs. Claris Pritchard, Denver, Colorado; Miss Pearl Ann Reeder, Editor, *Hobbies,* Chicago, Illinois; Mr. Albert Christian Revi, Dallas, Texas; Mr. Arthur H. Sanders, Deansboro, New York; and Mr. Norris F. Schneider, Zanesville, Ohio. In addition, most of these also made photographs available.

For making other illustrations available, the author expresses appreciation to Mr. George F. Adams and The Adams Company, Tulsa, Oklahoma; Miss

Ruth Shevin and Argosy Book Stores, New York City; Jerry G. Bails, Warren, Michigan; Mr. George Bennett, Jackson, Tennessee; the Brooklyn Museum, Brooklyn, New York; Can Manufacturers Institute, Washington, D.C., and Dudley-Anderson-Yutzy, New York City; Mr. and Mrs. Mike D. Cole, Smyrna, Georgia; Mrs. Ella Dearborn and The White Barn, Mason City, Illinois; the Dedham Historical Society, Dedham, Massachusetts; the Folger Shakespeare Library and Dr. Louis B. Wright, Director, Washington, D.C.; Miss Mary Earle Gould, Worcester, Massachusetts; Mr. Wayne G. LaPoe, Seattle, Washington; Leamington Book Shop and Mr. Sidney Hamer, Proprietor, Washington, D. C.; the Henry Ford Museum and Greenfield Village, Dearborn, Michigan; the Municipal Lightner Exposition and Mr. Cecil Zinkan, Director and General Manager, St. Augustine, Florida; Map Division, the Library of Congress, Washington, D.C.; the Metropolitan Museum of Art, New York City; the Middleborough Museum and Mr. Lawrence B. Romaine, Curator, Middleboro, Massachusetts; Old Sturbridge Village, Sturbridge, Massachusetts.

Also, Mr. Robert Rockwell and the Rockwell Gallery, Corning, New York; the Shelburne Museum, Shelburne, Vermont; the Smithsonian Institution and Mr. Paul V. Gardner, Curator of the Division of Ceramics and Glass, Washington, D.C.; the Society for the Preservation of New England Antiquities, Boston; Southern Bell Telephone & Telegraph Company, Atlanta; the Stephen Foster Memorial, White Springs, Florida, and Mr. Kendall L. Tolle, Lakeland, Florida; Henry Stevens, Son & Stile, Larchmont, New York; Mr. and Mrs. Frank K. Toney, Atlanta; Mr. David Vinar, Los Angeles; Mr. W. Porter Ware, Sewanee, Tennessee, and the Henry Francis du Pont Winterthur Museum, Winterthur, Delaware.

Acknowledgment and appreciation also are expressed to the following: *Antiques*, New York City, and Miss Alice Winchester, Editor, for permission to quote from an article appearing in that magazine; *The Antiques Journal*, Uniontown, Pennsylvania, and Mr. E. G. Warman, Publisher, and Don Maust, Editor, for permission to quote from articles in that magazine; Can Manufacturers Institute, Washington, D.C., for permission to quote from *The Metal Can, Its Past, Present and Future*; Card Collectors Company, New York City, for permission to quote from *The American Card Catalogue* by J. R. Burdick, Charles R. Bray, et al; Doubleday & Company, Inc., New York City, for permission to quote from *The New Antiques*: *Knowing and Buying Victorian Furniture* by George Grotz; Mr. Eric E. Ericson, Denver, for permission to quote from his *A Guide to Colored Steuben Glass,* 1903-1933; *Hobbies*, Chicago, and Miss Pearl Ann Reeder, Editor, for permission to quote from articles in that magazine; Mr. Norris F. Schneider, Zanesville, Ohio, for permission to quote from his *Zanesville Art Pottery*; the Society for the Preservation of New England Antiquities, Boston, for permission to quote from an article in *Old-Time New England*, and Mr. W. Porter Ware, Sewanee, Tennessee, and the Lightner Publishing Corporation, Chicago, for permission to quote from *Cigar Store Figures in American Folk Art* by Mr. Ware and A. W. Pendergast; and Thomas Nelson & Sons, New York, for permission to quote from Albert Christian Revi's *Nineteenth Century Glass*.

The author is especially indebted to Atlanta Newspapers, Inc., and Mr. William I. Ray, Jr., Executive Editor, for permission to draw upon certain material first published by the author in *The Atlanta Journal & Constitution*; to Mr. Tom Mahoney, of New York City, for numerous helpful suggestions and clippings; and to Miss Mary Earle Gould, of Worcester, Massachusetts, for suggesting the title for this book.

New Horizons in Collecting

1.
The Magic Wand

Among the hundreds of mementoes of the American past which have been literally thrust into the category of collectors' items in recent years are a score or more which have been touched by the wand of some fairy godmother. These are the "Cinderellas" of present-day collecting. They consist of items which have been suddenly "discovered" or rediscovered and whose values already have started soaring or will soon begin to ascend. These are articles for which astute collectors are keeping out a weather eye. Some collectors are buying with the expectation of being able to sell for a profit in the near future or over the long range, but there are more who are buying for the sake of possessing the articles themselves and thus becoming pioneers in new collecting paths.

Now one may say that folk who buy antiques and other collectibles with the expectation of profit are not collectors at all but are speculators. This is not necessarily so. Who can argue logically that buying things whose values may appreciate is either immoral or unwise — and particularly if the purchaser enjoys what he is doing, enjoys the article he purchases, and helps preserve for posterity intriguing, interesting, or useful relics of the American past?

The argument that one should not profit by one's hobby simply will not hold water. It is true that there is a difference between "acquiring" and "collecting." Anyone with money can acquire: Collecting assumes a purpose and the ability to discriminate. He who seeks to acquire without discriminating is not likely to profit, either financially or otherwise.

Today's "Cinderella Antiques" are nearly all items of some intrinsic merit. They may be inferior to antiques of long standing from the standpoints of rarity or artistic quality or sheer age; but they possess sufficient virtues of their own to justify their preservation. In some cases, a part of this merit lies in the simple fact that they *are* a part of this country's history and that they possess the magic quality of generating nostalgia. Many of the newer collectibles contributed to our forefathers' progress, or well-being, or happiness. Some contributed to the progress of the country itself.

Already some of these Cinderellas are finding their way into museums. Others now being bought by individuals undoubtedly will find their way into museums in the years to come; and almost invariably the museums will pay a higher price then than they would pay today. Of course, there are scores of articles being bought and sold today as "collectors' items of the future" which will never be entitled to that appelation. The ability to discriminate, therefore, becomes of paramount importance; for while the acquirer may clutter his premises with material few persons will ever want, the collector preserves articles of inherent worth — most of them things that he can appreciate and enjoy while watching their value grow.

This book, however, is not a treatise upon the morality of collecting or on the virtues of discrimination. It is a book whose purpose is to concern itself with certain items of the past which are just beginning to be collected in quantity by persons of discrimination (or perhaps even clairvoyancy) and which, in the opinion of experts and individuals of good judgment, ought to be preserved and whose values should be enhanced — and maybe considerably enhanced — by the passage of time. Interestingly enough, time seems to pass much faster today than it did last year and the year before.

Some of the Cinderella Antiques were discussed by this author in an earlier book, *Treasure at Home,* and these will not be belabored further in the present volume. Many of those which are discussed herein are still infants in the world of collecting, but they are lusty infants destined for maturity. Since the values of most, if indeed not all of them, are likely to increase, it must be borne in mind that the prices listed in this book are the values generally prevailing today. Even before the year is out, you may find some values have climbed. This will not mean that they still do not represent potentially good investments, because the chances are that ten years hence, many of next year's prices will seem extraordinarily low.

A few words about prices are needed. The values listed in this book represent price levels at which the articles discussed were selling in various parts of the country when the book itself was written. They reflect prices asked by dealers in shops and at antique shows and prices asked by dealers and individuals in advertisements in the various collector periodicals. One should be certain to remember that prices frequently vary from region to region, state to state, and sometimes at shops within the same locality.

Prices also vary according to the condition of the item itself, defects almost always detracting from value, sometimes sharply. A retail shop specializing in the higher-priced and rarer antiques may sometimes ask more for Cinderella collectibles than a shop specializing in the newer collectibles only, although this is not invariably so. A shop in a high-rent district may have slightly higher prices than one in a low-rent locality, but this is not always true either. The only way to find the best bargains is to shop around, and, after all, this is a large part of the fun of collecting. In the final analysis, prices often are set at a point which the lowest figure at which a dealer is willing to sell and the highest price which a potential buyer is willing to offer meet. When the two figures coincide, a sale is frequently consummated. Don't accept the values cited in this book, or any other book, as gospel. Use them as guides, which they are intended to be.

One of the best ways to keep abreast of values is to subscribe to one or more of the collector periodicals. Some of these may be found in your public library. And speaking of libraries, more of those operated by schools should find it advantageous to subscribe to one or more of the better collector publications, because teen-agers are entering the collecting field in ever-increasing numbers. This is a wholesome trend. Too many of us oldsters were permitted to grow up without ever seeing a bridle rosette or a daguerreotype or a sewing bird.

Since some of the Cinderellas you will encounter in this book are just beginning to attain collectible stature, very little has been written thus far about them. Many of them may be adapted to useful or intriguing decoration in the modern home. We have taken the liberty of suggesting certain of these usages. You will think of others yourself. This will provide an exercise in ingenuity — an exertion which needs to be encouraged.

Where are you likely to encounter these things of which we write? In antique shops, of course; in many stores specializing in used merchandise; and in basements and attics, lofts and garages, barns and other outbuildings, and a dozen other assorted hiding places. You will find that this is true despite all those "authoritative" pronouncements to the effect that one no longer need expect to find hidden treasures stashed away, that the whereabouts of all antiques of value are known, and that prices already have been fixed on these to the penny. Folk who make such statements, of course, are usually referring to rare antiques rather than to the newer collectibles, some of which one day will be rare antiques too.

The truth is that more Cinderella collectibles are emerging right now from hiding places than ever before in history, although at least 50 per cent of them would not have been considered treasures at all 25 years ago. More of them will emerge tomorrow. If you are interested only in such things as early English porcelains made by Thomas Toft and Ralph Simpson and Richard Champion, or the French china of Bernard Palissy and the faience made at Nevers and Rouen, or marquetry work by André-Charles Boulle, or very early Venetian, Dutch and Flemish glass — this book is not for you. It is for today's average collector who is willing to content himself with lesser but still fascinating treasures and who finds a real measure of happiness and pleasure in becoming a pioneer. It is designed for those who will enjoy discovering that this country of a century ago was a rugged, charming, and fascinating place and that its citizens then were people of remarkable ingenuity and inventiveness — a fact which seems somehow to have eluded even the parents of those who are now approaching middle age.

Shortly after the turn of the present century, a great many Americans assumed a disdain for many things associated with the middle and late Victorian era. In the 1920's we were caught up in a madcap postwar whirl of exciting and not infrequently reckless ways of spending our leisure. In the 30's, most of our energies were directed toward economic survival, and in the 40's toward any survival at all. Only since the 50's have we been able to settle down again, this time to something resembling an ebullient normalcy. It has been a normalcy, however, punctuated by increasing periods of spare time which need to be occupied to avert sheer boredom. And what could better occupy it than activity devoted to rediscovering the past one hundred years and prying into the customs and habits, the creations, the day-to-day routine, and even into the morals of our grandfathers and great-grandfathers?

The nineteenth century and the dawning years of the twentieth move farther from us day by day. They are becoming shrouded in the mist that cloaks all the centuries of the past, imbuing them with an aura of mystery which cries out to be penetrated. Who but the slothful and the unimaginative can resist that temptation? There are two great challenges today: to preserve the American future and to preserve the American past. The things discussed in this book were manufactured or otherwise fabricated during the 1800's and as far into the present century as about 1920 or 1930. Most of them are beautiful, or attractive, or useful, or mystifying, or intriguing, or somehow fabulous. While some of them already have been touched by that magic wand of which we spoke earlier, others are erstwhile ugly ducklings just beginning to blossom into swans. Of course, many of them weren't ugly ducklings to begin with: They were swans, but we declined earlier to see them as such.

In this book we have by no means exhausted the list of modern Cinderellas, but we have included many which become more attractive daily. We hope you will be spurred to discovery yourselves. All you need is curiosity and determination. Look around you when you enter a country store or a second-hand shop or visit an old home. If you see something with which you are not familiar, ask questions. The answers you get my be both enlightening and rewarding. Curiosity may have killed some cats, but it has made fat ones of others. How do you expect to learn if you're not inquisitive?

If you attend auction sales — and you should, at least occasionally, if for no other reason than to listen and learn — you'll find that some of the items discussed in this book will come up for sale from time to time. Excellent buys are frequently made at auction sales, but they are almost always made by persons who know beforehand the approximate values of the articles on which they bid, who have examined them to ascertain their condition, and who are able to restrain their enthusiasm when the bidding becomes excessively spirited. All one needs to do to get "stuck" is to permit his exuberance to reach such a pitch that he continues bidding well after the normal value of the article has been passed. Most dealers exercise such restraint, but there is magic in the chant of the auctioneer and the proximity of other enthusiasts.

The best way to buy at auction is to visit the establishment before the sale begins, decide upon which articles you would like to bid by examining them, and to make either a written or a mental note of the limit you should bid. Then don't exceed that limit. It's better to be disappointed than foolish.

A new version of the old-time country auction is becoming popular today. Instead of selling the contents of homes and estates on the premises, the new "country" auctioneers (who sometimes hail from the city and sometimes are country folk who have learned the ways of city traders) bring in van loads of antiques and collectibles from other areas. City folk, anticipating rare bargains, flock out to bid. Often they do get bargains. Sometimes they pay more than the goods are worth at retail. And sometimes they buy sheer junk. There is nothing wrong with such auctions. They afford fun and can be profitable for buyer and seller alike. But here again, the rule is not to let your enthusiasm get the better of your judgment.

So-called antiques "flea markets" also have been springing up around the country. Sometimes these are sponsored by civic or fraternal organizations which receive compensation for their sponsorship. Some flea markets consist of exhibits solely by dealers; others are composed of both dealers and individuals who want to sell a part of their collections. These can be profitable to attend if one knows values.

To reiterate, Cinderella collectibles will turn up in all sorts of unexpected places. When you visit friends in the country, poke around in their barns if they have no objection. You may find early tools and implements. When you stop in second-hand establishments, give the goods more than a cursory glance. You may happen upon such things as quaint iron doorstops or tobacco jars or foot warmers or old curtain tie-backs. Attend the rummage sales in your community: Thousands of dollars worth of collectors' items are sold at such sales every year. Remember, too, the church bazaars, the Good Will Industries which sell articles reconditioned by the handicapped, and even the junkyards. And don't neglect the antique shops, because they often turn up bargains.

Finally, take a trip once in a while into your own garret or basement. That stuff you stored away a decade or two ago may have suddenly acquired collectible status. These new horizons may be viewed from the very spot in which you hung your childhood.

2.
Early Ballyhoo:
Advertising Cards

Nineteenth-century advertising or trade cards constitute an integral part of American business history. Discovered earlier by collectors and then neglected for a while, they are now being "rediscovered" and are well on the road to becoming Cinderellas. Right now, thousands of them may be picked up for what may seem a pittance tomorrow.

These cards were published and distributed by the millions during the last half — and particularly the last quarter — of the nineteenth century by almost every conceivable type of manufacturer, as well as by wholesalers, jobbers, retailers and service establishments. In toto, they comprise an intriguing contribution to the history of mass advertising in the United States. By only a slight stretch of the imagination, some of the very best of them may even be considered a contribution to American art.

What appears to be a renewed determination to preserve these cards now stems in part from the American patriotic fervor which has been generated by the continuing cold war, the little hot wars, the abolition of men's rights in many areas of the world and the threat to freedom in others.

Numerous trade cards were given away free with the purchase of commodities. Many of the best were lithographed, and many of these are in color. Some of them were issued from the plants of distinguished lithographers of their day — Currier & Ives, Louis Prang, Burford & Sons. They were published for and distributed by soap and cigarette makers, thread companies, patent medicine concoctors, manufacturers of agricultural implements and horse goods, food processors, clothing makers, sewing machine works, and steam laundries. They were handed out to clients and customers by opticians, retail grocers, shoe emporia, dry goods merchants, organ sellers, and toy stores.

Some of the most desirable trade cards depict clipper ships, early aviation, shrines and other historic spots, famous Americans, early baseball stars and other sports figures. Others literally run the gamut from shoes and ships and sealing wax to cabbages and kings. In addition to the lithographed cards, there are cards with photographic depictions, particularly of individuals, including the pioneer motion picture stars. Winsome children seemed to have had a particular appeal, and many thousands of cards appeared bearing likenesses of babies smiling, laughing, pouting, and looking infinitely wise.

Many companies issued trade cards in series, and today the chief desire of hundreds of collectors is to find all cards issued in a particular series. Thousands of comic cards were issued as were many mechanical ones. The latter could be folded, pushed, or otherwise manipulated to effect a change in appearance.

In his booklet, 19th Century Advertising Cards: An Introductory Study, Herbert D. Loomis, of 127 Milford Drive East, Syracuse 6, New York, says that the most famous advertising card ever issued in this country was one given out by Paul Revere Silversmith. You know, of course, that Paul not only set a record riding a horse on a dark night in April, 1775, but that he also turned out some distinguished productions in gold and silver and did a bit of copper-plate engraving on the side. The Loomis study is available direct from the author.

Trade cards were not uniformly inexpensive productions. Some cost a pretty penny to produce, and among these were series issued by Wilson Spice Company, McLaughlin's Coffee, and the Singer Sewing Machine works.

Quite commonplace still and sometimes dreary or maudlin are cards with illustrations featuring flowers, children, and domestic animals. Most of these are worth comparatively little right now. But there are some rarities which fetch high prices. Some of the fine clipper ship cards are worth $20 to $100 and more. Other types which often will bring premium prices include those showing early modes of transportation, including balloons, automobiles, bicycles, and trains; early sports figures in color; and numerous cards lithographed by Currier & Ives, Burford, and Louis Prang.

Until quite recently dealers who handled advertising cards hadn't got together on anything really resembling standardized prices. One dealer would offer for a dime a card for which another asked $2. One who wants to collect these cards intelligently and to invest his money to the best advantage should familiarize himself with the whole field. In this connection, a fine reference work is The American Card Catalogue (Card Collectors Company, Box 293, Department H, Franklin Square, New York, New York,

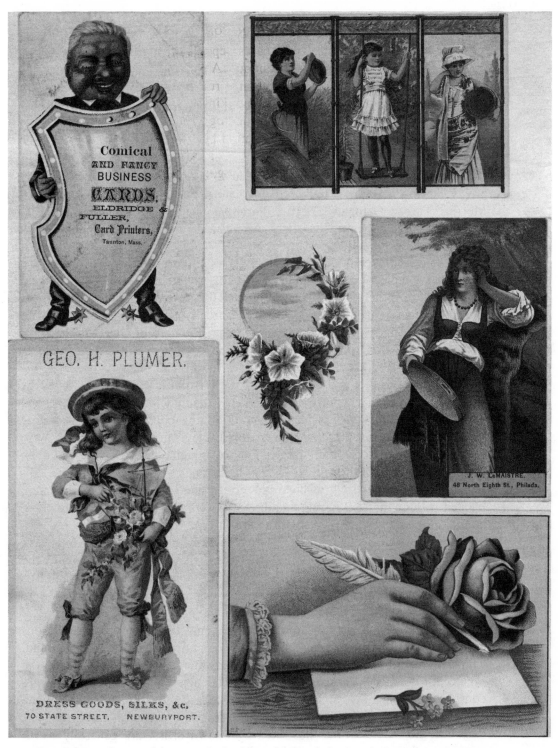

These advertising cards are typical of hundreds of thousands issued in the nine-teenth century. (From the author's collection.)

$4), by J. R. Burdick, Charles R. Bray and others. This lists the values of various types of cards. Another helpful publication in this broad field is *Baseball Gum Card Check List,* available from the same company.

Values of advertising cards generally will range from a few cents to several dollars each, the exceptions being the rarities such as the clipper ships cards mentioned and certain others.

Some of the companies which invested heavily in producing advertising cards, either singly or in series, included J. & P. Coats Thread Company, Singer Sewing Machines, Baker's Chocolate, Scott's Emulsion, Acme Soap, Merrick Thread Company, Bertier Parabola Spectacles, the Great Atlantic & Pacific Tea Company, Household Sewing Machine Company, and a number of tobacco companies.

The American Card Catalogue recognizes three primary divisions in the broad card collecting field. These are the advertising cards which were given away or otherwise utilized altogether for advertising purposes without a charge being made for them; insert cards which were packaged with merchandise and available only through the purchase of that merchandise; and souvenir cards which were intended to be sold. The last category is really outside the scope of this chapter.

Strictly speaking, trade cards comprise the smaller cards given away by retailers (though frequently furnished by manufacturers, processors and wholesalers). But some collectors also seek the considerably larger store cards which were used by merchants for display purposes and which were exhibited on counters or on large items of merchandise or were hung on the store or shop walls or were utilized as banners.

Most series cards, such as cigarette, coffee and chewing gum cards, were packed with or inserted in merchandise and were similar in purpose to those coupons which now are packed with certain types of goods and are redeemable for premiums. The former were generally not redeemable but were designed to be collected in series; therefore, they served to persuade the public to continue buying specific brands of merchandise. Although the majority of such cards were made of heavy paper or cardboard, some were of cloth or metal, as *The American Card Catalogue* points out.

As is the case with virtually all collectible items, the values of these various cards depend upon such things as quality, condition, scarcity, and demand. The majority of those easily available today date from the middle of the nineteenth century. Those issued during the first half of that century are considerably scarcer — and higher. It is exceedingly difficult for anyone except an expert to tell the age of the cards because, except in rare instances, they bear no dates. Cards illustrated by known artists are generally worth more than those by unknown artists. Poor printing detracts from the value.

Three charming advertising cards issued by the Woolson Spice Company for its Lion brand coffee (top row and bottom right), and one advertising Hire's Root Beer. (From the author's collection.)

Most colored cards date from the final quarter of the nineteenth century. Some print shops had supplies of stock cards which were similar and which could be imprinted with the name and address of any firm wishing to use them. In general, these are less desirable than cards made exclusively for one firm. However, as *The American Card Catalogue* points out, most Currier & Ives cards were stock cards, but these were limited in quantity and have become quite scarce. Consequently, their value is a good bit more than that for run-of-the-mill stock cards.

Unfortunately for buyers today, most of the early collectors pasted their cards in albums and, since a great many individuals collected haphazardly, an old album is likely to contain a score or two of different kinds of cards without regard to type or series. Some of these are difficult to remove without damage. The result is that one may often pick up an album containing a hundred or so trade cards for less than he would have to pay for half a dozen desirable cards in fine condition.

Just to give an idea of what some collectors' cards have sold for recently, here are prices taken from advertisements by dealers and individuals:

A lot of 22 different cigarette cards, $2; cigarette playing cards, 40 cents each; J. & P. Coats Thread cards depicting children and cats, 12 for 50 cents; Clarke's O.N.T. Thread cards with calendars, four for 50 cents; Arm and Hammer Soda bird cards, $1; Arbuckle Coffee cards, $4; "Honest Long Cut" Tobacco, 86 cards for $15; miscellaneous soap, thread and patent medicine cards, 15 for $1; King Bitters, 20 cents; Gordon & Dilworth Pickles, 10 cents; Currier & Ives cigar card, $3; Duke's Tobacco actor photo card, small, 5 cents; Fairbanks Fairy Tale card, 50 cents; Alden Vinegar calendar card, 50 cents; Currier & Ives colored comic card, $2.50.

While those prices may be fairly typical of those asked here and there around the country the individual who wants to buy or sell at fair prices should consult *The American Card Catalogue*. This book, incidentally, is nicely illustrated and contains a section of advertisers who buy and sell.

All kinds of other early advertising items and novelties also are being collected today and are of value. These include large prints, early calendars, games, puzzles and tricks, booklets, statuettes, tumblers, trays, and a host of other items which bear advertising of some type on them, sometimes merely the name of a manufacturer or other business.

The following advertised prices will give a rough idea of the diverse values of some of these:

Stoneware rolling pin made for Rhodes Burford House Furnishing Company, $12.50; Louis Brand Coffee tin tray with Buster Brown portrait, $8.50; California Cough Balm brown advertising jug, $2.75; Heinz tumbler with a pickle shape on its base, $1; tin container advertising Phosfo Nerve and Brain Food, $2; 13-inch-tall brass-and-bronze Indian advertising Round Oak Stoves, $8; verse booklet entitled "In the Swim," issued by Dr. Pierce's Golden Medical Discovery, 30 cents; and the Cardui Song Book, 50 cents.

Also, printed circular entitled "How to Make Lager Porter and Heavy Ale," advertising Crown Caps, 75 cents; "Walter Baker's Choice Receipts," a booklet by "Miss Parola" (1897), 48 pages, 75 cents; framed print on milk glass, 25x30 inches, in color and dated 1909, advertising Harper Whiskey, $75; steel engraving of Civil War soldiers with Lincoln, 25x31 inches, issued by the Travelers Insurance Company (1884), $6.50; and a tin zeppelin and hangar with small electric motor, $45.

You may find advertising cards and other advertising novelties in a variety of places, particularly in old stores — and especially old stores in rural areas. Keep your eyes open in such establishments for old counter display cards in particular. When you come across old albums, check their contents. They may contain trade cards of value. Scores of albums are sold at both city and country auctions, and usually for very small sums. But remember that it is inadvisable to buy anything at an auction without first examining it carefully.

Before leaving the subject, it will be of interest to note that the original J. R. Burdick collection of cigarette insert cards, post cards, and other pictorial advertising matter is now housed in a special collection in the Metropolitan Museum of Art and is the largest section of ephemeral printing in the Metropolitan's Print Department. The Burdick Collection has been supplemented by gifts from Mrs. Bella C. Landauer of European trade cards, billheads, labels and so on. The fine collection is described in a *Directory of the J. R. Burdick Collection . . . in the Metropolitan Museum of Art,* which also contains a tribute to the late Mr. Burdick by A. Hyatt Mayor, curator of the museum's Print Department.

Mrs. Landauer also presented a collection of 40 large scrapbooks of trade cards, primarily late nineteenth century, to the New York Historical Society, and in 1927 she published a book entitled *Early American Trade Cards* (New York), based on her outstanding collection. It is profusely illustrated.

Informative articles on trade cards include Harrold E. Gillingham's "Old Business Cards of Philadelphia," published in the July, 1929, issue of the *Pennsylvania Magazine of History and Biography,* and George Francis Dow's "Trade Cards," published in two instalments in the April and July, 1936, issues of *Old-Time New England,* the Bulletin of The Society for the Preservation of New England Antiquities.

Other institutions in the United States with fine collections of trade cards include the Essex Institute at Salem, Massachusetts, and the American Antiquarian Society in Worcester, Massachusetts.

Forerunners of the American nineteenth century-type trade cards were used in England as early as the seventeenth century. Those still in existence from both the seventeenth and eighteenth centuries indicate beautiful workmanship on the engraved copper plates from which they were printed. Noted English artists, among them Hogarth, Cole, Fourdrines and Sherwin, contributed to the art of the trade card in their day.

The early English cards showed far more painstaking work than their late nineteenth century American counterparts. Frequently the English cards depicted the signs which hung over the shop doors, and they often bore elaborately-embellished borders. There is a collection of several thousand early English trade cards in the British Museum.

Not the least important contribution which advertising cards make to history is their preservation of the appearance of early shop exteriors and scenes.

3.
Broadsides, Posters and Handbills

So-called "paper Americana" of various types has been growing in popularity among both collectors and speculators for several years. The Civil War Centennial sparked a renewed interest in Confederate currency. Trade catalogues have soared in value. So have interesting account books in manuscript form. Unusual greeting and special occasion cards, such as Valentines, and postcards have been edging upward in price. More recently, there have been offered for sale such a diversity of paper items as old stock certificates and railroad bonds, lottery tickets, ration cards of World War II days, vintage deeds and receipts, slave sale records, albums of clippings, and numerous other miscellaneous paper items.

Right now, there is a surging interest in eighteenth and nineteenth century broadsides and posters. Reduced to the simplest definition, a broadside is a large sheet of paper printed on one side only. Broadsides have been used for a wide variety of purposes. They have been issued to announce important meetings or events, to disseminate urgent news, for political announcements (or denouncements), for advertising purposes, to herald theatrical events, and even to announce slave sales.

Broadsides — sometimes called broadsheets — were displayed in public gathering places, attached to walls of buildings or posted wherever crowds were likely to assemble. Turned out by individual printers or printing establishments, and nearly always hurriedly, many were posted without the corrections of typographical errors made by the printers. Nearly all broadsides issued before 1900 are of some value, and those with historical interest are of special value, enhanced by the fact that, unlike newspapers, most of them were issued in small quantities. Rare broadsides may be worth $75 or

$100 or more. More commonplace types are usually worth several dollars each in good condition.

In the days before the advent of high-speed presses and the swift transmission of news, broadsides were utilized to announce the deaths of nationally-known figures. Recently, a rare broadside captioned JACKSON IS DEAD and containing 56 printed lines relating to the death of "Stonewall" Jackson was offered for sale at $100. It measured only 5x10 inches in dimensions.

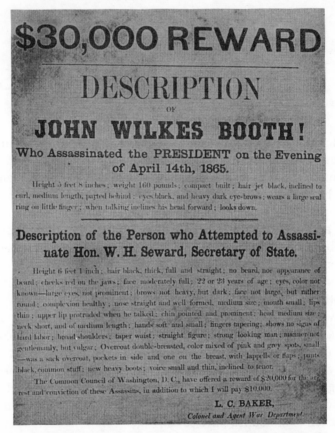

Facsimile reproduction of a reward poster issued after President Lincoln's assassination.

In today's collectors' market, the term broadside is sometimes used interchangeably with "poster" or "handbill." The last-named, whether printed on one or both sides, was designed, as its name indicates, for distribution by hand and was printed in larger quantities than were broadsides. Handbills and posters of historic or other special interest are definitely collectible. Early lithographed circus posters, for example, are eagerly sought by a growing circle of collectors of all types of circus mementoes.

As is the case with most collectors' articles, the condition of broadsides and posters is of major importance in relation to value. Tears, defective margins, and defacements detract sharply from worth. All other things being equal, a broadside or poster which has not been folded is worth more than one showing fold creases.

A. G. Lyon, Sr., operator of the Lyon Hobby Mart in Hartford, Connecticut, a specialist in paper Americana, says that American advertising posters dating between the 1830's and 1890's are particularly sought right now. He adds they could be characterized as "nineteenth century salesmanship at its best." The problem, he points out, is that many posters measuring more than 12x15 inches in dimensions are frequently found torn because they are bulky to handle. Many persons who did not realize their value have thrown scores of torn posters away. These, of course, are impossible to replace, and their loss is leading to a mounting pressure of demand against the available supply.

Between the 1830's and 1890's, Mr. Lyon says, a good many posters were issued by patriotic committees in various communities around the nation to commemorate Independence Day or the anniversaries of the births of such leaders as George Washington and Abraham Lincoln. He also recalls two fabulous railroad posters. One of these, "American Railway Scene, at Hornellsville, Erie Railway," was done in striking colors and featured wide smoke stack engines with train cars linking the country. The other was the Union Pacific Railroad's "Great Event" poster, which, on May 10, 1869, heralded through passenger service from Omaha to San Francisco.

Other highly desirable posters relate to medicine shows and the Civil War.

So much interest has been shown of late in collecting broadsides that some dealers in rare and out-of-print books have begun listing them in their catalogues. They also will be found offered for sale in the lists and catalogues of some dealers in autographs as well as in those of a relatively recent group of dealers in general paper Americana. Occasionally one will still find old posters attached to the sides of barns and other buildings in rural areas, but these have been rapidly disappearing. They are frequently difficult to remove without damage and, needless to say, permission of the property owner should be obtained before one tries to make off with them. Sometimes broadsides, posters, and handbills, together with other miscellaneous bits of paper, will be found stored away in old trunks and boxes where some of them have been untouched for decades. They will turn up from time to time at estate sales, often included in a lot with other articles because the auctioneer may not be

THE TICONDEROGA

Glorious

Steamboat Sails

on Historic
LAKE CHAMPLAIN

ABOARD THE LAST SIDEWHEELER IN NEW ENGLAND

The Ticonderoga is the Last Passenger Packet but one, with a
Walking Beam, Still Running in the United States

☞ *You Will Enjoy* ☜

THE MATCHLESS BEAUTY
OF THE

GREEN AND ADIRONDACK MTS.

AND THE

MARINE MUSEUM ABOARD THE STEAMER

Scores of interesting old prints and photographs of life on this Historic Waterway
The engine and ship models
The old-time barbershop exhibit
The massive steam engine run the paddlewheels, through special glass partitions

Sun-Bathed Decks, Commodious Lounges, Breeze-Swept Promenades, Souvenirs, Soft Drinks and
Tasty Snacks in Great Variety — Announcements of Points of Interest, Interludes
of Music — All To Give You

A Day That Will Live Long in Your Memory

YOUR TRIP will cover a segment of the famous NORTHWEST PASSAGE — the highway of
nations in the Revolutionary War, and of men — ETHAN ALLEN and BENEDICT ARNOLD —
Lake Champlain is the CRADLE OF AMERICAN LIBERTY — Its exciting history revived
aboard the Ticonderoga.

For all information, write or call the

SHELBURNE STEAMBOAT COMPANY

Dock at Foot of College Street

Tel. 4-7255
or 4-6211

192 College St. **BURLINGTON, VERMONT**

SERVING . . . TICONDEROGA, CROWN POINT, PORT HENRY, WESTPORT, PLATTSBURG,
ST. ALBANS, BURLINGTON, BASIN HARBOR

ON LAKE CHAMPLAIN

Sponsored by the Shelburne Museum, Shelburne, Vermont

The Shelburne Museum at Shelburne, Vermont on Route 7 includes a collection of old buildings
and structures selected for their beauty and historical interest. These buildings have been moved
and restored as nearly as possible to their original condition. Some are furnished and decorated
in keeping with their period and history. Others house antiques collected during the past forty
years by Mr. and Mrs. J. Watson Webb. Almost all of these antiques are American and include folk
art, carriages, sleighs, pewter, furniture, dolls, doll houses, toys, needlework, tools of the early
Craftsmen, farm implements, early cooking utensils for the open hearth kitchen fireplace and other
household utensils.

It is hoped when the Museum is completed that in addition to giving pleasure to the public, it
will become an educational and cultural center in Vermont and inspire a greater interest in our
American heritage.

aware of their value. It may pay you, therefore, to examine carefully before-hand the contents of trunks, suitcases, and boxes whose contents are offered as a single lot at such sales.

As opposed to broadsides, posters were used primarily for advertising purposes and therefore frequently illustrated, usually by the lithographic process which was invented in the closing years of the eighteenth century. The early "24-sheet" poster derived its name from the fact that 24 individual sheets were needed to complete it because of the limitation of the size of the lithographic stones used. Subsequently lithography utilized zinc plates instead of stones so that much larger sheets could be printed and fewer of them were needed to complete the large poster. Many nineteenth- and twentieth-century posters represent the work of distinguished and talented artists.

American poster advertising during the last quarter of the nineteenth century was largely devoted to the circus and theatrical events. Since about the end of the first quarter of the present century, posters have been used to advertise thousands of articles of merchandise and scores of services. Some of today's most artistic posters will undoubtedly be collectors' items in the years to come.

As for broadsides, many of those issued during the period of the American Revolution are of prime historic interest. One of these, printed in 1776 in the Colony of Massachusetts Bay, announced that those who had attached their signatures to it "profess, testify & declare . . . that we verily believe that the war, resistence [sic] & opposition in which the American Colonies are now engaged against the fleets & armies of Great Britain, is . . . just & necessary." This poster is valued by its owner at $135. Another small folio size poster issued in the same Colony in 1777 called upon the inhabitants to "frustrate the barbarous design" of Great Britain. This one was advertised for sale at $50.

A broadside denouncing Robert Toombs, the Georgian who served as Confederate Secretary of State, printed in New York in 1863 and signed "A Democratic Workingman," was tendered a few months ago at $50. A $25 price tag was recently attached to a 7½ x 15-inch broadside issued in 1845 in Boonsboro, Maryland, and announcing appointments made by the Baltimore Conference of the Methodist Episcopal Church. One announcing a Fourth of July celebration at New Albany, Kansas, and dated 1890 is offered at $20. A broadside containing news of the New York draft riots of July, 1863, is listed at $37.50, and another chronicling a mill disaster in Lawrence, Massachusetts, on January 10, 1860, is tendered at $12.50.

A rare book dealer's catalogue not long ago listed a group of scarce broadsides relating to Dorr's Rebellion at $15 each. This was a domestic rebellion in Rhode Island in 1842 led by Thomas Wilson Dorr, who ultimately was

is handbill in old-style type was issued when the Shelburne Museum in Shelrne, Vermont, was opened. It illustrates handbills of the nineteenth century. hoto by Einars J. Mengis, staff photographer, Shelburne Museum, Inc.)

Pictorial poster or store placard of 1898.

Reproduction of early poster advertising a Western show featuring Buffalo Bill.

A BRIEF, BUT WONDERFUL HISTORY.

Facts Verified by a Cloud of Witnesses!

As Florida is the natural home of a species of Pine which occupies much of her soil, the source of a perpetual aroma, which is pleasant to the senses, and invigorating to the systems of those who breathe it; as thousands of people, suffering from diseases of various kinds, are recommended by their physicians to visit this Italy of the United States; and as such visits, in a vast majority of cases, are productive of radical cures and new leases of life; it occurred to the inventor that nature, which had been so prodigal of her balsamic and invigorating odors amid the pine forests of Florida, could be persuaded to transfer them, in kind, to less favored regions, where both sick and well might breathe them, and be benefited thereby. If the balsam-laden air of a Florida forest brought an invalid back to health, why might not the balsam-laden air of his or her home produce the same desirable results? If the perpetual aroma of a Florida forest be purifying and revivifying, what better tonic and disinfectant could be provided for the sick room in the North, or for the entire house?

Question. How could these medicinal odors be transferred without impairment of their healing strength, or diminution of their pleasant effects on the senses. It was discovered that they were largely centered in the leaf of the pine, and that, if properly cured, they were perpetual. The cutting off and the drying of the leaves, and their preparation for the uses they were designed to subserve, did not diminish in the least their fine, invigorating perfume, but rather made it more pungent and agreeable. Here, then, was solved one important problem. The healthful balm of the native forest could be bottled up, as it were, and, like the odor of the musk, transported endless distances, to be let out as a remedy for the ills of those who breathed it.

These pines are commonly called "Fox-Tail Pines," because the leafy clusters bear a resemblance to a fox's tail. The characteristics of these "Fox-Tail" leaves are lengthy stipules, fibrous or feathery in texture, of great power of resistance; *i. e.*, elastic and durable, very aromatic and agreeable, permanent in their pungency. In them were found all the qualities of a first-class mattress and upholstering material. These characteristics decided the investigator. If the aroma and healing properties of the Florida forest were to be introduced into the distant home, and there made to do for the invalid what they undoubtedly accomplish when inhaled in their natural habitation, in what form could they be introduced so economically and comfortably, as in that of a mattress?

In this form, the aromas, perpetually exhaled, would load the atmosphere of the room and the entire house, and keep it continually disinfected. They would be ever present as a tonic to the sick and debilitated, and would constantly and quietly act remedially, as nature designed they should. They would be breathed in by those who sought their couch for rest or sleep, just at a time when medical remedies are most active on the system, and when a condition of repose greatly assists every curative agent. The result would be like transporting the invalid, with all his home comforts about him, to the balsamic forests of the South, and permitting him to partake, without cost of money or loss of time, of their health-restoring perfumes.

No mattress can be a genuine Pino-Palmine Mattress, unless it bears this trade-mark, and none should be bought without it.

Thus much is a history of the discovery. The process by which the Pine and Palmetto is converted into mattress and upholstering material, is protected by Letters Patent, issued June 18, 1878, to W. G. Benedict, of Orange Park, Florida. The Patentee has erected a large manufactory in the midst of the Pine and Palmetto section of Florida, and the State already boasts a new industry.

The Letters Patent only cover a process and not a name. Therefore Aromatic Pino-Palmine Mattress and Mattress Filling Co. having been vested by the patentee with the sole right to manufacture and introduce the Aromatic Pino-Palmine Mattress Filling in the United States and Canada, registered the trade-mark Aromatic Pino-Palmine Mattress, (which is here given) January 28, 1879.

We have given a brief history of the discovery, the patent and trade-mark.

NOW AS TO RESULTS:

In June, 1878, Mr. G. C. Stewart, of East Saugus, Mass., bought the first Mattress made of this material. On December 16, 1878, he sends us the following letter, the first positive proof of the medicinal virtues of the Pino-Palmine:

EAST SAUGUS, MASS., December 16, 1878.

Gentlemen:—For years I have suffered the most intense pains, and seemingly everything but death, from Neuralgia. For days together I have not been able to dress myself. Some five months ago I heard of the *Aromatic Pino-Palmine Mattress.* I at once ordered one, for I had tried everything known to the medical profession without permanent relief. To my surprise the pains commenced to subside, and in two weeks they were all gone, and they have never returned. That I am well now is due entirely to sleeping on the Mattress, a very pleasant medicine, I assure you. You are at liberty to use this in any way you choose, if you can benefit those who have suffered as I have. Respectfully Yours,

GEO. C. STEWART.

In September, 1878, Mr. William Hart, of 3703 Spring Garden Street, Philadelphia, having learned (through Mr. Stewart) of the merits of the Pino-Palmine as a curative agent, bought the first Pino-Palmine Mattress sold in Philadelphia.

In May, 1879, he gives the result of eight months' experience with the Pino-Palmine Mattress, in the following letter:

PINO-PALMINE MATTRESS CO.

Gentlemen:—After having used your Pino-Palmine Mattress for eight months, it affords me pleasure to inform you that I have received great benefit. The Lumbago and Rheumatic affections of the muscles with which I was so much troubled, have been entirely eradicated. To be cured of these without the aid of medicine or lotions, and while *sleeping*, is truly wonderful. The Pine aroma exhaled both night and day is very fragrant and agreeable. Yours Truly, WILLIAM HART,
3703 Spring Garden Street, Philadelphia.

What they say after a further experience of two years or more:

AROMATIC PINO-PALMINE MATTRESS CO. APRIL 15, 1881.

Gentlemen:—In answer to your inquiry as to my health remaining the same as when I gave testimonial, I will say my health continues excellent, none of my former ailments trouble me, but I continue to be a well man by the aid of your Pino-Palmine Mattress and Pillows. Truly Yours,

GEO. C. STEWART, East Saugus.

PINO-PALMINE MATTRESS CO. PHILADELPHIA, May, 1881.

Gentlemen:—As I have had your Mattress now two and a half years, it gives me pleasure to say that I have not had any return of the rheumatism, and I feel convinced of its beneficial effect on my general health. I like the Mattress now better than when I first purchased it. Truly Yours, WILLIAM HART,
3703 Spring Garden Street.

IGNATIUS SARGENT, M. D., Woburn, Mass.
"I can recommend it as highly beneficial in its health-restoring qualities."

Ex-GOVERNOR WM. A. NEWELL, M. D., of New Jersey, now Governor of Washington Territory.
"It is cool, comfortable, elastic, and, I believe, enduring and health-giving."

JOS. A. VERGE, Boston, Mass.
"I have derived more comfort from it than from any bed I ever used."

MRS. J. JONES, Aston Mills, Del. Co., Pa.
"I cheerfully recommend it to all who wish to sleep well and feel well."

J. A. McARTHUR, M. D., Lynn, Mass.
"I have used one for some time, and the result is, I am much benefitted of an asthma which has troubled me for years."

THOS. N. COOPER, Esq., Media, Pa.
"It is always cleanly and comfortable."

REV. B. D. CONKLING, late Pastor Congregational Church, Whitewater, Mich.
"One cannot resist the impression, even from its occasional use, that he is getting into a *bed of unusual neatness and cleanliness.*"

GEO. L. YEAGER, (Western Shoe and Leather Review,) Chicago, Ills.
"*I could not take one hundred dollars for it if I could not get another like it.*"

A. N. BRICE, Sunbury, Pa.
"They are cool and refreshing beds and pillows."

A. M. CUSHING, M. D., Lynn, Mass.
"It is a perfect non-conductor of heat, entirely relieving cold feet in bed; a priceless boon to the bed-ridden or fever-stricken patient."

S. S. WILD, 199 Eddy st., Providence, R I.
"It helped my rheumatism from the first. Outside its healing qualities, it is well worth the money it costs."

JAS. M. SHOEMAKER, (Cashier First National Bank), Jacksonville, Florida.
"Yours is something more than an ordinary discovery—it is a wonder."

W. W. BROWN, 96 Friend st., Boston.
"I believe it to be one of the greatest health-restoring agencies of the age."

SUSAN TAYLOR CONVERSE, Woburn, Mass.
"I do most earnestly recommend it as a *healthful, comfortable and cleanly* bed."

WM. PULLEN, (Furniture,) St. John, Mich.
"I would rather have it than all the hair, feathers, or anything else ever used."

S. WATERHOUSE, Boston.
"Its use has toned and invigorated my whole system."

H. L. BOWKER, (State Assayer,) Boston, Mass.
"Having tested the Pino-Palmine filling by actual use as well as by chemical test, I have no hesitation in giving to it the highest recommendation as one of the best materials for bedding that has ever been offered to the public."

F. H. PERRY, 49 North Main st., Providence, R. I.
"I would not be without it for any consideration."

GEORGE W. CADY, (Architect,) Providence, R. I.
"I have improved in general health, and would not part with it on any consideration."

MRS. A. L. SEYMORE, 219 East Worthing ton st., Springfield, Mass.
"I have received great benefit. The neuralgia is all gone. I sleep well, and am cured of all nervous complaints."

WM. HART, 3703 Spring Garden st., Philadelphia.
"Since using the Mattress the lumbago and rheumatic affections of the muscles with which I was so much troubled have been entirely eradicated."

L. E. PIPER, Springfield, Mass.
"I prefer the Mattress to any I have ever used."

W. H. HART, Philadelphia.
"It does not absorb dampness or heat. I find it the most cool, sweet and pleasant mattress I ever had."

H. H. LEWIS, Stonington, Conn.
"Were I unable to get another, I would not part with mine upon any consideration."

W. E. RICHARDS, M. D., Boston.
"When I retire with cold feet they soon become warm, and a gentle perspiration pervades the whole body."

WISTER H. STOKES, Germantown, Philadelphia.
"I have been using one, and could not be induced to go back to a hair mattress."

MRS. B. LUTHER, No. 7 Sheldon st., Providence.
"I am seventy years old. For twelve years and more I knew not a good night's rest. I now sleep well, and have from the first, since using the Pino-Palmine."

W. H. HENDERSON, Providence, R. I.
"I take pleasure in recommending it to any one wishing a perfectly sweet and wholesome bed."

J. T. SMITH, 52 Hudson t., Providence, R. I.
"It has been invaluable to us."

JOHN H. EDDY, 5 and 7 Exchange st., Providence, R. I.
"The most comfortable in summer we ever used."

Nineteenth-century advertising broadside.

convicted of treason, sentenced to life imprisonment, and later pardoned and restored to civil life. An extremely rare broadside dated June 12, 1820, signed by T. U. P. Charleton as Mayor of Savannah, Georgia, and asking for help and charity as the aftermath of a tragic fire which virtually wiped out that Southern city, is listed at $84.50. Another historic broadside, 9x14 inches in size, urging the promotion of the manufacture of firearms by the Continental Congress and announcing standards for their production, is valued at $225. It is dated November 4, 1775, and bears the printed signatures of members of the Massachusetts Government.

Another valuable one ($285) is a California-Oregon stagecoach broadside dated July, 1866. This one is printed in red and blue and is illustrated with a woodcut depicting a stagecoach and a six-horse team. It lists the stagecoach's stops and rest points and also bears the printer's signature.

Slave auction broadsides printed in the southern states prior to the Civil War are still not extremely rare but will bring $5 to $20. They are growing scarcer daily, however. A small Civil War recruiting broadside printed in the North around 1862 is listed at $7.50. One reporting a treaty of peace in the War of 1812, printed in Portland, Maine, is offered at $75 with a minor defect.

A poster dating back to the 1855-60 period and advertising "The Celebrated Oxygenated Bitters" is advertised at $10. It was of large folio size, lithographed in color.

As of this writing, there seems to be a great deal of variation in the prices asked for early broadsides, posters, and handbills of a similar nature; but as more collectors seek them and more dealers begin to handle them, prices are likely to become more stabilized.

Incidentally, broadsides have been reproduced in recent years. These reproductions are worth very little, and collectors rarely seek them, but some persons buy them for decoration and as conversation pieces.

4.
Sugar and Spice...

Since interior decorators are imaginative individuals, it is little wonder that they are making good use in home decoration today of the attractive spice cabinets which were so abundant in the nineteenth century. That is particularly true of the wooden cabinets which contained several drawers or compartments and were graced with stencilled decorations.

The nineteenth-century cabinets were fashioned of wood ranging from pine to nutwood. Some also were made of tole, or tin. The small cabinets resembled miniature chests. Most of the drawers had a small knob in the center by which they could be pulled open to permit access to their contents. The number of these drawers varied. The smaller ones contained two to five; the larger ones, six to a dozen. The little boxes were 6 or 7 inches tall and were designed to be placed on a shelf in the pantry or kitchen. The larger chests ranged all the way up to 24 inches in height, and many of these were hung on the kitchen wall.

The cheapest spice boxes were plain affairs, some of them home-made; but others were far more elaborate with painting, stencilling, and carving. A good many of those which are available today are dated and some bear the initials of their former owners. Spice boxes were used in the eighteenth century, too, but they are quite scarce now. In his book *Treen or Small Woodware Through the Ages,* (G. T. Batsford, Ltd., London), Edward H. Pinto pictures an eighteenth century English spice box of turned mahogany with radiating divisions. It is mounted on a foot and stem and is undoubtedly rare. He also pictures a group of circular birch column boxes which were relatively abundant in England a century ago. There were from two to six compartments in these, and each was labelled with a transfer. The compartments screwed into one another.

Technically, the larger chest-like containers are referred to as spice cabinets and the smaller ones, including the small round ones, as spice boxes. A good

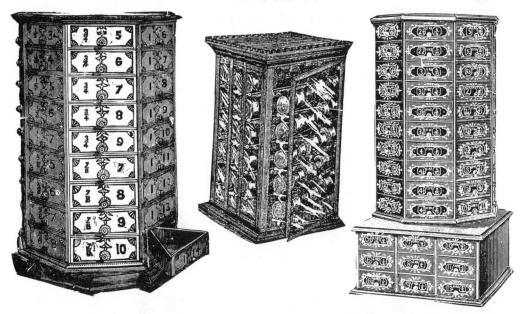

Coming collectors' items: screw, ribbon, and bolt cases shown here as offered at the opening of this century by Belknap Hardware & Manufacturing Company.

many of the spice boxes were fashioned of tin, some of it japanned. The boxes contained small receptacles in the form of smaller boxes or similar containers to hold the spices. Some wooden spice boxes were made with tin rims.

To what use can these old spice cabinets and boxes be put? If you have ever tried to locate such small items as pins, screws, tacks, rubber bands, and sewing devices for which you have no regular storage space, you'll realize how helpful one of these spice containers can be. The old cabinet knobs, incidentally, were made not only of wood but sometimes of porcelain or glass.

The small round containers (sometimes they were oblong) are easier to find than the larger spice cabinets and usually cost a good bit less. And although the cabinets are avidly sought by collectors now, the boxes also have become collectors' items. Sometimes you can find the containers with some of their original contents — cinnamon, ginger, cloves, pepper, nutmeg, all-spice, and so on — still intact.

Generally speaking, the value of nineteenth century spice boxes and cabinets will range from around $5 to $50, and it is difficult to find a cabinet type for less than about $15. Because there is such a heavy demand for them at this time, this pressure against a diminishing supply may force values higher.

A nice pine nine-drawer cabinet measuring 27x18x10 inches and equipped with porcelain knobs has recently been advertised at $40 in refinished condition. One of golden nutwood with eight drawers and round turned wooden knobs has an asking price of $15. It measures 10x15¾x4½ inches. A similar eight-drawer cabinet is advertised elsewhere at $22 and one of maple with eight drawers at $20. One cabinet measuring 11¼x9 inches and dated July 30, 1885, is listed at $34.50. It has white porcelain knobs and the drawers were carved from solid blocks. An eight-drawer cabinet of pine with the original iron pulls is tendered at $16.50, which is the same price asked for one of maple.

Late nineteenth-century spice box.

A spice box of heavy tin with a "Chippendale-style" cover and containing six round tin containers is offered at $5.50, and probably is a bargain. It measures 6x9½x3¼ inches and, of course, is oblong. A round wooden box with eight small containers is listed at $9.50. A round tole box with hinged cover and six round containers was recently on the market for only $4.50. Its paint had been chipped off, but it was otherwise in good condition. A box with six cans of its original spices still inside was tagged $10.50.

These handsome cabinets and boxes can be utilized almost anywhere in the house, but many homemakers prefer to place them in their native habitat, so to speak — the kitchen.

You can still come across a "find" in these cabinets and boxes in stores handling used furniture and household goods; but the demand for them is increasing at such a pace that you may not be able to do so much longer. You also will often find highly desirable ones in antique shops.

A sort of cousin to the spice cabinet — though not close enough to be a kissing one — is the spool cabinet, or thread cabinet. These, too, make excellent containers for small items. There was an article in the January, 1956, issue of *Spinning Wheel* magazine which related how Mrs. Arthur Schuster, an El Paso, Texas, souvenir spoon collector, used spool cabinets to house her collection. The cabinets actually can be used to house a wide variety of small, relatively flat articles, because the drawers themselves are not high.

These spool and thread cabinets were used originally in retail establishments to hold the spools of sewing thread the establishments sold. They were made for the thread manufacturers, the largest among these being J. P. Coats, and Clark's, and were sold to retailers by wholesalers or jobbers. The cabinets were made in sizes of from two drawers up to about fourteen. The average two-drawer cabinet will measure about 21x15¼x8¼ inches in dimensions. There also are rotary-type cabinets, some of them capable of holding 600 spools of thread.

Half a century ago, a wholesaler offered two-drawer cabinets for either J. & P. Coats or Clark's O.N.T. thread complete with 300 spools of thread for $11.75. Rotary cabinets measuring 22½x20¼x16¼ inches were offered complete with 600 spools of thread for $23.50.

In addition to the larger commercial spool cabinets, there also are smaller spool cases designed for use in the home. These, like the commercial ones, were usually made of wood, had folding doors, and contained spindles for holding spools of thread, a velvet pin cushion, and a drawer below for scissors.

The thread cabinets are selling today — without thread — for considerably more than they sold for filled with spools of thread 50 years or more ago. Prices have risen fairly sharply during the past three or four years. Those with the names of the original thread manufacturers still on the drawer fronts will bring a premium over those on which the lettering has been obliterated.

Here are some recently-advertised prices for two-drawer cabinets: oak, unfinished as found, $17.50; unfinished, $10; oak, unfinished, $12; walnut, with pilaster corners, painted, $18; walnut with teardrop drawer pulls, $20; walnut, 18½x14½x5 inches, $22.50.

Other sizes have been offered as follows: three-drawer, walnut, 23x16x9 inches, top corner broken, $25; three-drawer, walnut, 19x13x9 inches, $15; three-drawer, 20x12x18 inches, refinished, $19; three-drawer, walnut, 22x 14½x9 inches, good condition but needing refinishing, $28; four-drawer, oak, $30; four-drawer, walnut, 25x15x13½ inches, $22.50; five-drawer, oak, fine condition, $25; six-drawer, walnut, brass pulls, rough condition, $50; six-drawer, ash, $30; five long and two short drawers, walnut, refinished but one glass insert broken, $45; nine-drawer, eight of the drawers with glass fronts, brass pulls, minor defects, $28.50.

In some areas of the country, the larger sizes will often bring higher prices than those cited here. If you're good at refinishing, it would save you money

A highly desirable spice cabinet of walnut which is dated between 1850-1875. It is reproduced through the courtesy of The Henry Ford Museum, Dearborn, Michigan, of whose collections it is a part.

A mid-nineteenth-century spice cabinet of walnut, with porcelain labels. Courtesy of The Henry Ford Museum, Dearborn, Michigan.

to buy a cabinet in rough condition and then strip and refinish it yourself.

If you have spool cabinets to sell, you may get excellent results with a classified advertisement in your local newspaper. If you sell outside of your own community and have to crate and ship the larger boxes, your asking price should either include the shipping cost or specify that this is extra, because it can sometimes amount to a sizable sum.

Finally, if you want to do a bit of pioneering yourself, watch out for old store ribbon, screw, and bolt cases. These provide excellent storage for small items.

5.
"Hello, Central"...

Contrary to popular belief, Don Ameche didn't invent the telephone. It was Alexander Graham Bell. Don Ameche probably popularized its use. The chances are, however, that neither of these gentlemen visualized the uses to which early telephones are being put today.

Early phones are Cinderellas of the collecting field right now. Business in them has been booming for a couple of years. The telephones being sought are the old crank ones, long since outmoded by technological developments.

You used these crank phones earlier only if you're well along in years. And if you used them, the chances are that you carried on many informal conversations with the operator (we used to refer to her as "Central") as well as with the persons you intended calling when you decided to chat with the operator a while first.

For the edification of those of you who missed the horse-and buggy days, dial phones are relatively new contrivances. It was June 2, 1875, that Bell confirmed his theory of the electric telephone and he obtained his first patent on his invention the following year. Teen-agers may not realize fully just how deeply they are indebted to this one-time Boston University professor, but the parents of teen-agers who rarely get to use the telephone do.

In the very early days, the box telephones were used as both transmitters and receivers. A little later modifications were made so that the box was hung on the wall and was used primarily as a transmitter. Various inventors, among them the renowned Thomas A. Edison, contributed to the development of the telephone. When the box phone first came into use, callers used to tap on the diaphragm with pencils or other small instruments to signal the party at the other end of the line. This was easier than dialing, though not as effective. Later, a hand-operated hammer mechanism was developed to give a sharp blow on the diaphragm. This blow was transmitted to the station at the other end of the line. Thomas A. Watson, who worked with Bell, finally developed a ringer and magneto-generator to enable a user to call another party by turning a crank.

Still later, there were developed switchboards and all sorts of refinements for easier contact and improved reception. But before the refinements came into use, persons making calls were supposed to use the generator to signal the operator when they had finished talking so the lines could be disconnected. They often forgot to do this, which resulted in the operator frequently butting into the conversation with the question, "Are you through?" This was a nuisance, but it gave proof that the operator wasn't sleeping on the job.

That's enough about the history of the telephone. If you want to know more, you'll just have to consult a good treatise or an encyclopedia. What we set out to say was that there is probably more business right now in the old wall hand-crank telephones than there was in Grandmother's day. These old wall cases are being converted into radio cabinets, for one thing. One company recently offered old wall phones in which a five-tube, two-speaker radio had been installed for $59.95, or you could purchase the radio chassis for installation yourself. These telephone-radios make interesting decorative and utilitarian accessories in just about any room in the home.

Other firms are converting old desk-stand telephones into lamps, which was only to be expected. And the French-type phones which were used in the 1920's are regaining popularity for decorative use in the home today. These include those with the solid brass dials and similar types with ornate trim. One company offers these phones with a four-prong plug and an extension cord at prices ranging from around $30 to about $40.

Dealers in the new collectibles all around the country are offering both the wall-type and the French set phones for sale, and they still haven't got together on standard prices. You can find oak cases, for example, offered at prices ranging from less than $6 to more than $30.

If you have any mechanical ability, you can convert one of the old phones into a radio yourself; you can also hook it up so that it serves as a doorbell. Most persons who do this clean the metal parts and replate them with brass so that they are nice and shiny-looking.

Here are some of the prices which have been recently asked for old telephones: 1900 model, $17.50; 1895, $20; old desk phones, upright, with brass under the original enamel or nickel plate, $15; complete wall phones with plain oak cabinets, $33; similar ones with paneled cabinets, $42; European cradle phones without dials, $39; similar ones with dials, $49; old French phones with dial and jack, $49.50; old double-decker phones, $10; and candlestick phones and ringer box, $3. When you figure in the transportation charges, which the buyer must usually pay, the prices move upward a bit.

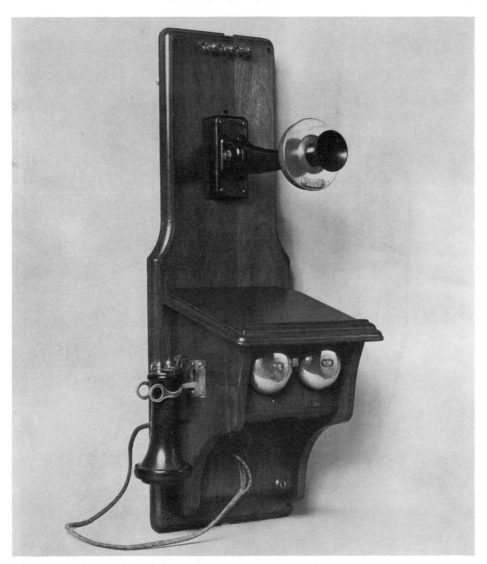

Common battery wall set. This model dates back to 1900. (Courtesy of Southern
Bell Telephone & Telegraph Company.)

Some companies sell not only complete phones but parts for old phones.
One of these advertises mouthpieces at $1 and receivers at $5. Cranks are
worth $2 or $3.

One firm which specializes in converting phones to lamps offers brass
phone lamps without shades at $35. You can buy or design your own shade.

Magneto wall set. This is the 1907 version of the telephone with a built-in generator mechanism to provide current for signaling the operator. (Courtesy of Southern Bell Telephone & Telegraph Company.)

Relatively new collectible items are telephone pole insulators. Most of these are of green glass, but some have turned a purplish color. They are being used as paperweights and are fetching about $5 each.

The old phones with their outmoded equipment do not work satisfactorily as a rule on present-day telephone hookups, and, generally speaking, most telephone companies do not make provisions to connect them to their advanced equipment. They much prefer that you convert them into radio cabinets or lamps or simply hang them on the wall as decorative items.

A good many of the old phones being traded now come from the old farmers' cooperative lines which have since gone out of business. One major telephone company in this country reported that it had "absolutely no wall telephones for sale." Some of the phone companies do have museums of their own, featuring many items of equipment used in earlier years.

This "new improved acoustic telephone" was offered by *The Youth's Companion* in 1887 at a price of $1.25.

A word of warning, too: Just because a good many old telephones are moving into the category of "antiques," think twice before you try to remove the phones in your home and cart them off with you when you move. The telephone company, which in all probability owns the phones in your home today and rents them to you, will look with a jaundiced eye upon the removal of its property.

You may be interested in knowing, too, that trading is beginning to start now in old radios and radio equipment. Collecting of these items is relatively new, so few prices have become stabilized. A number of folk who have bought early radio sets are looking for parts to fit them. Early simple tubes, for example, have recently been advertised at prices ranging from 75 cents to $2 each. Early speakers will bring several dollars.

Just to give you an idea about such things, here are some other prices of early radios and related equipment which have been asked during the past year:

The magnificent collection of early radio paraphernalia shown here was assembled by Wayne M. Nelson, Concord, North Carolina, a veteran radio station operator and builder.

Old tube tester, $25; 1914 model battery radios, $20 to $25; 1920 three-tube headset battery radio, $7.50; 1924 Crosley Musicane radio receiver, $4.50; model 100 Radiola speaker, $6; Atwater Kent model 30 receiver with six good tubes, $20; Everyman DT600 crystal set with earphones, $75; De-Forest seven-tube battery radio with large speaker and headset, $15; Cocka-day radio, $12.50; early Zenith battery police radio in working condition, $50; Myers tubes, $3; Western Electric head phones with head bands, about 1920 vintage, $20 a pair; Auditoron 1915 tube with wires coming out of each end, $35; and Radiola 111-A with tubes but no batteries, phones or speaker, $50.

And don't throw away those old radio magazines issued before 1925. There's a market for these too, as there is for early radio catalogues.

Undoubtedly thousands of old radios are stored away and forgotten in homes around the country and probably many of these can be picked up for a pittance if their owners haven't read this chapter.

There is one organization called the Telephone Pioneers of America. Its members are interested primarily in the history of the telephone business. There are chapters in various areas of the United States.

In the radio field, there are a couple of organizations. One is The Radio Club of America, Incorporated, 11 West 42nd Street, New York City. Another is the Antique Radio Guild of America, with headquarters at 6913 Westmoreland Avenue, Takoma Park 12, Maryland.

One of the finest private museums of radioana (a perfectly terrible appelation) is owned by Wayne M. Nelson, of Concord, North Carolina, a pioneer radio station operator. Some of his equipment, books and catalogues date back to around 1908. In 1936 his bookkeeper turned over to him a package of his father's effects, including an early coherer-decoherer.

Some of his paraphernalia can boast interesting associations. A Radiola semi-portable super-heterodyne, for example, was once the personal set of a man paralyzed from childhood and who depended solely upon the set (and a bit of photography) for diversion and entertainment. One of his transmitting tubes was confiscated by a radio inspector who participated in enforcement of the Volstead Act in the 1920's. It had been used illegally to direct the operations of an off-shore whiskey runner. Mr. Nelson also has several tubes used in the transmitter and receiver of the U.S.S. *George Washington* which transported President Woodrow Wilson to and from the Versailles Peace Conference.

Many other pieces of equipment owned by Mr. Nelson also have historic associations. He seeks, as do many other serious collectors, early and rare equipment rather than the far more commonplace items dating from the 1920's. He told the author:

It takes the devil of a lot of sifting to find the one item in about every two dozen offers that represents something I do not already have on hand, and it's a one-in-a-hundred shot to find that really rare piece. But a true collector develops a sense of expectancy that must parallel that of the inveterate gambler, who always anticipates that the 'next time' will be the payoff. When you have just about despaired of anything worth while turning up — bingo! It comes in, and often it's more interesting than your fondest dream about it.

In turn, many persons have contributed rare items to his collection, which is displayed in a nine-room house near his home.

Mr. Nelson has his own definition of a radio "antique," and he contributed it to the spring, 1965, issue of *The Old Timer's Bulletin*, the official journal of the Antique Wireless Association, edited by Bruce Kelley, Holcomb, New York. Here it is:

"A radio antique is a wireless or radio transmitting or receiving apparatus, or set, or some part thereof, made for, used in, or representative of the art of wireless telegraphy and/or telephony, as practiced before the beginning of radio broadcasting in 1920, though specimens of some of the early battery operated sets used as late as 1925 are often included by collectors and museums."

Of course, some collectors go farther afield and collect later items, and, as Mr. Nelson himself adds, "There is always a borderline, often crossed over."

The American Radio Relay League, Incorporated, headquartered at Newington, Connecticut, has published its official journal, *QST*, for members since 1915. Books of interest to collectors in this field will be found in the Selected Bibliography at the end of this volume.

6.
That Great Game of Politics

Wise old Disraeli once said, "There is no gambling like politics." Today a bit of gambling is being done by collectors of political memorabilia: They're betting that the value of their collections will be up sharply within a few years. They probably will win.

Interest in political campaigns of all types has spread in the United States in recent years as more persons have become aware of their individual responsibilities for good government. The activities of the political parties themselves and of such organizations as the League of Women Voters have contributed to the growing interest in exercising the franchise and taking sides.

With the mounting of interest in politics, there also has been a rapidly-growing interest in collecting various types of political campaign materials. This has been especially true among the newer collectors, which doesn't necessarily mean only the younger ones. In recent years, too, there have been more campaign materials to collect, made available in large quantities by the political parties themselves and by enterprising manufacturers and processors.

Collectible items in this field cover a wide area and range from the early 1800's right up to the present day. They include campaign buttons, pins, and badges; lithographed prints (including a number by Currier & Ives) and cartoons; ballots and printed lists of candidates; china and glass items such as plates, mugs, bud vases, trinket boxes, and the like; posters, flags, and photographs; sheet music, song books, and campaign instruction printed material; canes, umbrellas, hats, and caps; earrings and other items of jewelry; combs, comb cases, scissors, and clothes brushes; tokens, toy animals, handkerchiefs, lanterns, banners, and a host of other items.

Twenty-five years ago there were only a handful of political campaign collectors of any consequence around the country. Right now their ranks are swelling weekly. A. G. Lyon, Sr., who operates the Lyon Hobby Mart in Hartford, Connecticut, and who is mentioned earlier in this book, relates

53

This McKinley-Roosevelt poster, used in the campaign of 1900, is printed in red, white, and blue and measures 16½ x 23 inches. (From the collection of Wayne G. LaPoe, 11986 Lakeside Place, Seattle, Washington.)

an interesting story of himself which indicates the sharp increase in values of many desirable political items over a period of a relatively few years.

"About sixteen years ago," he says, "I was offered for sale a George Washington inaugural button, the type with 'G.W.' in the center and 'Long Live the President' embossed in print on the outer edge. The price was $15, and was

considered a bargain, since the 'going rate' at that time was $25. I didn't buy the button as I thought the price too high and extravagant for one button. But today, this same type of button will bring $100 and will attract almost any serious button or political collector who will be happy to pay it if he does not already have one like it in his collection."

But Mr. Lyon didn't make the same mistake twice. Shortly after the Washington button incident, he was called on the telephone by a friend who dealt in antiques and who had picked up more than 100 Lincoln medals and campaign medals. He wanted $30 for the lot.

"I bought the collection and was able to turn it over quickly to one customer intact, and for a much better than average profit," he recalls. "The customer was delighted with the collection, and I was happy with the quick sale and the profit. This collection today would retail for about $400 to $500. Collecting Americana items — carefully purchased at the right price — can be amazingly profitable as well as a great deal of fun."

This veteran dealer says that only a few years ago many dealers in miscellaneous antiques, especially in the New England region, could be expected to have on hand cards with celluloid pins of Wallace, Dewey, Thurmond, Franklin D. Roosevelt, Willkie, Norman Thomas, Al Smith, Hoover, Coolidge, Davis, LaFollette, Wilson, Hughes, Harding, Cox, Taft, and Bryan which they would have been happy to dispose of at a lot price of 10 cents each or less.

"The problem today," Mr. Lyon adds, "is to find a dealer who has a sizeable lot of such pins for sale — even half a dozen of them. An even greater problem would be to get such a dealer in the mood to sell them at any kind of a 'reasonable' price."

In the November, 1952, issue of *The Antiques Journal,* James H. Winchester in an article entitled "Political Americana" related how Mrs. Damon G. Douglas, of East Orange, New Jersey, had been inspired by her son (a freshman at Cornell University), who was collecting Lincoln-head pennies, to start her own collection of Presidential campaign material in 1941. By the time Mr. Winchester wrote his article, Mrs. Douglas had assembled a magnificent collection composed of more than 5,000 separate items, covering every President or Presidential candidate since George Washington.

Mrs. Douglas's collection included, the author wrote, such a diversity of items as torch lights, carved pipes, jewelry, collar and sewing boxes, medals, ribbons, bric-a-brac, match books and boxes, china, canes, prints, buttons, toby mugs, bottle tops, lanterns, games, pencils, and other materials.

Even starting today, a collector can assemble a first-rate collection of political memorabilia for a relatively modest investment. Whether he can begin ten years hence and do so is more doubtful. The more unusual items and scarce ones relating to the popular or dramatic Presidents are usually more costly. Generally speaking earlier items are more valuable than recent ones.

Most collectible campaign items available today will date back to about 1840 and the vigorous campaign between William Henry Harrison and Martin Van Buren. As Mr. Winchester points out in his article in *The Antiques Journal*, Harrison's campaign managers capitalized on the rumor that their candidate was born in a log cabin and publicized him as "the exponent of

Group of ribbon badges from the political campaigns of 1886, 1896, and 1900, representing a small part of the collection of more than 4,000 items of Wayne G. LaPoe, Seattle, Washington.

Republican simplicity and hard cider." Harrison campagn items are highly desirable today, but they are hard to come by. An Ohio newspaper which carried a campaign ad for Harrison was recently advertised for $5. A campaign token of hard rubber with a portrait of Harrison in the center and the inscription "I'm for Harrison, R-U" on one side and "The Plymouth Rock Arts Co." on the other is offered at $15. Another Harrison token is priced at $12.50, and a small brass one at $5.

Shortly after the assassination of President Kennedy, collectors began buying all the available mementoes related to his campaigns and his tenure of office, and prices soon ascended sharply. Prior to his death, however, his campaign buttons and badges could be picked up at low prices.

Excellent prices are brought for lanterns and torch lights used during the Lincoln campaign in 1860 and for similar ones which were used about 20 years later. There is also considerable activity in the campaign items associated with the colorful Franklin D. Roosevelt, and some years ago an F.D.R. Collectors' Association was organized.

Many campaign items associated with another Harrison — Benjamin — are considered quite desirable by collectors. A political silk handkerchief bearing portraits of Harrison and Morton and the words "Full Vote-Fair Count" was recently tendered for sale at $20. An 1888 Benjamin Harrison token is offered at $6.50, and a Harrison medal with a view of the Capitol on the verso at $5.

A group of novelty pins issued during the national political campaigns of 1880, 1888, and 1896. (From the collection of Wayne G. LaPoe, Seattle, Washington.)

As for Lincoln items, not long ago a private collector offered to pay $100 to $500 for dated Lincoln-Hamlin political posters. An 1864 Lincoln cartoon measuring 13 x 16 inches in size is valued at $37.50. An 1864 Lincoln token bearing the phrase "Good for another heat" is offered at $12.50 and another scarcer Lincoln token at $15.

Going farther back than 1840, one can find buttons of considerable value with the likenesses of James Monroe, Andrew Jackson, Franklin Pierce, and other Presidential candidates, successful and unsuccessful. A valuable 1840 button issued in behalf of the William Henry Harrison campaign bears the slogan "Tippecanoe and Tyler too." "Tippecanoe" refers to the place where American troops led by Harrison defeated Indian warriors commanded by Tecumseh.

The following recently-advertised prices will give a rough idea of values of some collected political items:

Woven silk American flag with portrait of Ulysses S. Grant and bearing the words "General Grant Our Next President," $27.50; large colored portrait of unsuccessful candidate Eugene V. Debs, issued in 1920, $22.50; 1908 Taft campaign ribbon with his portrait and a depiction of the White House, $6; Kansas City Democratic convention ticket dated July 4, 1900, with stub still attached, $3; Taft-Sherman tumbler with the words "Free Coinage" engraved on it, $4.75; red and white handkerchief with faded portrait of Theodore Roosevelt and the printed words "Progressive Roosevelt 1912 Battle Flag," $3.50; 1864 General McClellan token, $12.50; James A. Garfield token, $5; two-piece delegate badge to the 1948 Democratic convention with the words "Phila." and "Delegate," gold-washed, $3.50; 1916 "The Democratic Text-book," 480 pages, with a picture of Wilson on the front cover and of T. R. Marshall on the back, published by the Democratic National Committee, $4.50.

Also, political pin in the shape of an elephant's head with the phrase "Hoover & Curtis 1928" in the center and a ribbon attached, $2.75; milk-white glass Uncle Sam's hat advocating Taft's candidacy, $8.50; red cloth-covered pin with the inscription "Cleveland and Thurman," $7.50; lapel button with a portrait of D. Russell Brown (an 1896 Vice Presidential candidate), $2.50; ornate document certifying that a donor had contributed $5 to the 1912 Wilson-Cox campaign fund, $5; 10-inch Garfield memorial plate, $8.75; Landon pin, 75 cents; lithographed Taft-Sherman campaign plate, 9½ inches in diameter, $12; assorted Eisenhower pins and earrings, $2 each; William Jennings Bryan covered portrait mug, $8; linen handkerchief with portrait transfer print, boosting the candidacies of Bryan and Sewall, $4.

A 1904 advertisement depicts caps for boys and girls which could be purchased with the name of either the Republican or the Democratic Presidental candidate on them. The price was 35 cents each, and the caps were made by the Big Cap Factory in Brooklyn, New York. Another advertisement dated 1888 shows campaign plug hats offered at $12 a dozen untrimmed and $13.50 a dozen trimmed with either a large bandanna handkerchief of a campaign banner handkerchief. These were made of wool felt by Jordan, March & Co. in Boston.

There are now several dealers around the country who specialize in political campaign collectibles. The collectors themselves often advertise their wants

Group of medalets, ferrotypes, brass stickpins, celluloid buttons, and lithographed tin buttons from political campaigns covering the elections from 1860 to 1948 in the United States. (From the collection of Wayne G. LaPoe, Seattle, Washington.)

in hobby and collector periodicals. Undoubtedly many collectible campaign articles are stashed away in attics and elsewhere in some of the older homes. They will frequently be found, too, in establishments operated by purveyors of second-hand miscellany.

A good collection of this material can make an eye-catching display for the den or playroom. Many items can be mounted flat on the walls. Others, such as plates, mugs, and jewelry, can be housed on shelving or in glass-front display cases.

A serious collector won't stop with merely assembling the campaign items; he will delve into the history of the campaigns themselves. And the most astute collectors will jot down on file cards not only the date and price of each acquisition but also pertinent facts relating to the campaign in which it was utilized. If the collection is ever sold, this data will certainly add to its value.

One of this country's outstanding collectors of political Americana is Wayne G. LaPoe, of Seattle, Washington, an official of the American Political Item Collectors, a national association, whose secretary-treasurer is Robert Sterling, 412 Taft Avenue, Charleston, Illinois. Mr. LaPoe, who has been collecting since he was a high school student about 30 years ago, has more than 4,000 political items ranging from the campaign of Andrew Jackson to the present day.

7.

Statuary for the Masses: John Rogers

As typically American and almost as typically for the masses as were Currier & Ives prints are the figure groups made primarily of plaster of paris during the latter part of the nineteenth century by a New England sculptor named John Rogers.

Once turned out in large quantities, the so-called Rogers Groups are becoming difficult to find today, and just at the time that a vogue for them is beginning to be revived. The groups created by this Massachusetts artist can scarcely be billed as great art, but they may be assigned to the category of folk-type art with a whimsical appeal and a charm of their own.

Born in Salem, Massachusetts in 1829, John Rogers did a bit of modeling in clay during his teens. At the age of twenty-nine, he went to Europe and studied art under masters in both Paris and Rome. After a year there, he returned to the United States and began modeling the statuary that was to make him famous. He was both gifted and lucky, for the very first group he modeled, "Checker Players," attracted rather widespread attention. Encouraged by its reception, he decided to plunge into business on a fairly sizeable scale. His next production, "The Slave Auction," marketed in 1860, also caught the public's fancy, and he was on his way.

He engaged in business in New York City under the trade name of John Rogers. His first studio was on Broadway, but he subsequently moved to 212 Fifth Avenue, where he remained for about ten years. During the same period, he maintained a workshop on Centre Street. He moved to several other locations in New York City prior to retiring, and an 1882 advertisement for his wares indicates that his place of business at that time was at 23 Union Square.

Dorothy C. Barck in an article reprinted in the January, 1933, issue of

Old-Time New England, the Bulletin of the Society for the Preservation of New England Antiquities — with additions from the *Quarterly Bulletin* of the New-York Historical Society, says that from 1889 until his permanent retirement to New Canaan, Rogers resided at 14 West 12th Street, which later became the church house of the First Presbyterian Church. In 1895, the Salmagundi Club rented this house and, until it was reconstructed for the club's specific needs, used Roger's studio for its meetings, dinners, and exhibitions.

Rogers developed a secret formula for his hard plaster works, which were pressed in molds and turned out by the thousands. For the most part, they were smaller than life-sized statuary but were larger than the Staffordshire cottage figures so they could not be displayed easily on the ordinary mantelpiece but required a table or some similar sturdy support for display.

The "Checker Players" was exhibited in 1860 at the annual exhibition of the National Academy of Design in New York, together with two other Rogers Groups, "The Village Schoolmaster" and "The Auction." The following year Rogers displayed a clay group at this exhibition and a year later offered an exhibit in clay and another group in marble, according to Dorothy Barck.

Though Rogers himself was a highly competent modeler, he also had several talented sculptors working for him, foremost among them being Daniel Chester French, who produced a number of distinguished creations on his own, including "John Harvard" for Harvard University and "The Republic," which was shown at the Chicago Exhibition of 1893.

The Rogers Groups, most of which were decorated with a rather drab-colored paint, all bore names or titles, which alone will serve to identify the type of appeal they possessed, primarily sentimental mid-Victorian. In addition to the colored groups, his works also turned out some statuary in white Parian or unglazed biscuit without color. Also, Rogers sold carved ebony pedestals in various sizes and with revolving tops on which his groups could be displayed. Rogers figures may be identified by the impressed name "John Rogers."

Estimates are that Rogers turned out altogether between 75 and 100 different groups with thousands of reproductions made from the original molds. A number of his most popular groups relate to the Civil War. One of these, titled "Council of War," depicted Abraham Lincoln, Edwin M. Stanton and General Ulysses S. Grant. Another entitled "Taking the Oath, Drawing the Rations," depicts a Civil War soldier, Bible in hand, surrounded by his wife and his child and a Negro lad with a basket on his arm and a barrel by his side.

The only group Rogers ever produced that was derived entirely from

TAKING THE OATH
DRAWING AND RATIONS

This is an 1866 Penfield engraving of a well-known Rogers Group as published in the July 21 issue of that year by *Harper's Weekly*.

imagination was one called "The Fairy Whisper." The work consists of a winged fairy bending over to whisper to an attentive child. A copy of this may be seen in the Essex Institute in Salem, Massachusetts, which also has other Rogers Groups.

One favorite with nineteenth century families — and a highly desirable one for today's collectors — was called simply "Chess." It represents two men in costume seated at a chess table and a standing woman pouring tea. This was produced in 1889. A rather large group, 40 inches high, is called "Bubbles." This one, weighing a little over 200 pounds, was designed for

This is a Rogers Group in marble. Entitled "Air Castles," it is in the possess of the Society for the Preservation of New England Antiquities, Boston, by wh permission it is reproduced.

use in the garden and was made of a composition formulated to withstand the weather. It is the life-size figure of a young boy blowing bubbles. Two other groups for garden use also are said to have been turned out by Rogers. One of these, "Hide and Seek," with tall figures of a boy and a girl, was advertised for $50 in 1876. This was $30 to $40 more than the price of the majority of the smaller parlor groups.

The groups illustrating homely, everyday incidents and scenes were the favorites with nineteenth-century purchasers. But some groups which also were popular depicted figures well known in literature, including "Rip van Winkle" and several from "Faust." Rogers issued catalogues of his statuary, and these are invaluable for proper identification, sizes, and descriptions, and particularly because some plaster groups produced by other companies have been erroneously attributed to him. Except for the larger garden figures, most of the other groups fell within an original price range of $10 to $20.

In 1952, *Spinning Wheel* magazine published a list of Rogers Groups with descriptions and dates of production, and those who wish to collect this ware will find this list of great interest and importance. Descriptions of Rogers Groups for the garden will be found in an article in the July, 1938, issue of *Hobbies*. *Spinning Wheel* for May, 1952, reported that Rogers made two garden flower containers and that he sold a three-tiered table, mentioned earlier (which he did *not* produce), on which his groups could be displayed. A splendid list of Rogers Groups and photographic reproductions of many of them were published in *Old-Time New England* issued in January, 1933, and this list also is of great value.

Among the most desirable Rogers Groups are a few casts which were not offered for general sale and a few which were cast in bronze.

About a quarter of a century ago, an Arlington, Massachusetts, sculptor, Prescott W. Baston, decided to reproduce some of the original Rogers Groups in miniature. His first production was "The Favored Scholar," which he reproduced after the copy in the collection of the Society for the Preservation of New England Antiquities in a clay version 3¾ inches high on a base 2½ by 1⅞ inches. It weighed less than six ounces. He sent one of these to Miss Katherine R. Rogers, daughter of John Rogers. She and other members of the family gave Mr. Baston permission to reproduce the groups in miniature. These miniatures also are desirable collectors' items today, even though they are only about 25 years old.

Among organizations possessing collections of Rogers Groups in addition to the two already mentioned are the New-York Historical Society; Manchester (New Hampshire) Historic Association; Manchester Art Association, and the Municipal Lightner Exposition, St. Augustine, Florida.

The late Benjamin W. Arnold, of Albany, New York, had a fine collection of the groups, and this was exhibited in 1928 at the Albany Institute of History and Art.

This original clay Rogers Group, "The Checker Players," helped establish the fame of John Rogers. It is in the possession of the Society for the Preservation of New England Antiquities, Boston, by whose permission it is reproduced.

John Rogers lived until 1904, spending his last years at his summer home in New Canaan in poor health.

Right now desirable Rogers Groups can be found in some areas at prices approximating those for which they originally sold. Those interested in this statuary are picking them up rapidly at such prices, because they believe values are going to increase considerably if more collectors continue to seek out the wares. A good many other groups have been offered during the past year or two at less than double the original selling prices.

The once-popular "Rip van Winkle at Home" has been advertised at prices ranging from $22.50 to $87.50. A group entitled "Family Cares" is offered at only $20, which is the same price asked not long ago for "The Neighboring Pew" in defective condition. Here are a few other recently-asked prices:

"A Capital Joke" (with a small repair), $15; "The Favorite Scholar," $55; "Union Refugees," $40; "School Examination" (defects), $15; "Going for the Cows," $25; and "The Wounded Scout," $30. Other groups may be found at prices ranging from around $20 to $125 with some of the finest ones being worth more.

A competitor of Rogers was the West Statuary Company, which operated in Chicago simultaneously with the Rogers operation in New York City. Their figures also are collectible, although they don't possess the magic of the Rogers name.

Of course plaster of Paris figures had been produced for many years before John Rogers began making his groups. The material dates from the middle of the eighteenth century. Slip statuary cast in plaster of Paris molds was turned out in the eighteenth and nineteenth centuries in England, Germany, France, Italy, and other countries, as well as in the United States. Hundreds of these earlier items are worth collecting.

During the past year there has been an increase in the number of advertisements placed in various collector periodicals by individuals and business establishments seeking Rogers Groups. This may be the tip-off that a boom is in the making. At any rate, the groups are worth collecting for themselves whether or not values increase.

Sometimes they may be found in antique shops, but you may be more likely to encounter them in private homes and at antique auction sales. Don't pass up a group with a minor defect if it can be obtained at a low price. This statuary was often chipped or broken in handling, and small defects can be repaired.

8.
American Art Pottery: Weller Ware

American pottery in the so-called art nouveau mode was first popularized by the Rookwood Pottery, established in Cincinnati by Mrs. Maria Longworth Storer. Fine examples of Rookwood now fetch fancy prices, and for a discussion of these wares one can consult the book *Treasure at Home*.

Right now other American art pottery turned out in the late nineteenth and early twentieth centuries is moving into the spotlight, none perhaps more rapidly than Weller wares produced in a pottery founded by Samuel A. Weller, a country potter who made the "big time."

Sam Weller learned the art of potting in the country potteries of Muskingham County, Ohio, which made milk crocks, cuspidors, flower pots, and similar simple household wares. In 1872, he started his own pottery in Fultonham, his home village, and peddled his wares himself. Comparatively little had been written about the Weller production and Weller himself until Norris F. Schneider, of Zanesville, Ohio, published a booklet based on his own researches in 1963. The booklet, *Zanesville Art Pottery*, which is now available from White Pillars Antiques, R.D., Norwich, Ohio ($1.25 a copy), has probably done more than any other single source to popularize Weller pottery all over again during the past few years. The author is indebted to Mr. Schneider and his booklet for a good bit of the information about Weller in this chapter.

Ten years after starting his own pottery, Sam Weller moved it to Zanesville and set up business under the name S. A. Weller. A good businessman with a vision, Weller employed salesmen who soon were sending him so many orders that he was forced to expand. In 1890 he built a large new factory to turn out umbrella stands, jardinieres, and cuspidors. But in 1893, Weller attended the Chicago World's Fair and saw glazed pottery of a much better type than he was turning out. This was the work of William A. Long, of Steubenville, Ohio. Long and two associates operated the Lonhuda Pottery Company in Steubenville, and their wares with underglaze decorations bore a close kinship with types produced by the Rookwood Pottery.

It was not long until Weller bought control of the Lonhuda company, and Long remained with him for several months before joining the J. B. Owens Pottery Company, also of Zanesville. Weller continued the production of the Lonhuda-type wares, renaming them Louwelsa. The best pieces, according to Mr. Schneider, feature artistic slip decorations on a blended mahogany-colored background.

Shortly after the turn of the twentieth century, Weller expanded his business facilities again, making the Louwelsa line in scores of different shapes, including vases, jardinieres, umbrella stands, clock cases, and other articles. Louwelsa was marketed from 1895 to 1918, and marked pieces of it are now beginning to be avidly collected.

About the turn of the century, Weller began producing his Dickens-ware, decorated largely with characters, incidents, and scenes from the works of Charles Dickens. This was a sgraffito-type pottery, the designs having been scratched in the clay with a needle, but this technique, because of its cost, was soon abandoned for casting. The cast pieces were coated with a clear glaze and were marked with an embossed head of Charles Dickens on a small black disc.

Other wares with underglaze decoration turned out by Weller included those which were given the names Aurelian, Eosian, Auroral, and Turada.

The type of pottery best known to more collectors than perhaps any other made by Weller with the exception of Louwelsa and Dickens was designated Sicardo ware and was designed by a French craftsman, Jacques Sicard, and an associate, whom Weller employed in 1901. This metallic luster ware, featuring floral and other conventional designs on a dark iridescent background, is marked "Sicard Weller."

In an article in *The Antiques Journal* for September, 1964, Kenneth H. Markham reports that Sicard brought with him a secret process for making this metallic luster pottery which bore a striking resemblance to glass. Today, marked Sicard pieces bring high prices in comparison with most other types turned out by Weller. They include such small items as bon bon or candy dishes, jewelry boxes, candle holders, lamp bases, and plaques. At one time these were sold by Tiffany's in New York City.

Much of the early production of the pottery was marked "Weller," impressed on the bottom of the articles, together with the name of the particular trade line in curved lettering above. About 1915, says Mr. Schneider,

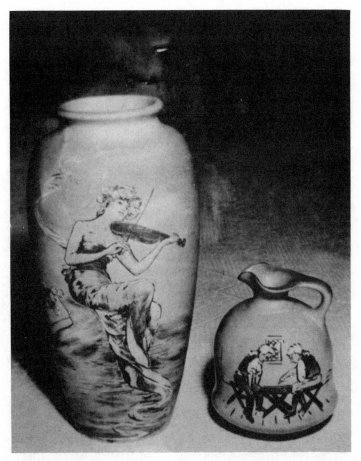

Two pieces of Weller Dickens Ware. (Photo through the courtesy of Norris F. Schneider, Zanesville, Ohio.)

the line name was dropped and only the word "Weller" continued to be impressed.

Mr. Schneider lists among the lines turned out during the period of World War I those bearing such names as Forest, Roma (a classical design type), Flemish, Blue Ware, Blue Drapery, Ivory, Knifewood, and Pearl. For fuller descriptions of these and other lines one should consult *Zanesville Art Pottery*.

Following the end of the war, Weller made lines named Zona, Hudson, Lassell or LaSa, Baldwin, Fairfield, Barcelona, Chengtu, and Lamar. Still later trade names included Bonito, Cornish, Classic, Dorland, Floral, Gloria, Ivoris, Patricia, Velva, and Cameo.

Two Weller vases from the collection of Mr. and Mrs. Mike D. Cole, Smyrna, Georgia. (Photo by author.)

In 1920, Weller acquired the Zanesville Art Pottery, and five years later he reorganized as the S. A. Weller Company. He died later that year, but his company continued to be operated until 1948, when it was closed permanently.

In addition to the types of articles already mentioned, Weller manufactured such things as creamers and sugar bowls, planters, plates, bowls, tankard pitchers, and powder boxes. But vases were produced in the greatest abundance.

Almost all of the better pieces of Weller's early production are worth collecting, and many of the later pieces also are. Much of the Dickensware (and also a good bit of other Weller types) is characterized by a crazing or crackling of the glaze. A Dickensware vase 11½ inches tall and entitled "Dombey and Son" is offered at $30. A Dickensware mug 5½ inches tall and signed with the name of the decorator is valued at $14.50. Another Dickensware piece — a cavalier's figure 13 inches high in colorful costume — is offered at $35. A Dickensware tankard pitcher 12 inches tall, depicting an Indian, is marked $18, and a 7-inch-high vase with white seagulls on a blue-green background is priced $25.

To indicate the generally higher values of Weller's Sicardo wares, here are a few advertised prices: tri-cornered vase, 7 inches tall with an all-over design of long leaf sprays with highlights of blue, green, and burgundy, $42.50; two-handled candlestick with a green, gold, and purple iridescence, 6¾ inches high, $40; round powder box, 5¼ inches in diameter, iridescent purple and green, with a carnation, and lead decoration on the lid, $45; 5-inch-high tri-cornered vase, burgundy to green, $27.50; and a 9-inch iridescent vase with a decor of blue bells and leaves, $70.

In the Louwelsa wares darker colors generally predominated and decorations featured flowers, berries, and fruit. A good many vases and mugs were made. The following examples will indicate general value ranges for these: mug with cherries, $9.50; squatty, handled vase, 3 inches tall, with pansies on brown background, $15; 17-inch-tall vase with yellow rose decoration, $29.50; candlestick, green top and brown body with flower and leaf decor, $12.50; handled brown jug with blackberries and green and yellow leaves in glazed brown and yellow background, $12; and vase 17 inches tall with rose decor, $32.50.

An Eosian vase, green to gray with large open lilies, 12¾ inches high, is valued at $28, and a smaller one with four handles at the neck and grape decor at $27.50.

Items merely signed "Weller" are worth from around $5 to $15 for vases, creamers and similar items. There are a few rarities which are worth more. One of these — a lily pool with frogs and pond lilies — is advertised at $38.50, and an unusual pitcher with a full-length figure of a woman done in relief is offered at $52.

There has been very little published research on the Weller Pottery, except for Mr. Schneider's work. When more has been undertaken, the values of the best pieces of this ware could go up. Certainly they are worthy of preservation and can grace the home. Because Weller is not nearly as well

Lavender and tan vase made by the S. A. Weller Pottery Company, Zanesville, Ohio, beween 1896 and 1905. (From the Marcus Benjamin collection at the Smithsonian Institution, Washington, D.C. Reproduced through the courtesy of the Smithsonian Institution.)

known at this time as are Rookwood and a few of the other art potteries of the United States, pieces can often be found in antique shops and at auction sales for prices lower than those quoted in this chapter. If they are good pieces, they could prove a sound investment. Here, one simply must exercise judgment and select items which are graceful, and tastefully decorated with interesting colors.

One thing seems certain: Weller is going to be "discovered" by more collectors in the next year or two.

9.
Up and Coming:
Roseville Pottery

Whether the price trend in American-made art pottery will follow that of American art glass remains to be seen. Early examples of Rookwood pottery are bringing good prices, and, as we noted in the preceding chapter, Weller pottery is rising in value. By comparison with Rookwood and Weller, art pottery produced at the Roseville Pottery Company, which operated in Roseville, Ohio, has been relatively neglected except by some astute collectors. It's our feeling, however, that many of the finer pieces turned out by this company deserve closer scrutiny and are well worth preserving.

Roseville Pottery Company was organized by an Ohio sewing machine salesman named George F. Young and a group of associates and was incorporated in 1892. Young became its general manager and secretary, and C. F. Allison was elected president. The company's first act of importance was to purchase the simple pottery plant which had been operated by J. B. Owens. Owens had been making painted flower pots and cuspidors, and the new owners continued this line for the time being. Three years later, Roseville acquired the Midland Pottery, also located in the same community, and in 1898 the Clark Stoneware Company's plant in Zanesville was purchased. From then on, expansion was the order of the day.

General Manager Young was acutely aware of the growing markets of the Weller Pottery and he decided to invade them by turning out art pottery in his own plants. Very little has been written about the Roseville Pottery Company and its operations and production except by Norris F. Schneider in his booklet, *Zanesville Art Pottery*; and once again we are indebted to him for much of the information contained in this chapter.

Young employed one Ross C. Purdy about 1900 to develop an art line

Roseville Pottery Company's Rozane Ware. (Photo through the courtesy of Norris F. Schneider, Zanesville, Ohio.)

for his company. The result was Roseville's Rozane ware, which was copied from Weller's Lonhuda and Louwelsa lines. It was underglazed decorated ware cast in molds. The ground was sprayed on and slip colors were used to paint the decorations. The pieces were fired, the glaze then applied, and fired a second time. These pieces are marked with the name Rozane ware and a rose contained within a circle.

Rozane became a highly successful line and the company advertised it in a number of high-class magazines around the turn of the century. In an effort to keep pace with continuing developments at Weller, the Roseville company hired a Japanese artist, Fugiyama, to create a line of incised ware which it called Rozane Fugi. Soon thereafter two additional lines of incised pottery were put on the market, one called Woodland and the other Della Robbia. This incised pottery is extremely scarce today.

After Weller's big success with Sicardo, Roseville employed a former Weller artist, John J. Herold, who perfected a Chinese-red type of pottery which was named Rozane Mongol. It was attractive but failed to win popular approval, so Roseville came out with still another line which it termed Mara. This was a metallic luster type, also in imitation of Sicardo.

Three pieces of Roseville pottery. (From the author's collection.)

Other types of pottery produced at Roseville prior to World War I included Rozane Royal, which had a light background; Rozane Egypto, which featured embossed Egyptian designs with a matte green glaze; Pauleo, which imitated Chinese luster wares; and Donatello, produced in shrunken plaster casts from original figures by an Italian sculptor of that name.

Mr. Schneider reports that many pieces of Pauleo were offered for sale in Roseville's New York City retail store at prices as high as $500. The

Donatello pieces had deeply fluted borders at top and bottom separated by half-round molding from a wide strip of embossed cherubs and trees extending around the pieces. Donatello was a smash hit and was on the market for ten years prior to World War I.

Lines made during the period of the first World War included Carnelian, Mostique, Imperial, Rosecraft, Volpato, and Corinthian.

Pottery from this company marked "Roseville, U.S.A." was made after 1917, when fire destroyed one of the company's plants and all operations were consolidated in the plant on Linden Avenue in Zanesville. Russell T. Young succeeded his father as general manager in 1918. Between that year and 1954, when the company ceased operations, the Roseville Pottery Company turned out two lines annually, molded by Frank Ferrel as art decorator, according to Mr. Schneider. These included lines known as Sylvan, Dogwood, Florentine, Corinthian, Cremona, La Rose, Normany, a new Imperial, Savona, Tuscany, Victorian, Pine Cone, Ferella, Blackberry, Baneda, Cherry Blossom, Luffa, Laurel, Morning Glory, Primrose, Sunflower, Apple Blossom, Ming Tree, Snowberry, Zephyr Lily, Gardenia, Lotus, and Silhouette.

Roseville's matte glazes established the company's popularity. Mr. Schneider points out that the firm changed to gloss glazes during its last ten years, but these failed to attain the popularity of the earlier matte glazes. The Mosaic Tile Company bought the plant in 1954.

For a fuller description of the various lines and greater details of the company's operations, one should consult *Zanesville Art Pottery*.

The plant's later productions, with certain exceptions, are not as desirable as many of the earlier pieces, but it probably is an educated guess that Roseville pottery will gain increasing favor with collectors within the coming years. To Mr. Schneider's researches and his booklet and several newspaper articles he authored must go a large part of the credit for calling public attention to the art pottery manufactured in the Zanesville area.

Prices right now vary widely in different areas of the country. In sections in which little is known about the Roseville production, vases, candle holders, and a good many other pieces may sometimes be picked up for a pittance. A Rozane cider mug in brown and olive green with a spray of berries was offered not long ago for $3.50. A pair of candle holders was offered at $5. A Roseville jardiniere and pedastal, 25 inches tall, tan with yellow flowers, was advertised at $25.

Other prices asked for certain pieces during the past year or two will give some indication of prices at which much of the ware is still available. These include the following: a Pine Cone vase 11 inches tall, $8; vase in the shape of a handled basket in green and brown, $6; small bowl, $6; Rozane ewer, 7 inches tall, dark brown with berry decorations, $14; red-marked jardiniere

Sang de Boeuf vase made by the Roseville Pottery Company, Zanesville, Ohio, about 1905. (From the collections of the Smithsonian Institution, Washington, D.C., by whose courtesy the photograph is reproduced.)

in greens, yellows and black with geometric decor on an ivory matte background, $7.50; and a bulbous handled vase with a large flaring lip with lily decorations, $10.

One should judge Roseville pottery by the same artistic standards by which one judges other art pottery or fine glass. Some pieces will prove inferior and others superior. Roseville could be a sleeper.

10.
Dedham Pottery: Rediscovered

Just as has been the case with various other collectibles, Dedham pottery has been discovered and rediscovered several times since the beginning of this century. Right now, it is the apple of many ceramics collectors' eyes.

Prices of good pieces are not yet exorbitant, compared with pieces of roughly similar age and quality made by other well-known American potteries, but they appear on the way up.

The Dedham Pottery actually didn't cease production until 1943. As the "Dedham Pottery," it was opened in Dedham, Massachusetts, in 1894; but its roots go much farther back. Mabel M. Swan, in an article in *Antiques* in August, 1926, and Frederick W. Allen, in one in *Hobbies* in September, 1952, agree that the story of this pottery had its real beginnings in 1853 when James Robertson, a Scotsman with potting experience in both Scotland and England, arrived with his family in this country.

In 1866, one of his sons, Alexander, started a pottery in Chelsea, Massachusetts, and one of his brothers, Hugh C. Robertson, became associated with him the following year, according to the two authorities cited above. The firm name became A.W. & H.C. Robertson. The father, who had been associated with the Plympton & Robertson Pottery Company, of which he was a co-founder in East Boston, Massachusetts, joined his sons in the Chelsea pottery in 1872, and, according to Mabel Swan, the name was changed to Chelsea Keramic Art Works. More decorative wares were produced and were identified with the impressed mark: "Chelsea Keramic Art Works Robertson and Sons." Greek examples were imitated.

When the father died in 1880, the sons continued in partnership until 1884 when Alexander moved to California, and Hugh continued the operations alone.

Mr. Allen reports that when Hugh attended the Philadelphia Centennial

Exposition in 1876, he was greatly impressed with a Korean exhibit which featured Chinese Crackle and Dragon's Blood vases of the Ming period, and he returned to his own pottery determined to reproduce that color, the art of making which had been long lost. Mabel Swan says that his determination to reproduce that color arose after he had seen it on a piece of ware in the East Boston Pottery. But no matter how he obtained his inspiration, he succeeded, after several years of experimentation, in obtaining it and, reports Mabel Swan, actually improving upon it. She points out that whereas the Chinese glaze was opaque and the vases had streaks of purple on them, Hugh Robertson's color, which he called "ruby," was transparent, without the streaks. He produced only 300 pieces of this ware.

The Dedham pottery shown here is in the possession of the Dedham Historical Society, Dedham, Massachusetts. (Reproduced through the courtesy of the Dedham Historical Society.)

During his experimentations, both authors report, Robertson also discovered the process for making crackle ware (or "Cracquelware") which is
characterized by a sort of spiderweb in glazed marking, resulting, Frederick
Allen says, from his secret process of kiln baking. Table and similar practical
wares were turned out by this process.

Because so many of the fine wares turned out by this pottery were high
in price, they did not find the mass market necessary for financial success,
and the pottery was forced to close in 1889. Two years later, however, it
was reopened with funds supplied by a group of Bostonians and with Hugh
Robertson as manager. The name adopted was Chelsea Pottery, U.S.A.,
and the production of crackle ware was expanded.

In either 1894 or 1895 (Mr. Allen gives the former date and Miss Swan
the latter), the pottery was moved to Dedham, Massachusetts, and was re-
named Dedham Pottery. Of the work there, Mabel Swan wrote in her
article in *Antiques*:

"From 1896 to 1899 experiments were conducted in high-fire colored
vases — red, slate, green, yellow — and in Chinese crackle vases, all simple
and heavy to stand the great breaking strain of high-fired colors . . .

"These vases have been spoken of by French and German ceramists as
'forty to sixty years ahead of public appreciation which has as yet advanced
only to the flower and figure period.' "

Upon the death of Hugh Robertson in 1908, his son William succeeded
to the managership. Upon the latter's death in 1929, the business was continued by his son J. Milton Robertson until the company ceased operations.
In his fine study *The Pottery and Porcelain of the United States,* originally
published in 1893 by G. P. Putnam's Sons, New York, Edwin Atlee Barber
says that while Robertson was experimenting in his efforts to obtain the
Chinese blood red or *Sang de Boeuf* color, he produced varieties of a deep
sea green, "peach-blow," apple-green, mustard-yellow, greenish blue, maroon,
and rich purple. Wares with any of these glazes are extremely desirable
collectors' items today. So, too, are the crackle wares.

Marks used by the Robertsons in their various potteries included:

C

K A

W

which was impressed in their art wares starting in 1866; the letters C, P, U, S
impressed in a cloverleaf design from 1891 to 1895; an impressed rabbit
with a head-on view, used in 1895; a blue-stamped mark with a side view
of a rabbit and the words "Dedham Pottery" above, used in 1896 and for
some time thereafter; the same design with the addition of the word "Registered," used from 1929 to 1943; and also two rabbits impressed (head-on

views). Certain wares made personally by Hugh C. Robertson bear his initials scratched on them.

The decorations on the crackle ware in blue were all done free hand. Dedham pottery was made in a variety of patterns, of which Rabbit is said to have been the most popular. Other patterns were given the names Azalea, Butterfly, Clover, Duck, Grape, Horse Chestnut, Magnolia, Apple, Turkey, Dolphin, Lobster, Owl, Elephant, Iris, Turtle, Swan, Water Lily, Crab, Polar Bear, Chicken, Bird in Orange Tree, Lion, and Snow Tree.

Among the artists who created these patterns, according to Marguerite R. Leander in an article entitled "Dedham Pottery" in the March, 1949, issue of *Hobbies*, were Charles Mills, Denver Ross, John G. Low, Mr. Robertson himself and students of the Boston Museum of Fine Arts School.

Generally speaking, the fine earlier Dedham pottery wares are of greater monetary value than those produced during the years of its existence in the second quarter of this century. A series of plates in various patterns has recently been advertised as follows:

Rabbit, 6¼ inches in diameter, $12.50; Azalea, 6¼ inches, $14; Rabbit, 8½ inches (minor fleck on edge), $16; Pond Lily, 8½ inches, $19.50; Duck, 8½ inches, $18.50; Iris, 8¼ inches (minor fleck on edge), $18; Polar Bear, 8½ inches, $22.50; Rabbit, 10 inches, $20; Horse Chestnut, 6 inches, $12; and Butterfly, 10 inches, $20.

Relative values of other Dedham items include these:

Early heavy vase, dark brown and green glaze, 7 inches high and 4½ inches in diameter (small rim flake), $60; Rabbit round tea tile, $12.50; Rabbit creamer, $31; Rabbit sugar and creamer, $48.50; another Rabbit creamer, $38; Rabbit bowl, 6 inches in diameter and 2¾ inches deep, $27; salt and pepper shakers, $42.50; and a pair of rare small Dedham pottery rabbits, $135 a pair.

11.
Household Necessities: Boxes

You'd certainly be surprised at how many persons collect boxes but you would be even more surprised at how many kinds of boxes are being collected. In fact, there's a "box boom" under way right now, and literally hundreds of thousands of boxes are finding their way into collections.

The wooden box is a favorite. It was one of the most commonplace items in the household of 50 or 75 years ago. Wooden boxes have been made in almost every conceivable size and shape and for hundreds of different purposes. They once served as containers for everything from pills to buttons and herbs to cheese.

Cardboard, plastic, and other materials have replaced wood for hundreds of thousands of boxes today, though thousands of the wooden ones are still being made. But the old wooden boxes are taking on new interest and new values. Of particular interest are the hand-made ones which were used before the advent of the factory-made box about the middle of last century. Many of these early boxes were put together with hand-made nails or with wooden pegs.

Interestingly enough, many collectors are intrigued by shapes. Right now the focus is on round boxes. Don't ask me why. The early ones came in scores of sizes from tiny boxes designed to hold pills and other very small items to much larger ones for meal, butter, and cheese. Nests of small boxes hold a particular fascination. From the collectors' standpoint, they are of interest not only because they are becoming scarce but also because a large collection of them can be assembled in a small space. The hand-made boxes all differed in some respect for the simple reason that they were made by hand. The later machines eliminated these differences for boxes of the same shape and size.

Many different woods were utilized for fabricating the old boxes. Those more commonly used, according to Mary Earle Gould, an authority on

FINE ANTIQUE OAK BOXES. BEST CABINET FINISHED.

These Boxes are the very best quality on the market. All are made from selected quartered oak, polished and finished in antique. All lined with best quality satin, except Cigar Boxes, which have Moistening Pad.

PRICES EACH.

No. 190. Jewel Box........ ....$4 75
Fine silver plated trimmings, best satin lined.
Size, 8x5¼x3 inches.

No. 191. Jewel Box............. ....$7 70
Fine silver plated trimmings, best satin lined.
Size, 8x5¼x5 inches.

No. 192. Jewel Box.....................$6 25
Fine silver plated trimmings, best satin lined.
Size, 8x5¼x3 inches.

No. 193. Handkerchief Box..........$7 00
Fine silver plated trimmings, best satin lined.
Size, 7½x7½x3 inches.

No. 194. Necktie Box......................$5 50
Fine silver plated trimmings, extra fine satin lined.
Size, 13½x4x3 inches.

No. 195. Handkerchief Box..........$5 60
Fine silver plated trimmings, best satin lined.
Size, 7½x7½x3 inches.

No. 196. Glove Box....................... $5 50
Fine silver plated trimmings, best satin lined.
Size, 13½x4x3 inches.

No. 197. Photograph Box.. $4 50
Fine silver plated trimmings, best satin lined.
Size, 7½x5x3 inches.

No. 198. Glove Box........ .... $7 70
Fine silver plated trimmings, best satin lined.
Size, 13½x4x3 inches.

No. 199. Cigar Box for 50 Cigars $8 50
Silver plated trimmings and linings, with moistening pad.
Size, 10x6½x4 inches.

No. 200. Collar and Cuff Box... ....$6 40
Silver plated trimmings, best satin lined.
Size, 7½x7½x5 inches.

No. 201. Cigar Box for 50 cigars.........$5 50
Silver plated trimmings and lining, with moistening pad.
Size, 10x6½x4 inches.

ALL TRIMMINGS SILVER PLATED, LACQUERED AND WILL NOT TARNISH.

Wooden boxes for everything from neckties to cigars. From a 1900 catalogue of Otto Young & Company, Chicago.

woodenware, writing in the October, 1962, issue of *The Antiques Journal,* were maple, curly maple, birds-eye maple, birch, ash, beech, and pine. Here is how Mrs. Gould describes the production of the early wooden boxes in her informative article:

To make a box a strip of wood was cut of the desired width and length, with an extra length to form a lap. This strip was placed in boiling water to make it pliable. Then it was shaped at one end for a lap. Every box-maker cut his lap point as he wanted it and this is what makes handsome boxes so different and interesting to collect. . . .

The cover and bottom of the wooden box were generally made of a single flat piece, soft pine if it could be had. These round shapes were marked out with a wood compass, generally hand-made, which consisted of two arms joined at one end with a sharp point at the opposite end of one arm and a steel marker or a pencil at the end of the other arm. Marking a round cover was a simple matter but to make an oval cover took longer because of the geometrical shape of the oval arcs. Old wooden boxes often show the marks of these arcs and compass circles on both cover and bottom.

Where nails were not available, wooden pegs such as early shoe cobblers had were used to fasten the bottom to the side and the top to the rim. The pegs were made by first cutting strips of birch to a square, pencil-lead size, which was then smoothed and cut into short pegs and pointed.

Early American boxes. (From the collection of Miss Mary Earle Gould, Worcester, Massachusetts.)

Incidentally, Mary Earle Gould is the author of the book, *Early American Wooden Ware* (Charles E. Tuttle Company, Rutland, Vermont), which should be of major interest to all persons who collect in this field.

Among the types of wooden boxes which are more easily located today are those designed for such things as cigars or tobacco, collars and cuffs, gloves, buttons, and jewelry. Scores of desirable ones in these categories can be purchased for a few dollars each. For example, ordinary wooden handkerchief boxes with some sort of decoration are currently valued at three or four dollars each with undecorated ones a bit cheaper and the more ornate ones a bit higher. In about the same value range are wooden glove boxes.

The larger and better-made handkerchief, jewelry, gloves, and cigar boxes will bring premiums. Scores of factory-made boxes of this type were offered in wholesalers' catalogues issued during the closing years of the nineteenth and the opening years of the twentieth centuries. One of these catalogues, issued in 1906, pictured a cigar box with a green Mission oak finish and heavy lacquered brass trimmings. It was described as "full zinc lined with patent moisture pads" and was fitted with a lock and key. The box, which had a capacity of 50 cigars, measured 10 inches long, 6¾ inches wide and 4 inches high and was offered at a retail price of $5.65.

The same catalogue offered an attractive handkerchief box with lacquered polished brass trimmings, a moiré silk lining and a reproduction of an oil painting on the cover for $4.65. A wooden collar and cuff box with brass trimmings and measuring 7¾ inches long and wide by 5¾ inches high was tendered at $6.75. It was set with ten amethysts.

Silk-covered glove and handkerchief boxes dated 1902.

A large floral hat box dated 1839 was offered for sale recently for $15. Wooden knife-and-fork boxes, which may be pressed into service advantageously in the modern home, are of much interest and will bring from $2 to about $10 for more commonplace types.

All kinds of trinket boxes were produced during the nineteenth century, and since these may still be used to accommodate trinkets and provide "show pieces" as well, they are highly desirable if they are interestingly made and decorated. One in burled walnut and measuring 7 by 12 inches was offered not long ago for $6.50.

A few other types of collectible wooden boxes include those made for sealing-wafers, collar buttons, hat pins, stamps, patches, meal, food items — including pies and spices — sewing items, pens, and pencils.

Of major interest in the wooden box field are boxes which are painted and still have most of the original paint intact and those which were covered with colored paper. Favorite early colors were red, green, blue, and yellow. Some boxes still have their original owners' names or initials on the covers. Hat boxes (as well as some others) were occasionally lined with old newspapers, which help to date them. A hat box of this type (18 by 10 inches in size), lined with a newspaper dated 1839, was offered about a year ago for $9.50.

Some button collectors, incidentally, also collect button boxes. These were turned out in a great variety of shapes, sizes, and designs.

Three-piece collar, glove, and cuff boxes dating to 1891.

Because there were so many different types of wooden boxes made, the collector will find it advantageous to specialize in a certain type. Generally the smaller boxes hold a wider appeal than the large ones. The latter can pose a space and display problem.

Of course boxes were made of all sorts of materials in addition to wood, but we are concerned primarily with the latter in his chapter. It should be pointed out that a good many modern-day boxes are being made in the styles of the early ones. That is why it would be advantageous for the collector to consult a good reference work such as Miss Gould's book mentioned earlier so as to be able to distinguish readily between the old boxes and the modern reproductions.

This bandbox, owned by the Shelburne Museum, Shelburne, Vermont, commemorates General Taylor's Palo Alto victory over Santa Anna's Mexican forces. (Photo through the courtesy of Shelburne Museum, Einars J. Mengis, staff photographer.)

Another type of box well worth collecting is the wooden dresser box, which was usually equipped with a tray divided into compartments and a storage space beneath. Some of these were elaborately decorated. Others were lined with cloth or colored paper. Some had owners' name plates on the tops. In external appearance, many of these are similar to the old lap desks or portable writing boxes (which also are extremely desirable items and which are described in some detail in the book *Treasure at Home*).

Old boxes turn up in all sorts of places; and if you look hard enough, you may find some of them on your own shelves. If the brief discussion in this chapter stimulates you to go out and look for desirable old boxes, it will prove advantageous for you to read some of the collector magazines. These often publish articles on various types of boxes which will aid you in identifying collectible categories.

12.
"Knock, Knock...Who's There?"

The advent of the electric door bell and the buzzer led to a diminishing use of the old-fashioned door knocker in the earlier years of this century. In recent years, however, the knocker has been regaining much of its former popularity and has been giving the electric chime, for example, a run for its money.

You can't beat the ornamental molded knockers used years ago as a decorative accessory (or necessity) for outside entrance doors; and right now they are also coming into wider use for inside doors as well. This is an expression of the desire for and need of indoors privacy — a desire being recognized by architects who once again today are acknowledging it by utilizing more doors between rooms in the modern home.

Don't be surprised if a boom develops soon in ornamental door knockers of the eighteenth and nineteenth centuries. If this should happen you just might find it more and more difficult to locate a desirable old knocker at what you may think a desirable price. What may well happen is that collectors will seek the more attractive metal knockers for use on both outside and inside doors.

This new desire for greater privacy represents a reversal of a trend which began some years ago for more open spaces within the home and resulted in the abandonment of doors between some of the areas in which they had been used half a century earlier. It is true that the majority of modern homes do not utilize doors between kitchen and dining areas, for example, and the Victorian parlor whose doors were opened only when company arrived has long since been abandoned. But the move now is for more doors between sleeping areas; doors for "dens" and studies to help serve as a barrier against outside noises and doors for playrooms to help keep the noise which often originates there from disturbing other members of the household.

This trend is leading to the use of indoors knockers of wrought or cast iron and less frequently of brass or bronze. These knockers are not only utilitarian; they also are ornamental and can lend charm to the home's interior.

Door knockers have been used for centuries. The earliest ones, usually of wrought iron or bronze, normally consisted of a large metal ring and a striking plate. These were in commonplace use in the seventeenth, eighteenth, and nineteenth centuries, although by the 1800's cast iron knockers had largely replaced those of wrought iron.

Most likely to be encountered today are knockers of the nineteenth and early twentieth centuries. A favorite design on these was the eagle. Another popular motif featured an arrangement of flowers, and shell and vase designs also were widely used. Many early indoor knockers are quite charming. They depict such things as animals, children, ships, birds, flower baskets, and fictional characters. Thousands of these were cast in the 1800's in the nation's metal foundries, and especially in those of Pennsylvania and some of the New England States.

A check of stocks in dealers' shops and of advertisements in collector periodicals discloses that these designs, among others, are available: cats, dogs, parrots, sailing ships, baskets of flowers, frogs, golfers, children, hands, leaves, lions, eagles, human heads, and monkeys. Most of the brass knockers date from the eighteenth century. Many English knockers were cast in the form of a lion's head.

Probably the oldest door knocker known is one in the shape of Medusa with a ring which was located in ancient Capua, near Naples, and which is cited by Franz Sales Meyer in his *Handbook of Ornament,* (Dover Publications, New York), to prove that they were used in antiquity. Meyer cites three primary classes of historical door knockers as follows:

A ring, usually suspended from a lion's jaws (so that it also serves as a door handle).

A hammer moveable on a hinge.

Figures, animals and so on.

In all cases the moveable part, whatever its shape, is lifted to permit its falling back against a metal plate or stud. Meyer points out that in the first two classes, the plate itself is often the major feature of the design while in the third class, it is the moveable part which features the primary design.

In the Gothic period, Meyer adds, ornately-decorated plates of pierced work were devised, and these carried over into the period of the Renaissance. In the latter period, double-headed eagles were often employed as motifs. In the *Handbook of Ornament* Meyer shows a plate with eleven designs of door knockers from ancient times. Perhaps the most intriguing of these is an Italian one of bronze, measuring 13½ inches high, depicting David with the head of Goliath. This was found on a house in Ferrara.

At left is a brass door knocker cast in the form of the head of Medusa. It was made between 1850-1875. At right is a knocker of cast iron in the form of a lion's head. (Courtesy of The Henry Ford Museum, Dearborn, Michigan.)

Actually, little literature on the history of the door knocker is available, and this is a field to which an earnest researcher can make a real contribution. To do a thorough job, one would have to delve well back into history, because knockers probably date as far back as the bolted door itself. In the Middle Ages, the iron or bronze handles of outside doors served double duty as knockers. They took the shape of heavy iron or bronze rings undoubtedly devoid of decoration; but simple decoration, such as chasing, did follow after some years. Still later, varied shapes were evolved and the knocker became an adjunct of the primitive ring. By the Renaissance, door

Old sailing-ship door knocker. (Courtesy of The Adams Company, Tulsa, Oklahoma.)

knockers were being made in all sorts of decorated shapes — mermaids, dolphins, dragons, mythological figures, and others. Some of the knockers were of rather mammoth proportions but by the dawn of the Victorian era the size diminished, and so did the cost. Incidentally, door knockers are commented upon several times in the novels of Charles Dickens.

One reason for the trend to smaller and less expensive knockers or rappers is said to be that these objects were frequently detached from doors by petty thieves, who probably made enough from their surreptitious sale to buy a glass or two of suds.

One of the most famous door knockers which was copied in the early twentieth century is described by Fred W. Burgess in his book *Chats on Old Copper and Brass* (published by T. Fisher Unwin, London, 1914). This was a knocker used on the sanctuary door of Durham Cathedral in England, having been placed there prior to the reign of King Stephen. This knocker was in the shape of an animal's head with two empty eye sockets behind which lights are said to have been placed. Mr. Burgess also describes another much-copied knocker — a brass lion of Brazenose College, Oxford, which was in use prior to the fifteenth century. The lion's head was the traditional English design, and the cast iron eagle became the favorite in the United States. Designs of vases and shells also were highly popular.

Some of the interior door knockers were painted, and to be in collectible condition these should have their original paint. In the great majority of nineteenth-century knockers, the moveable part is the one which features the design, and the plate is of secondary importance.

Nineteenth-century knockers, excluding the more intricately-designed ones, will range in value from $4 or $5 to around $25. A solid bronze knocker in the shape of a hand 7 inches long has been recently offered for $14.50. A small one in the shape of a monkey, in brass, 2½ inches tall, is tendered at $8.75, and a brass one in the shape of a woman's head at $20. Here are a few other typical current prices:

Bronze lion, $13.50; heavy brass eagle (7x5½ inches), made in China for export, $12; small cast iron basket of flowers, painted, $3; brass urn (2x4 inches), $2.50; 3½-inch-tall brass eagle, $6; and early Oriental brass knocker featuring a half-human, half-animal head holding a knocker in the form of serpents, $22.

One may still find desirable knockers on some of the older homes; and if you can talk a stranger out of giving you the shirt off his back, you probably can talk the home owner out of selling you such a knocker. An easier way to acquire them would be to advertise in the collector publications if you cannot find them in the antique shops.

The Antiques Journal in its November, 1963, issue published two pages

A variety of door knockers and bells.

of photographs of perfectly charming interior door knockers, including a rare woodpecker, from the collection of Mrs. Lon Twinem.

More museums could render a service to posterity by assembling representative collections of eighteenth-and nineteenth-century knockers.

In addition to the knockers, early door bells and buzzers also are worth salvaging and saving. Many buzzers of ornamental cast iron are quite interesting. Thus far, very little attention has been paid to these early rotary bells, but one day we may see an interest suddenly awakened in them and will look back with regret — as we so frequently have the occasion to do — upon the times when we could have picked up intriguing examples for little or nothing.

These rotary bells frequently consisted of a gong, or convex metallic disc, which emitted a resonant sound when struck, and a turn key which operated a metallic device that struck against the disc. The turn keys, which were made in various shapes and designs and often quite ornamental, were a part of the frame, which also was frequently ornamented. The majority of the gongs used at the opening of this century ranged from about 2½ to 3½ inches in diameter. These were offered in 1900 at wholesale prices of $4 to $6 a dozen! An antique copper was a favorite finish for these rotary door bells.

Of course many older homes still have their outside rotary bells, but electrically-motivated push buttons or lift handles, which operate just about everything from gongs to chimes, have replaced them in the majority of modern houses. You might want to watch out for these bells when you see old homes being wrecked or dismantled.

13.
Doorstops –
Collect and Use Them

One might consider the doorstop a sort of remote cousin to the door knocker, so it seems logical to consider the former in this chapter.

Just as door knockers may be used today for the purpose for which they were originally created, so may the nineteenth-century stops. Doors often swing shut for a variety of reasons when one would prefer to have them open. Some doors are designed to return to a closed position after they have been opened, and they are equipped with springs or mechanisms for this purpose. Sometimes doors which should remain in an opened position once they have been placed there swing shut or partly shut because the house itself is a bit out of kilter; and of course strong winds will blow opened doors shut. The doorstop, therefore, is an effective ally in keeping doors open when one wants them that way.

The majority of collectible doorstops available today date from about the third quarter of the nineteenth century although earlier ones can sometimes be found. The majority of these were made of cast iron or other metals, although some were made of wood and glass and some consisted of various types of hollow ware filled with stones or pebbles. About the middle of the nineteenth century or a little thereafter some intriguing doorstops were fashioned of glass in the form of a turtle in some of the factories in New England.

Scores of the early cast iron doorstops are delightful to behold. They were contrived in the shape of animals, birds, flower baskets, children, story book characters, houses, ships, stagecoaches, and so on. Many were decorated in colors. When the original paint is found still in good condition, it adds to their monetary value.

The weights of the old doorstops varied considerably. Some were cast as

This small lady in the extremely long dress is actually a doorstop. Beneath the head and shoulders is a bag filled with sand. (From the author's collection.)

full figures; others carried a lifelike representation of the figure on only one side, the reverse being flat. Some figures are mounted on oblong or, occasionally, oval bases of metal; others are not. Some are higher than they are long, and others are longer than they are high. If variety is indeed the spice of life, then there's plenty of spice in the category of early doorstops.

About 1920 and even earlier, Thayer & Chandler, a Chicago firm specializing in artists' materials and supplies, china for home painting, and similar items, advertised iron doorstops for sale.

A group of iron doorstops offered early in the twentieth century by the Chicago firm of Thayer & Chandler.

When used for the purpose for which they were originally intended, the quaint old doorstops can lend decorative charm to any room in the house which has closing doors. But they have other uses also. Smaller ones with one flat side can be used in pairs as book ends for heavy volumes, for example. Or, one may wish simply to assemble an intriguing collection of them for display alongside a wall. They should be placed preferably on the floor because of their weight.

Because they are really just beginning to be collected, many fine doorstops made during the final quarter of last century can be acquired at very low prices, particularly from second-hand furniture stores and at church bazaars and sales of miscellaneous household goods. Some desirable ones have been offered for sale during the past year or two for only three or four dollars each. One, in the shape of a German Shepherd dog in cast iron, was advertised for $2.50. Offered recently at $3 each were one measuring 7x5 inches in the shape of a house, one in the shape of a flower pot, and another in the shape of a basket of flowers.

A doorstop or holder with a rubber floor bolt to prevent slipping. Known as "The Little Giant," these sold at about $4.50 a dozen in 1900.

Here are some other advertised prices for cast iron stops found in various geographical sections of the country:

Chesapeake Bay retriever dog, $8.50; blacksmith, $8; sailing ship, $5; Red

Riding Hood, $6.50; basket of tulips, $4; large wolf's head with a high handle, $15; large lion's head, $4.50; lamb, $10; squirrel, $10; kitten with yellow eyes, $9; parrots, $4 and $9.50; owl, $18; lady with bonnet, $5; large setter dog, $12; Scottie dog, $12; frogs, $3.50 and 4.25; cats, $5, $5.75 and $6; and a Negro "mammy" figure, $9.

A bronze bulldog stop was offered at $9; a caricature of a cat in glass at $5; and a box weighted with pebbles and covered with fabric and needlepoint at $8.

There's one more place in which you may want to look for old doorstops. It's a place where the darnedest things sometimes turn up — the junk shop.

14.
Guideposts to the Past:
Old Maps

Military eruptions, internal revolutions, and even nature's own upheavals have literally scrambled the world in the past half century. Once-independent countries have been absorbed by their erstwhile neighbors; former dependencies have been granted their freedom and sovereign rights, and even the United States has been enlarged by the addition of two new states.

It's getting so that you can't trust the accuracy of a map published earlier than a year ago. Old maps are rapidly becoming collectors' items. They portray the world's geography as it was and not as it is, as such they are significant contributions to an understanding of the history of empires, countries, and nations.

But attractive old maps are serving other purposes as well today, and decorators are beginning to turn to them as wall embellishments which will lend both color and fascination to a room. One reason for this may stem from the mass reproduction of great art which has made available to the average person copies of masterpieces which retain great faithfulness to the originals but which also is making great art rather commonplace. We hasten to add that this procedure of making reproductions of distinguished paintings available at a low cost is certainly all to the good. But decorators, professional and homebody alike, eternally seem to be seeking innovations. Right now old colored maps are providing just that.

Neatly framed maps can be used to advantage in virtually any room in the home. Moreover, they make excellent decorations for waiting rooms of doctors, dentists, attorneys, and other professional people as well as for private offices and factory corridors.

As good a way as any (and better than most) to start collecting old maps is to seek those of your own state, or even of your own county or city. Visualize, for example, the home study of a California resident with a wall devoted to early California maps, or the wall of a doctor's office in Michigan devoted to maps of the Wolverine State.

Some of the interesting maps now beginning to be collected come out of old atlases. Some were published years ago by map-publishing firms. Others were drawn originally for history or other books, and a number of those you stand a good chance of encountering were drawn by famous map-makers of an earlier day. Some maps were printed in colors; others are hand colored. They will be found, of course, in many sizes, some large enough to cover a small wall by themselves but the majority of a size suitable for individual framing and small enough so that half a dozen or so may be placed side by side along the wall of an average room.

Values of maps vary considerably and depend upon such things as scarcity, general desirability, the name of the maker, age, and condition. Unless it is quite rare, it is seldom advisable to buy an old map which lacks adequate margins or whose margins are badly frayed, torn, or deeply soiled. And be careful if and when you frame a map: If you trim the margins very much, you'll reduce its value, perhaps considerably.

There are several specialists in old maps who advertise from time to time in collector periodicals. A number of print shops carry maps as do some shops which specialize in old and rare books. And back to those atlases: It's a real joy to pick up a good-sized one for a relatively small sum and find it contains a profusion of good colored maps. The Library of Congress has an extraordinarily fine collection of maps, and its collection is described in a book compiled by P. Lee Phillips and entitled *A List of Maps of America, in the Library of Congress, Preceded by a List of Works Relating to Cartography.*

Cartography, simply put, is the art of making maps or charts.

Maps are worth anywhere from a few dollars to hundreds of dollars. A great many desirable ones which would lend interest to the home or office can be found now at prices from $5 to $25. Some very early and well-drawn maps of America are valued at $100 and more. One book dealer, who also sells maps, advertises the following, among others:

American map, published about 1800 in Amsterdam, with allegorical cartouches featuring Indians and with small ships and whales adorning the seas (dimensions 21⅜ x 17 inches), $125; map of America by A. Arrowsmith (Aaron Arrowsmith was a famous English cartographer and achieved fame for his *London Atlas* published in 1834), 56½ x 47½ inches, published in London in 1804, colored and mounted on linen, $135; map entitled "A New and Exact Map of the Dominions of the King of Great Britain on ye Continent of North America," measuring 24 x 30 inches and published in

CARTE TRES CURIEUSE DE LA MER DU SUD CONTENANT DES REMARQUES NOUVELLES ET TRES UTILES NON SEULEMENT SUR LES PORTS ET ILES DE CETTE MER.

This American map (1719) is valued at about $750. (Reproduced through the courtesy of Henry Stevens, Son & Stiles, Larchmont, New York, and Burnham, Surrey, England.)

London in 1715, $125; and an American map, 19½ x 15 inches, colored, published in Amsterdam in 1631, $135.

Maps published in this country during the War between the States are desirable, and those published in the Confederacy are of special value. For example, a map entitled "Map of the Seat of War in North and South Carolina," published by James T. Paterson, probably in Augusta, Georgia, about 1863, is valued at $125. It is colored and measures 23½ x 17 inches, not including the margins. Confederate maps are very scarce.

Even a good many colored maps of states published during the first half of the nineteenth century may be bought now at prices under $25. Here are some typical values recently advertised:

Georgia map, 8 x 10 inches, by T. G. Bradford, issued in 1835, $6.50; "New Map of Alabama with Its Roads & Distances from Place to Place along the Stage & Steam Boat Routes," 17¼ x 14 inches, colored, published by Thomas, Cowperthwait & Co. in 1852, $7.50; "New Map of Illinois, with its Proposed Canals, Roads & Distances," etc., by H. S. Tanner, colored, 17¼ x 13¼ inches, issued in 1845, $10; "A New Map of Kentucky with its Roads and Distances," etc., by S. A. Mitchell, colored, 13½ x 17 inches, published in 1846, $7.50; and a small map of Maine, 8½ x 6 inches, drawn and engraved by Joseph Scott and published in Philadelphia in 1795, $20.

Other earlier state and territory maps and even some very fine later ones are worth $25 and more. A scarce map of the Battle of New Orleans entitled "Plan of the Operations of the British & American Forces below New Orleans, 8 January, 1815," published by William James Mutlow in 1818 and measuring 20½ x 8 inches, is advertised at $35. A 30 x 23 map of Florida by Tanner, colored, published in Philadelphia in 1825, is offered at $50. This one shows grants in St. John's County, the track of Indian hunters across the peninsula and other paths.

Of major interest to American collectors are old maps which show such things as Indian and other paths, mail and pony express routes, canals and steamboat routes, and early turnpikes. Of special interest also are those showing various territories before they became states; city maps which show thoroughfares and sites of public buildings which have since disappeared, and maps which are quaintly decorated with allegorical and mythological figures and creatures. Among those treasured by historians and advanced collectors are those which contain inaccuracies reflecting the imperfect geographical knowledge of their times. The astonishing thing is that so many early maps were as accurate as they are. Those printed on rag paper have an added charm.

It is not always easy to determine the publication dates of maps; sometimes the only date listed is a copyright date, and the map may have been issued after that time.

Historians and genealogists frequently seek early maps which show such things as residences, landmarks, and property lines. These, of course, are usually maps of cities or counties.

One source of maps now being turned to consists of early magazines which sometimes utilized them as illustrations. This was particularly true during the Civil War when battlefield maps were drawn and published.

It may be of interest to cite a few examples of higher-priced maps as listed in recent catalogues. These include the following:

A rare sixteenth century map of America, entitled "Americae sive Novi Orbis, Nove Descriptio," woodcut, colored, 13½ x 16½ inches, published in Basle in 1598, $175; "A Map of ye English Empire in ye Continent of America," 23½ x 19⅝ inches, published in London about 1685 and engraved by W. Binneman, $350; maps of the City of Detroit drawn by John Farmer, the district surveyor, and engraved by C. B. & J. R. Graham, issued in four parts measuring 34 x 45 inches assembled, published in New York in 1835 and showing the lots numbered, $150; North American map published on four sheets in Paris in 1777, measuring 76 x 43 inches assembled, and consisting of a French translation of a famous map by Dr. Mitchell of the French and British Dominions in America, $250; and a pictorial world map by Hondius, 18 x 22 inches, colored, published in 1636, $250.

In addition to maps, plans of cities, fortifications, battles, and the like are also valuable when they are originals.

With certain exceptions, maps issued since 1900 are of small value. If they are not framed, maps should be kept flat wherever possible. Avoid folding and creasing them since this detracts from both appearance and value.

15.
Signs of the Times

Construction crews, real estate dealers, rental agents, and shopkeepers in almost every city in the United States are tossing thousands of dollars into the municipal incinerators every year without realizing it. This is the value represented by old signs and signboards removed from stores and shops, taverns, hotels, office buildings, and a host of other establishments when these structures are either demolished or rented to new tenants.

Almost any painted signboard made prior to the turn of this century is of value. Some are worth hundreds of dollars. Effigies, such as wooden Indians and other carved figures, and shapes and designs — animated or inanimate — are also of value. Of special interest are any of these carved or painted by well-known artists of their time.

Just as many do today, dealers, tradesmen, and professional men of past years hung signs representative of the articles they sold or the services they rendered outside their offices or shops. Thus, a locksmith might have hung a sign in the shape of a huge key above the entrance to his place of business, or a hatter may have erected a large wooden hat above his door. Some inns and eating establishments featured signs in the form of coffee or teapots of tremendous size. Tobacconists, as well as certain other types of establishments, frequently displayed carved wooden Indians or similar effigies in front of their doors.

All of these early signs are part and parcel of America's advertising art and thus a part of the country's business history. Aside from the fact that they are of monetary value now, they should be preserved for their own sake, and to toss them into the trash heap is almost a sacrilege.

One of the most familiar of all signs, of course, is the barber pole, already disappearing rapidly from the American scene. Generally, these stood 3 to 7 feet tall. The early ones were simply painted with the recognizable circular

A metal casting of a cigar-store Indian. (From *Cigar Store Figures in American Folk Art*, by W. Porter Ware and A. W. Pendergast. Reproduced through the courtesy of Lightner Publishing Corporation and W. Porter Ware.)

stripes, usually in red and blue. Later, other ones were animated in such a manner that the stripes appeared to revolve around the pole. The early painted poles in fair to good condition are currently worth from $25 to around $150. In the late nineteenth and early twentieth centuries the stranger in a small community didn't have to ask the location of a barber shop. He could stand on a street corner and see a barber's pole from two blocks away.

Many early barber poles were implanted in the sidewalk. Later, city ordinances prohibited such use, and the poles were attached to the shop itself. These poles derived from the days when barbers also were minor surgeons, engaging in such tasks as blood letting and dressing wounds. Several centuries ago barbers were known as barber-surgeons, and their sign consisted of a striped pole from which was suspended a basin. The stripe or band running around the pole was intended to represent a bandage around the arm or leg. The basin, of course, depicted the vessel into which blood was let. After barbers and surgeons were separated, the former began to discontinue the use of the basin but retained the striped pole.

Early opticians' signs are particularly fascinating. Most of these were in the shape of a pair of huge wooden eye glasses, painted, but others simply featured a big wooden (or sometimes metal) eye. Many jewelers used to (and some still do) sell spectacle frames; and some jewelers also were opticians. One interesting sign consisted of two large globes, one above the other. One globe represented the human eye, the other a clock with painted numerals, hands, and often, the jeweler-optician's name. These were sometimes made of glass heavy enough to withstand abuse, and the eye was animated so that it appeared to wink. Not long ago an auctioneer offered a large pair of wooden eyes for sale which had once hung outside an optician's shop, but he was unable to get a bid on the sign because his audience, apparently, was unaware of its value. Had anyone been interested, it undoubtedly could have been purchased for a song. And in another city the sign might have been snapped up by an alert collector or dealer who recognized it for what it was and knew that it would be of increasing value. At about the same time, a dealer in these old store and shop signs advertised a pair of wooden eye glasses for sale measuring 4½ feet long and 17½ inches high. The price asked: $95.

Carved wooden Indians, commonly known as cigar-store Indians, and other similar effigies, are in a class by themselves and are worth up to several hundred dollars each, depending upon the quality of the carving and painting, the size, condition, and date. Modern effigies are being produced, but only the older ones are being collected.

Obviously, the use of wooden Indians by tobacconists stems from the fact that it was the Indian who introduced tobacco smoking to this country's pioneer settlers. The earliest of these Indian effigies were small, usually standing

Combination sign for optician and jeweler. Advertised in an early catalogue of Swartchild & Company, Chicago.

no taller than about 2½ feet. They were usually carved of elm or oak wood, and, later, of pine.

A great deal has been written about these cigar-store figures. Among the more interesting and delightfully-illustrated books is *Cigar Store Figures in American Folk Art*, by A. W. Pendergast and W. Porter Ware (The Lightner Publishing Corporation, Chicago). In their book, published in 1953, the authors point out that the early effigies were given bright colors in their ornamentive parts and the remainder of the figures were frequently coated with tar to serve as a preservative. A medallion resembling the seal or brand of some tobacco was usually suspended from a carved band around the neck.

Messrs. Pendergast and Ware quote John L. Morrison, writing in *Scribner's* magazine for October, 1928, as reporting that the first wooden Indian in this country made its appearance in 1770 outside the tobacco shop of Christopher Demuth in Lancaster, Pennsylvania. But it was not until after 1840, they say,

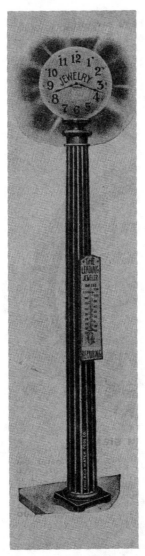

Jeweler's post sign. Pictured in early catalogue of Swartchild & Company, Chicago.

that the vogue of such effigies really began in the United States. The earliest tobacco-shop effigies used abroad, according to the authors, were figures of Negro boys, and these were adorned with feathered headdresses a bit later on.

Not all tobacconists who utilized effigies wanted Indians; some boasted classical figures — and, of course, these too are highly collectible. Those in-

terested in knowing more of the history of these early cigar-store figures will find a wealth of information in the book quoted above, in Kate Sanborn's, *Hunting Indians in a Taxi-Cab* (Gorham Press, Boston, 1911), or in the materials which are listed in the bibliography of the volume you now hold.

As for values, a 4-foot-tall wooden Indian chief on a 9½-inch-square base, with feathers around the waist, a pipe by the side, and a cigar in one hand, is offered at $675. The asking price for a squaw, 5½ feet tall on a 3-inch base, with yellow hair and a painted yellow dress and a wigwam at the bottom of the skirt, is $875. A smaller squaw figure holding a bunch of cigars in one hand and carrying Havana cigars and a box of snuff in the other is valued at $785.

Carved figures also were utilized by other tradesmen and specialists, notably harness-makers. For the latter, the horse was most commonly used. Recently, a full-sized harness-maker's horse, painted gray with white on canvass over a frame, was offered at $875. An antiques dealer in Atlanta, Georgia, has had a full-sized carved horse outside his place of business for many years. This has been "abducted" and later returned or located on half a dozen or more occasions during the past decade or so, and the figure's disappearance rarely fails to result in newspaper publicity.

Another quite familiar sign is that used by pawnbrokers and featuring three balls. This sign is derived from the three golden balls which were featured by the armorial bearings of the Medici, that fabulous Florentine family which rose to such great wealth and power in the Middle Ages. Signs of this type have been used by pawnbrokers for many generations and are still in use today. Early ones are of value, their worth depending on the material of which they are made, their general quality, size and condition. Two such signs, both of forged steel, one with a set of three gilded balls made of tole and the other set of wood, were advertised for sale some months ago at $135 each.

Watchmakers' signs have been particularly abundant and are beginning to be eagerly collected. The majority of the more interesting ones are in the shape of a watch (some depict clocks instead) with painted dials and hands. Similar signs, as already noted, were often used by Jewelers who sold watches and often had watch repair shops. One of these handsome watch signs was listed for sale recently for $125. It consisted of a large piece of block tin in the shape of a thick stem-wind watch with a large ring at the top and the name of the watchmaker on each side, plus a notation to the effect that the establishment was founded in 1892.

Numerous other types of early signs and signboards are of value. Here are some prices noted in dealers' shops or taken from dealer catalogues or adver-

cigar-store figure — Sir Walter Raleigh, owned by Brown & Williamson To-
cco Corporation, of Louisville, Kentucky. (Reproduced through the courtesy
W. Porter Ware and Lightner Publishing Corporation.)

Early advertising signs and effigies. (Photo through the courtesy of Mrs. Ella Dearborn and The White Barn, Mason City, Illinois.)

tisements, and these will serve as a very rough guide to current values, even though prices may start climbing soon:

Primitive post office sign 5 feet wide by 13 inches tall with a hand-forged bracket by which to screw it to a wall, $15; shoemaker's sign measuring 23 by 17½ inches in dimensions, consisting of a large man's boot and a woman's high-button shoe with the word "Maker" below, $17.50; butcher's cast iron sign measuring 19 by 20 inches in the shape of a knife and saw, $45; optometrist's sign in the shape of a large glass eye, $60; locksmith's sign in shape of a wooden key 97 inches long with cutout designs to form an "R" and a "Y" in the key and bearing the date 1795, $85; an early Dutch sign featuring a carved mermaid about 12 x 28 inches in size, attractively painted, $45; tailor's sign reading "Allen the Tailor" and measuring 23 inches wide by 39 inches high, painted in green, black and yellow, wood, $85; an Austrian naval officer figure standing six feet tall on a 2-inch base with wheels and clothed in a red coat with yellow buttons, blue trousers, blue cap, and holding a sword and a billy (the inside of the figure is hollow so that a bee hive may be housed in the belly, and there are holes for the bees to make their entrance and exit in the belt buckle, ears and billy), $175; tobacco store figure dating to about 1860 and consisting of the figure of a carved Turk 29 inches tall with a musket in the hands and mounted on a base on which the word "Cigars" is lettered, $275.

Early Vermont tavern sign, now owned by Shelburne Museum, Shelburne, Vermont. (Photo through the courtesy of Shelburne Museum, Inc., Einars J. Mengis, staff photographer.)

Many smaller and more recent signs are worth several dollars each. Most individual collectors specialize in the smaller signs because of the space required for display of the big ones. A number of museums have collections of signs and effigies, and, of course, some individuals have a cigar-store figure or two as conversation pieces. If you have intriguing early signs for sale, query

This huge boot, outside the Jesse Hitchcock Boot Shop in Old Sturbridge Village, is typical of the type of early advertising signs now so eagerly sought by collectors. (Photo through the courtesy of Old Sturbridge Village, Sturbridge, Massachusetts.)

one of the museums or similar institutions which preserve Americana.

A fine reference on the subject of very early signboards is the book, *The History of Signboards*, by Jacob Larwood and John Camden Hotten, published by the latter in London in 1866. It is a collector's item itself, and a copy fetched $20 at auction a few years ago. Another good reference in a single field is Fritz Endell's *Old Tavern Signs, an Excursion in the History of Hospitality*, published in a limited edition in 1916 and now valued at about $15.

16.
Don't Kick the Can – Save It

A surge of interest in collecting antique tin cans has arisen within the past couple of years and it is one which, conceivably, could reach the peak which has now been attained in the field of bottle collecting.

Can making goes back to the start of the nineteenth century, and the French and the English share the credit for stimulating an industry which today is of major proportions the world over.

Back in the days of the French Revolution, many thousands of soldiers died on the battlefields as a result of starvation and spoiled foods. The French Directory, becoming gravely concerned over the problem, offered a reward of 12,000 francs to any one who devised an effective method for food preservation. In 1810, that prize was claimed by one Nicolas Appert, who had invented a bottle in which heated food could be sealed and protected from spoilage. No one less than Napoleon Bonaparts presented the award to him.

Incidentally, Appert wrote a book about his discovery. It was published in Paris in 1810 and was entitled *L'Art de Conserver, pendant plusieurs Années, toutes les substances animales et végétales.* It is illustrated with a folding plate, and the first edition is worth about $150.

In the same year, however, King George III granted a patent to an Englishman, Peter Durand, for his principle of using "vessels of glass, pottery, tin, or other materials." Durand is said to have invented his principle after reading Appert's treatise But Durand substituted a cylindrical cannister made from tin-plate (iron coated with tin) for Appert's unbreakable French bottle; and thus, the can-making industry had its real birth.

Naturally, the first cans were made by hand. The earliest ones were cylindrical in shape for the packing and sealing of cooked foods. Interestingly enough, this is the shape still used today for thousands of products put into "packers cans."

It was not long, however, before items which did not have to undergo a

A few choice items from the antique tin can collection assembled by the Can Manufacturers Institute, through whose courtesy this photo is reproduced.

heat-sealing process (such as biscuits, tea, coffee, and tobacco) presented a challenge to the artistic abilities of the can makers insofar as design was concerned. Since no classic pattern in can making had been established, there was none to follow, and the artisans were free to exercise their imaginations to the utmost. Many of the early cans which survive today will be found in an intriguing variety of shapes and designs.

The English biscuit makers, in particular, came up with some quaint and delightful designs. They devised tin boxes which resembled sets of books, fishing hampers, clocks, and even roulette wheels. All of these are of considerable value today and are eagerly sought by those who have turned to this new field of collecting.

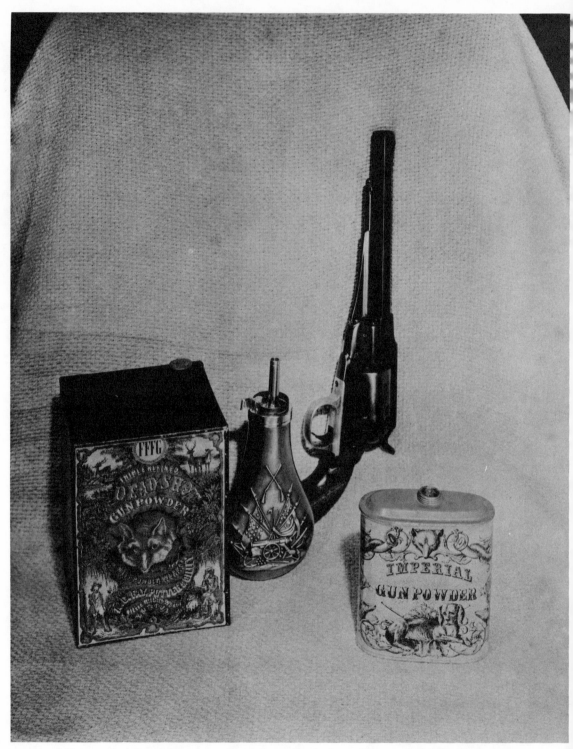

Tin cans fashioned into containers for gunpowder. (Photo through the courtesy of Can Manufacturers Institute.)

Cans were produced by hand for a good many years, but eventually the first steps were taken toward mass production. It became increasingly evident that the perfect and the ageless barrier to the deteriorating effects of light, air, and moisture was the metal can.

The first canned fruits and vegetables appeared in the United States about 1812 when Thomas Kensett opened a cannery in New York City and William Underwood a few years later began canning operations in Boston. President James Monroe granted patents in 1825 to Kensett for preserving food in "vessels in tin."

In those early days of can making, the skilled artisans hammered out their cans in forms shaped to produce the desired container. It was a laborious process, and even the expert craftsmen could produce no more than a few cans an hour. This was indeed a far cry from the present day when more than 600 cans a minute can be formed by our advanced machinery.

The early hand-made cans were of heavy-gauge tin-plate. In those days there were no standard sizes, and the cans came forth in a great variety of odd shapes which required considerable skill in forming. The variety was expanded still further as cans came into use for gunpowder and a great diversity of other non-food products.

The production of tin-plate was expanded sharply as a result of the discovery by Henry Bessemer in England and William Kelly in America in the mid-nineteenth century of the process for converting cast iron into steel, because it meant that tin-plate could be made of a mild carbon steel covered with a thing coating of tin, rather than of iron coated with tin.

About 1847, a patent for a pendulum press was granted to one Henry Evans. Combined with a die device contrived by William Numsen, a Baltimore canner, the press could make a complete can end in a single operation. Other developments and improvements proceeded apace.

Between 1880 and 1900, the development of a semi-automatic turret type of can bodymaker with automatic side seam soldering enabled a production rate of 2,500 cans per hour and marked the beginning of the end of the production of cans in canneries and the start of the can manufacturing industry as a separate entity.

Between 1900 and 1910, the open top cylindrical can was perfected. Theretofore, the can in common use was one with a hole in the cap similar to the first tin cannister invented by Durand. In those early cans, food had to be forced through a small opening in the can. The cap was sealed on by soldering, and heat was used to drive the air from the can through a vent in the cap, which was subsequently sealed. In the newly-perfected cylindrical can, a machine crimped on the lid.

By 1948, cans were being produced at the rate of 20,000 an hour. More

One of the most sought-after "can antiques" is this cookie tin made in the form of a set of books. (Photo through the courtesy of Can Manufacturers Institute.)

recently, improvements have been made in both machinery for can-making and in the materials from which cans are made so as to keep the cost of the tin can down.

Through the years, since it was first invented, the tin can has served man-kind in many ways. The can was of yeoman service during the Civil War when the need for food that could be preserved for long periods of time was so great. Pioneers who opened the American West took their food with them in metal cans packed in the East.

It is the early differentiation in size and design which really whets collector interest now. There is, for example, a cookie tin in the shape of a group of books created by Huntley and Palmers of England. These reusable containers were part of a truly fascinating line of tin cans and boxes turned out by this enterprising firm.

About the middle of the last century, Somers Brothers, of Brooklyn, New York, devised a technique of applying a lithographed design directly on the can instead of on the paper wrapper, and this represented a development of great significance for the metal can industry. Many of these lithographed cans were so attractive that they were saved by their original purchasers and have been handed down from generation to generation. Incidentally, the Somers method is still in use.

Other late nineteenth century milestones for the metal can industry included the invention by A. K. Shriver, of Baltimore, in 1874, of the pressure cooker which enabled canners to control temperatures accurately while cooking the sealed cans. This opened a still greater potential for an industry that was to develop into a giant.

Back in 1819, Thomas Kensett, mentioned earlier, canned lobsters, sal-mon, and oysters in his New York City facilities. Seafoods were being canned in Maryland in 1841. Tuna was first canned in 1909, and today 99 per cent of the tuna catch goes to canneries. Meat was among the first items ever canned, and canned pork converted Cincinnati into a meat-packing center in 1820.

The drug industry began utilizing tin cans before the middle of the nine-teenth century, and the first metal can for consumer use to appear on drug-store shelves was a round green one with a conical roof tapering to a cylindri-cal dome. When the dome — a telescopic affair — was pulled out, a small dispensing hole was pulled out with it. This was the can used by Dr. I. W. Lyon to hold his Dr. Lyon's toothpowder. Another pioneer user of the drugstore-type of tin can was Gerhard Mennen, who utilized a cylindrical can with a disc top for his Mennen's Baby Powder. Round, seamless metal boxes were introduced in the 1880's to hold all types of salves and ointments. Chipwood boxes had been used earlier but were difficult and more expensive to make.

The aerosol can was first developed during World War II as a result of the Army's need for an insecticide to attack malarial mosquitos in the South Pacific. Today, the first examples of these aerosol cans are being collected, as are the log-cabin shaped cans of the 1930's which held syrup.

The earliest cans adopted by numerous other industries, including tobacco, beer, oil, and others, are now beginning to be collected, and it would not be at all surprising if many of the new types of cans being introduced today will become collectors' items some decades hence. The tin can not only contributed immensely to the world's economy and welfare in earlier years but continues to do so today.

The collecting of cans has been spurred during the past year or so as a result of the building of so-called "restoration villages" and the creation of replicas of old-time country stores in various areas around this country.

One of the largest and most interesting collections of early metal cans has been assembled, logically enough, by the Can Manufacturers' Institute, a national trade association. This collection was sent on a tour of metropolitan areas in 1964 and 1965.

The values of the more interesting early cans have increased greatly in the past few years, and more modern cans also are rising rapidly in value right now. A can does not have to be a hundred years old to be collectible, but it should be interesting in shape or design, and the quality of the lithography has a bearing upon its desirability. A good many cans worth collecting are undoubtedly still in storage somewhere in older homes. Often they will be found at "flea markets" and sometimes in the antique shops. You probably will be able to find a good number worth saving at prices of from 50 cents to a dollar. But it is not uncommon to find more unusual ones now valued at $5 to $100. A set of the can books mentioned earlier is worth $75 or a bit more if the paint is in first-class condition.

An early lacquered tin powder can with a screw top and a large, bright, orange-colored label reading "Sharps Rifle Co. — Bridgeport," etc., has been offered for sale at $17.50. One book-shaped tin box labeled "The Herold, Norway," and with an illustration of sardines inside was advertised at $12.50. An early red tin chocolate box 7½ inches in diameter and with a domed cover is tendered at $2.50.

The modern can industry is now turning out more than 48 billion cans a year and is continuing to improve both design and lithography. Many of these may be collectors' items a few years hence. There is no reason, in fact, why you should not save a few of the more attractive tin containers in which you are buying both food and non-food items today. While they are not yet

An oil can with a pump for filling lamps. (Photo through the courtesy of **Can Manufacturers Institute.**)

of value monetarily, they will provide fine contrast when displayed side-by-side with a collection of earlier cans.

Here is one new field of collecting in which it may pay you to literally search through the rubbish heaps. Naturally, the more fastidious people will have certain objections to this procedure, but you just can't stop the adventuresome spirit displayed by certain collectors.

Much of the story of the fascinating development of the tin can through the years is related in a booklet published by the Can Manufacturers Institute, and entitled *A Pictorial History of the Metal Can.* A good bit of the historical background in this chapter was drawn from that source. Some of the other material has been drawn from an article on tin can collecting by this author first published in *Hobbies.*

17.
The Fireplace Makes
a Comeback

The open fireplace is making a comeback in the modern home. That's the word from architects who report that few things can lend greater charm to a living room than just the kind of fireplace which provided a focal point in the homes of our grandfathers. True, some fireplaces are being utilized today which feature gas heat and artificial logs, but the clamor seems to be for the genuine thing — an open fire feeding upon logs of wood. For heating efficiency, it simply can't compare with a modern furnace or other contemporary heating devices; but for creating an atmosphere of friendliness, conviviality, and inner warmth, there is no substitute for the old-fashioned fireplace. And with its resurgence, there has come a renewed interest in nearly all types of fireplace accessories which were used by our forebears.

A year or two ago, most of these accessories, save the quite elegant ones, were being handled primarily by specialists in primitives; but today many of them are finding their way into the better antiques shops. On the other hand, thousands of them may still be found in homes less than half a century old, many of them still in use and others stored away. Others will be found in salvage yards and in used-furniture stores.

Even if you don't have an open fireplace in your home, you will find that there are literally dozens of ways in which you can use the old accessories as decorative and utilitarian features in almost any room in the house.

Take the decorated coal hod and the coal vase as examples. Many thousands of these were in use in America well before the middle of the nineteenth century and their widespread use continued until architects and home builders decided, not many years ago, that homes no longer needed fireplaces with grates, and the enclosed heating stove gave way to more efficient heating devices.

A number of early fireplace accessories are shown in this photograph of the interior of an early log cabin which has been recreated at the Shelburne Museum, Shelburne, Vermont. (From the Shelburne Museum, Inc., Einars J. Mengis, staff photographer.)

Nineteenth century hods and vases were made of such diverse materials as wood lined with sheet iron, copper, japanned, and otherwise decorated sheet iron, steel, brass, gunmetal, bell metal, bronze, and even Sheffield plate. Coal vase was the name customarily given to small bins, and these were used for the storage of more coal than could be held in the ordinary hod. An early twentieth-century hardware catalogue issued by Belknap Hardware and Manufacturing Company (which is still in business, by the way, in Louisville, Kentucky) pictures a group of good-looking brass coal vases ranging in price from $20.50 to $27 each. Brass coal hods were offered in a $13.50 to $22 price range.

Both the hods and the vases were quite often japanned — that is to say, given a coat of hard, durable black varnish or lacquer — and then decorated by painting on various designs or figures or by using gold leaf. Most of the decoration was professionally done. In addition to such things as scrolls, leaves, and geometric designs, the decoration frequently pictured objects, scenes, and figures. Among the more desirable decorations were depictions of such things as sailing vessels, early agricultural machines, locomotives and trains, buildings, and the like.

Of course, these coal hods and vases can be pressed into service now for the same purpose for which they were originally intended and the decorated ones will grace the fireplace area. But they also can be used for the storage of other materials, including magazines; and the vases (which had tops) can be used as clothes hampers or for the storage of small linens. Hods also can be converted into planters for use inside the home. Moreover, those with artistic abilities can take the undecorated hods and vases and do their own decorating, which is always a delightful way to occupy leisure time. Scores of the nineteenth- and twentieth-century hods and vases can still be found for only a few dollars each with the elaborately-decorated ones and those of brass, bronze, and copper coming a good bit higher.

Eighteenth-century fire grate (English).

Firesets, which consisted of a coal shovel, poker (sometimes two or three different types), coal tongs, and a hearth brush, lend a homey appearance to the hearth and are still needed when an open fire is built in the fireplace. These were made chiefly of iron or brass. In 1900, an attractive and serviceable set of polished brass fire tools consisting of four to six items could be purchased from $8 to $10. These come a good bit higher in the better shops now. A pair of chamber-type tongs 17 inches long was recently offered at $6 and a pair of hand-wrought iron, 15 inches long, at $7. A brass hand shovel is advertised at $6, and not long ago one individual advertised a set of three brass fire tools for only $10.50, which is probably quite low if they were in good condition.

Fireplace dog irons for holding logs were fashioned in an intriguing variety of designs throughout the years of their abundant use. Our favorite motif for the front upright was a Hessian soldier. This design, by the way, is being reproduced today. Oriental designs also were quite popular late in the nineteenth century. One of the old Belknap catalogues pictures these designs on a lacquered iron ground surface, offering one pair for only $3.25 and another for $3. Simple dog irons with open handles on the front uprights and adorned with the simplest designs, such as stars, could be bought at the turn of this century for as little as $1.25 to $2 a pair. Dog irons were made in extremely heavy and elaborate designs and shapes in the seventeenth and eighteenth centuries.

The terms fire dogs and andirons are frequently used interchangeably but today fire dogs usually have heavier supports to hold logs while contemporary andirons are somewhat lighter in weight. There are a few andirons which survive from the old Roman days, and these terminate in a representation of a deer's head, complete with antlers. The very early English fire dogs were simple iron bars with vertical fronts a few feet in height. The tops were often of a scroll-like character. Quite elaborate designs were utilized during the Middle Ages. Later, dogs of brass, bronze, and silver were used on the Continent and in England and were sculptured by outstanding artists. Rococo designs came still later and were popular over a long period of time. Some of the very early elaborate andirons are now worth thousands of dollars a pair. These are out of the financial reach of the average collector, but many late nineteenth century andirons are available at prices from $20 or $25 to $75 a pair.

Fireplace fenders of cast or wrought iron or brass also are coming back into use. Some of the nineteenth-century fenders consisted of several relatively simple bars of metal, one atop the other, attached to end supports, while others were more artistically fashioned with scrolls and other designs on both front and sides. About 1900, the iron fenders could be purchased at about

A dog grate made early in this century for liners of the Cunard fleet. It is constructed in sixteenth-century style by the Carron Company, a British firm founded in 1759.

$5 to $15 each, depending upon size and design; and fairly simple but attractive brass fenders were roughly in the same price range. Now, their values are substantially more.

Fireplace grates and fronts, which could be used as closures when the fireplace was not in use, were often elaborately and beautifully made. The fronts were fashioned of bronze, nickel brass, copper, and iron. A late nine-teenth-century catalogue issued by the Chattanooga (Tennessee) Roofing and Foundry Company illustrates some magnificent fronts, many with embossed figures, including cherubs and angels and classic figures, and others with embossed scrolls and flowers. Grates and fronts were often made as combina-tion pieces and came in various sizes, one standard size being 20 inches wide. Except for their bulkiness, one could assemble a perfectly delightful collection of the decorated summer fronts, At the turn of the century many of these beautiful fronts could be bought for as little as $5 or $6 each.

Ventilating grates, which brought in fresh air from the outside and heated it, were widely used in the 1890's and early 1900's. These had a hot-air chamber which could throw out warmth into a considerable area of the room.

Firebacks were used at the back of the fireplace to throw heat out into a room. These iron shields, which also were often decorated, further served as a safeguard for the rear wall to keep it from crumbling under intense heat.

Of course, mantelpieces a century ago were show places. Their tops held an astonishing array of articles, including clocks, vases, urns, candlesticks, articles of colored glass, glass domes housing treasures inside, and so on. The more ornate mantelpieces were carved, gilded, and otherwise decorated. Per-haps the most famous of mantlepiece designers were the Adam brothers of the eighteenth century. Large mirrors were often placed just above the mantlepiece in the living room or the parlor. Paintings also were frequently hung there.

Mantles were made of cast iron, wood, marble, stone, and other materials. Some had carved pilasters. The large mantlepieces are generally considered too cumbersome to use in the smaller living rooms of today, but are adaptable to larger homes, and some choice ones have come in recent years from old homes and from hotels and hostelries which have been torn down and dis-mantled.

Late nineteenth-century coal vases from a catalogue of Belknap Hardware and Manufacturing Company, Louisville, Kentucky.

Summer fireplace fronts (top) and grates with fire tile backs and sides (below) from an old catalogue of the Chattanooga Roofing and Foundry Company, Chattanooga, Tennessee.

In farm homes of not too many years ago, the fireplace not only was used for heat but also for cooking purposes, and the major fireplace was, as often as not, to be found in the kitchen. This was equipped with a variety of accessories, such as an iron crane to which kettles could be attached, long-handled "slices" for removing bread from the fire, iron "S" hooks used for attaching kettles and pots to the crane, tin ovens for food, bellows for perking up the flames, and firescreens to shield one from the heat which sometimes was intense.

All of these accessories are in demand today for purposes of decorating the modern fireplace and hearth. Wrought-iron cranes may be picked up at prices from about $8 to $15, depending on size and condition. The pot hooks are worth $1 to $3.50. An iron slice is offered at $10, and a long fireplace fork at $4. These forks are ideal for toasting marshmallows, and some have a gadget which may be used to push the marshmallows from the tines without burning the fingers. An iron skewer a foot in length is advertised at $7.50.

Brass-bound bellows come in a wide price range, the value being governed by size, condition, and ornateness of decoration. One of brass and wood with an embossed scene on the brass is valued by its owner at $14. It is a large one, 17 inches long. Some are worth more, others less. An early tin oven with a swing hood is offered at $16.50 by an individual; it may cost more in shops. Don't forget the old iron pots. Attractive round ones of medium size with bail handles are worth from $5 to $25.

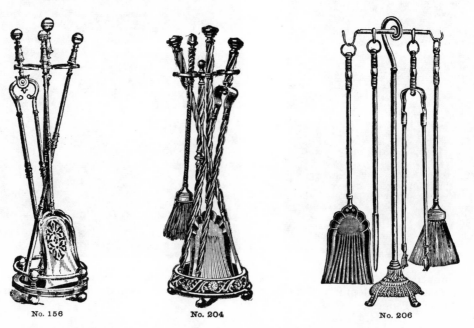

No. 156   No. 204   No. 206

Attractive fire tool sets advertised about 1900 by Belknap Hardware and Manufacturing Company.

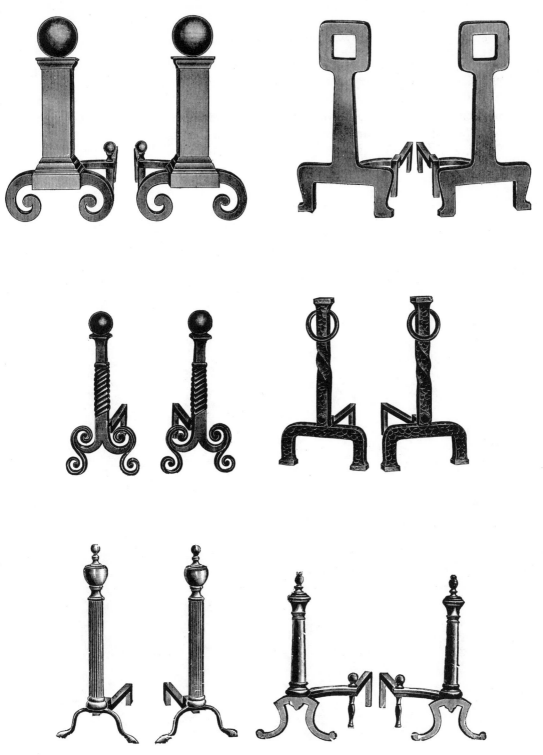

Cast iron and polished brass andirons offered about 1900 by Belknap Hardware and Manufacturing Company, Louisville, Kentucky.

A splendid reference for those interested in these old fireplace implements and accessories is J. Seymour Lindsay's *Iron and Brass Implements of the English and American House*. First published in 1927, this book has been supplemented and reissued with 480 illustrations by Alec Tiranti in London with distribution by Carl Jacobs, of Deep River, Connecticut, in the United States.

18.
Saving Grandpa's Whiskers: The Mustache Cup

In grandfather's day, almost every man with a mustache had his own mustache cup. This means a lot of cups because in grandfather's day, almost every man had a mustache; and those who didn't have a mustache at least had sideburns.

Mustaches today have lost favor. Those who do wear them keep them tiny and tidy except for a relatively few robust souls and our so-called "beatnicks" who simply don't give a hoot when the girls complain that they tickle. Back yonder, all the mustaches were robust — so robust that they would have been dredged alarmingly every time grandfather tried to drink a cup of coffee or a spot of tea if it hadn't been for the cups with the little shelves on one side. These were mustache cups, and the ledge-like devices built in near the top on one side kept the coffee (or other liquids) from soaking grandfather's whiskers. The liquid flowed through an opening in the shelf while the mustache rested on the shelf itself.

Mustache cups, like so many other household items in those days, were fairly inexpensive. Today, it's a different story, because collectors are latching on to them, and prices are rising. These cups have been collected for some time, but right now there is a sudden spurt of interest in them. You'll find it difficult to pick up one for less than $5, and the range goes on up to about $25 for prettily-decorated ones.

There are still a large number of mustache cups (and saucers) around, but they are beginning to grow scarcer because so many collectors have become addicted to them in the past year or two.

Pottery and porcelain factories once turned out these cups and their matching saucers by the thousands. Some were produced by factories whose

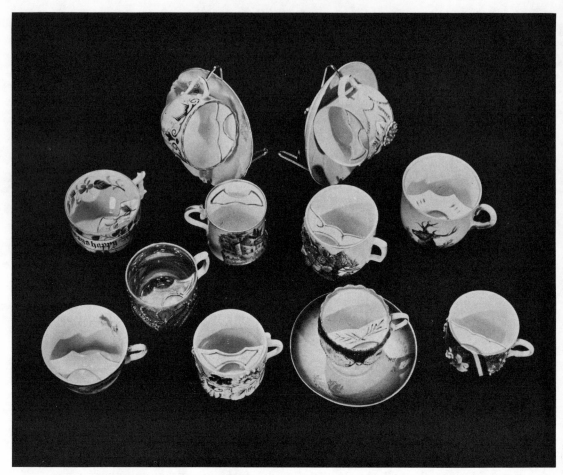

Mustache cups from the collection of George Bennett, Jackson, Tennessee. (Photo through the courtesy of Mr. Bennett.)

wares have since become famous and are eagerly sought. These will bring excellent prices. Many mustache cups have raised or embossed decorations. Others are lettered, sometimes with a single word, sometimes with an inscription. Decorations are frequently in color, and many of the cups are oversized, not at all like the dainty thin porcelain cups which the family used to break out when company came for dinner.

A great many of the heavier cups were produced during the latter part of the nineteenth century by factories in Germany and have "made in Germany" stamped on the bottom. But United States potteries and those in other countries also made them. For special occasions and families of wealth, there were quadruple silver-plated mustache cups and saucers. About 1900, many of these sold for prices ranging from $5 to $10. One early twentieth-century trade catalogue pictured an octagonal cup in "Colonial" pattern, gold line, which, together with its octagonal saucer, sold for $6. Many of the silver-plated cups also were embossed with flowers, geometric designs, and curley-cues of one type or another.

Now in view of their popularity in the nineteenth and early twentieth centuries, you'd expect *The Youth's Companion* to have offered them as premiums, wouldn't you? After all, that magazine offered as premiums just about anything you can name for which there was a widespread demand, as well as a lot of things which were not in demand. Well, that publication did offer them. In 1900, it tendered a set consisting of "1 Mustache Cup and Saucer for a gentleman and 1 Cup and Saucer for a lady" in exchange for one new subscription and 40 cents additional for postage and packing. They were made of porcelain with gold-decorated edges, gold linework on the embossed relief and a floral decoration in color. In 1891, the same periodical had offered a large mustache cup and saucer of Carlsbad china in exchange for one new subscriber plus 35 cents, or for $1 plus 35 cents postage when purchased outright.

Favorite inscriptions on mustache cups made as gifts were "Remember Me," "Think of Me," and "Papa." Scores of older homes have a mustache cup or two still around somewhere, but more and more of the attractive ones are gravitating to antique shops. The cheapest cup-and-saucer set we have seen advertised in a long time was one of Bavarian china listed not long ago for only $3.75. If the set was in good condition, it was below the current market price.

A green iridescent mustache cup and saucer, made in Germany, with gold trim and the inscription "Remember Me," is listed at $10. A similar one is offered for a dollar less. A set in moss rose with additional violet decor is tendered at $7.50. Nine dollars is asked for a swirled cup and matching saucer with the word "Papa" on the side of the cup.

One dealer advertised 30 mustache cups and saucers at $10 a set or the cups alone at $5 each. A majolica cup and saucer with fan and scroll decoration is a choice item at $20. A pink luster cup, minus saucer, dated 1902 is priced $12.50. Silver-plated mustache cup and saucer sets will sell from about $12.50 to $20. One private collector some time ago offered for sale a lot of 12 mustache cups and saucers, including one marked Haviland and one described as triple-plated, for $150.

Some of the cups bore historical scenes, and many of these are choice. One depicting the Clarke House and the Old Munroe Tavern at Lexington is priced $10.50. A pink lustre cup and saucer are offered at $25, but good lustre ware generally comes high.

QUADRUPLE AND TRIPLE SILVER PLATED
CUPS AND SAUCERS.

Prices Each.   **Cuts about One-half Size.**

No. 2211. $5 80
Ladies' Cup and Saucer, beaded border.
Quadruple plated, fluted, hand burnished, gold lined.

No. 2212. $5.00
Gents' Cup and Saucer, with mustache guard,
Satin, hand engraved, beaded border.
Gold lined Cup.   Quadruple plated.

No. 2213. $4.50
Gents' Cup and Saucer, with mustache guard.
Satin, hand engraved.
Gold lined Cup.   Quadruple plated.

No. 2214. $3.50
Ladies' Cup and Saucer, gold lined.
No. 2215. $3.75
Gents' Cup and Saucer, with mustache guard.
Quadruple plated, fine hand engraved, burnished rim.

No. 2216. $3.60
Ladies Cup and Saucer, gold lined.
No. 2217. $4.00
Gents' Cup and Saucer, with mustache guard.
Quadruple plated, satin, bright hand engraved, beaded border.

No. 2218. $3.25
Ladies' Cup and Saucer, gold lined.
No. 2219. $3.50
Gents' Cup and Saucer, with mustache guard.
Quadruple silver plated, rich satin, hand engraved.

Fancy-plated mustache cups and saucers of 1900, plus a couple of ladies' cups and saucers. These were offered by Otto Young & Company, Chicago, in its catalogue at the turn of this century.

Although the mustache shelf was normally a permanent part of the cup, Donaldson & Company, of Detroit, Michigan, offered in an advertisement in 1899 a detachable mustache guard which could be put on or taken off any size cup. It was a sterling piece with an ornamental design on the top and was advertised at only $1, or $1.15 with a monogram. Similar silver-plated detachable guards were offered for only 60 cents.

These matching cups and saucers are great fun to collect and are not too expensive for the average collector. A collection of decorated ones arranged along a shelf can be most attractive. You can collect the cups by themselves, of course, and then continue the search for saucers that will match. There's scarcely an antique shop in the country that doesn't have a batch of odd saucers around.

If you're interested and can't find these cups in your own bailiwick, pick up any of the collector periodicals and scan the For Sale advertisements. This will also provide you with an opportunity to compare prices.

You may also be interested in knowing that pressed glass goblets and beer mugs with mustache guards were produced during the late nineteenth century. These are far scarcer than mustache cups.

19.
Wars to End Wars:
Military Mementoes

Military mementoes have been collected for many years. Somehow the souvenirs of conflict, and this includes even the gruesome and awesome implements of destruction, have held a fascination for thousands.

The centennial observance of the Civil War sparked a renewed interest in relics relating to the battlefields and camps of the War between the States. But at the moment there is a special interest among a widening circle of collectors in military articles of all types utilized during or somehow pertaining to World Wars I and II. Purveyors specializing in this category of collectibles report a brisk trade in articles ranging from medals to bayonets, from mess jackets to helmets, from carbines to autograph letters by distinguished commanders.

The sensational development of atomic weapons, of course, has changed the complexion of war and has outmoded many of the weapons of the past, including those used in both World Wars. Scores of military items used earlier this century are no longer being produced and are, therefore, from the collectors' standpoint, desirable for that reason, among others. Nevertheless, many military items associated with the two World Wars of this century are still plentiful, so scarcity and abnormally high prices have not yet been reached to serve as a deterrent to those whose interest lies in this direction.

So many military items are collectible — and available — that specialization is advisable. For example, some persons collect military medals only; others limit their acquisitions to bayonets and knives; still others concentrate solely on rifles or pistols or insignia or canteens and so on. Incidentally, there is an American Society of Military Insignia Collectors, of which Ira L. Duncan, 744 Warfield Avenue, Oakland, California, 94610, is secretary. There also is the Society of Medalists, of which F. Kimmerle, 115 East 40th Street, New York, New York 10016, is secretary.

Because the area of military collectibles is actually so vast and could not possibly be covered adequately in a single chapter, the present discussion will be limited to World Wars I and II.

There are, of course, scores of collectors of firearms — all kinds of firearms, and this in itself is a specialized field. Some of these individuals are now focussing their major attention on firearms of the two World Wars. Unless one knows what he is doing, he can work himself into a financial hole by buying indiscriminately, so he had best bone up beforehand by consulting works in this field by some of the authorities. There are a good many books available. Two outstanding ones recently published are *Encyclopedia of Firearms,* edited by Harold L. Peterson, staff historian of the United States National Park Service (E. P. Dutton & Company, New York), and *The Gun Collector's Handbook of Values,* by Charles Edward Chapel (Coward-McCann, Inc., New York). Specialists in both the United States and Europe have contributed chapters to the former, and the latter is a revised edition of a book first published earlier. If neither of these is easily available, your public librarian undoubtedly can recommend other good ones.

As for medals, there are thousands available. United States Federal awards are not supposed to be sold, but some collectors swap them. Medal, ribbon, and special occasion Award values start at about $2 and range up to around $5 for those which are easily available. The scarcer ones are higher. The simplest way to ascertain current values is to write for one of the dealer lists or catalogues and check the prices. Dealers advertise in most of the collector periodicals. Here are a few typical values for decorations taken from some of these catalogues:

Missouri World War I Victory medal, $4; 1949 convention badge of the Veterans of Foreign Wars, $2.75; American Legion convention medals for various years, state and national, $2.75 each; Armed Forces Reserve miniature, $3.75; Richmond, Virginia, World War I medal, $4.75; French World War II medal, $4; World War I Croix de Guerre, lacking ribbon, $3.75; Nazi "Spanish Cross" bronze for service in the "Condor Legion" in Spain, $22.50; Nazi Iron Cross, $5; Austrian World War I Merit Cross, $4.

Military uniform insignia of all kinds are sought. These are worth from a dollar up with a few items at around 50 cents.

Uniforms bring widely varying prices. A United States Navy Warrant Officer's hat is offered at $5; a World War I United States Army uniform at $10; a United States Marine Corps jacket and trousers at $7.

Other collectible items relating to the two World Wars include all types of equipment, soldiers' diaries, printed books, buttons and patches, ratings,

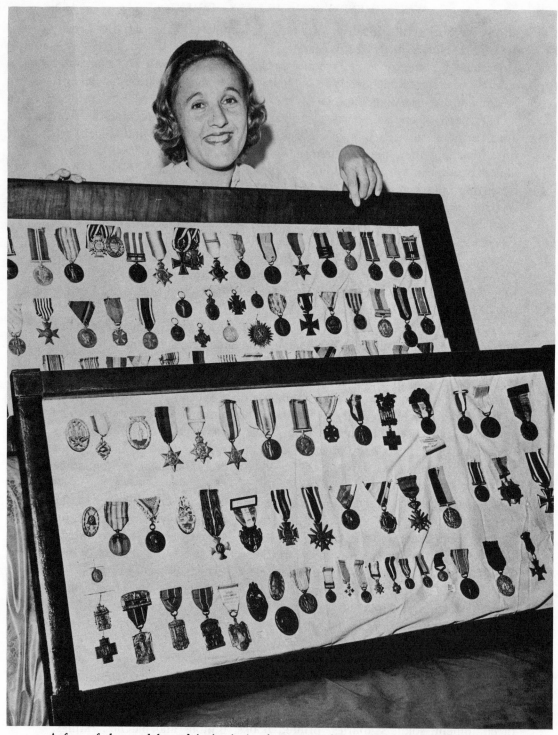

A few of the medals and insignia in the outstanding collection of David Vinar, 4621 Coliseum Street, Los Angeles, California. Mrs. Vinar is shown in the photograph. (Photo through the courtesy of Mr. Vinar.)

shells and shell fragments, swords, flags, flare guns, parachutes, bomb sights, ship's bells, compasses, etc., medical kits, gun holsters, all kinds of edged weapons, various items relating to aircraft, and trench shovels, to mention only a few.

Because this field is so vast, we list here the recently-advertised prices of a group of miscellaneous items pertaining to World Wars I and II, and it should be borne in mind that these will serve only as a rough guide to some values:

Nazi army officer's dagger and sheath (silvered), $19.50; Italian World War II military dagger and iron sheath, $24.50; World War II Italian officer's cap insignia, $9.50; United States doughboy's trench shovel from World War I with canvas cover and clip belts, $7.50; Nazi flags, $6.50 to $14.50; World War I United States Navy ship's bell, iron, 7 inches tall and 9 inches in diameter, with mounting arm, $27.50; World War I doughboy's uniform, winter wool, $39.50; German Wehrmacht World War II field compass with band, $12.50; German Wehrmacht hand grenades, $4.50; United States Cavalry World War I metal canteen with screw cover and case, $12.50.

Also, World War I heavy wool overcoat, $22.50; World War I custom-made artillery officer's uniform, $27.50; World War I signal flag outfit with carrying case, $14.50; Luftwaffe flight helmet, $9.50; Japanese World War II signal outfit, $22.50; World War I brass artillery shell case, $7.25; Luftwaffe World War II bomb sight, $94.50; World War I doughboy's trench helmet, steel, $9.50; World War II Japanese .30 calibre infantry rifle, $24.50; and World War I Naval officer's sword and scabbard, $15.

Many items in this field will be found today in establishments selling used merchandise, including stores of the so-called "Army and Navy" type, and individuals frequently offer them for sale. However, the more desirable and scarcer articles are gravitating largely to the specialized dealers. Most of these dealers are constantly in the market for good World War mementoes. Some of them advertise regularly in various collector periodicals, where their addresses may be found.

Although this brief discussion has been limited to the periods of World War I and II, military relics from wars throughout the ages are collected, and museums here and abroad house collections of ancient armor, weapons, and other reminders of man's inhumanity to man.

20.
Magazine Collecting
Can Pay Off

For the magazine collector, there is certainly no dearth of basic material, unless, of course, one is choosy and confines his collecting to the so-called "little magazines" and the experimental publications which flourished only for a brief time before passing to their reward — whatever it was.

Magazines designed for mass circulation began springing up in the United States late in the first quarter of the nineteenth century, though not too many of them were long-lived. But midway in the century magazine reading caught on in this country, and hardier periodicals (with more adequate financial backing) began their emergence from editors' minds. True, some of the old standbys have had their props knocked out from under them in the past few years, but others have sprung up to keep the ranks from thinning.

Early magazines are collected now for a variety of reasons. Some collectors seek them for their illustrations; some for their editorial content, and still others for their advertisements. Some individuals buy single copies; others want only long bound runs of issues.

Periodicals with colored fashion plates are avidly sought by a growing group of collectors. Outstanding in this category were *Godey's Lady's Book,* founded in 1830 by Louis A. Godey and co-edited from 1837 until 1887 by Sarah J. Hale, and *Peterson's Magazine,* founded in 1842 by Charles Jacobs Peterson as *Ladies National Magazine.* The name was changed six years later. *Peterson's* was edited by its founder, who, until 1853, had the assistance of Ann S. Stephens, the lady who wrote the first of the Beadle Dime Novels, *Malaeska,* and who at times utilized the pseudonym "Jonathan Slick."

Framed fashion prints from these magazines are now being sold at $2 to $10 each.

These were widely-read magazines as the twentieth century dawned.

Also eagerly sought are early magazines with paper doll cutouts and those with illustrations by such artists as Kate Greenaway, Palmer Cox (of "Brownies" fame), A. B. Frost, Frederic Remington, Charles Dana Gibson and Howard Pyle, to mention a few.

Issues of magazines which contain the first printing of literary work which later became famous are always of value, and some of these are of considerable worth. For example, a tabloid publication, *Contempo,* published in Chapel Hill, North Carolina, under the editorship of a couple of young intellectuals in 1932, devoted one issue almost exclusively to work written by William Faulkner. This particular issue consisted of only four pages, but it was offered for sale by a book dealer in 1963 for $12.50, later that year by another dealer for $15, and in 1965 it was advertised by a well-known bookseller for $75!

Of substantial value are certain magazines which first printed well-known works of such authors as Edgar Allan Poe, Ernest Hemingway, William Cullen Bryant, John Burroughs, Thomas Wolfe, Nathaniel Hawthorne, and other literary peers whose fame seems, for the moment at least, established.

A great many persons who collect such things as early automobiles or automobile parts and accessories, early sewing machines, and pioneer photographic equipment buy old magazines containing pictorial advertisements for these articles.

Magazines published during the Civil War and containing Civil War prints are of great appeal. These include *Leslie's Illustrated Monthly, Harper's, Century,* and others. These usually are of greater value when assembled as complete volumes (either six or 12 consecutive issues) than as individual miscellaneous issues.

A number of the experimental magazines which lasted for only a short time are sought because they first published the work of then-obscure authors who subsequently became famous.

Of interest, too, are issues of magazines which contained several illustrated pages of premiums offered in exchange for subscriptions. The reason is that so many of these premiums are now collected. Magazines containing premium lists are virtually always worth more than they sold for originally, and sometimes they are worth a good bit more.

Comic magazines are in a category by themselves and comprise a relatively new area of collectibles. The first issues of many of these so-called "comic books" are mounting rapidly in value. These include such titles as *Famous Funnies, Whiz,* and *Superman.* The nation's foremost collector of these magazines is reported to be Billy Joe White, a St. Louis, Missouri, fireman. A sixteen-year-old youngster, Bill Placzek, was the subject of a feature article written in 1965 by Judy Klemesrud for the *Chicago Daily News Service,* because he has a collection of comic magazines reportedly worth about $40,000. There is now an Academy of Comic Book Fans and Collectors, founded interestingly enough by Jerry Bails, a professor at Wayne State University.

Fads come and go, and the collecting of comic magazines may go — but right now the interest is strong and the prices are rising. Remember, too, that the great surge of interest in early "dime novels" is fairly recent and that prices in this field are continuing to rise.

Scholarly magazines are frequently sought by college and public libraries and institutions. Because most of these were not published for mass consumption, their early issues are scarcer than those of popular magazines. There are several firms which specialize in handling scholarly magazines and technical periodicals. Here are some typical values:

American Journal of the Medical Sciences, 63 volumes, bound, covering the years 1919 to 1950, $250; *American Ornithology,* six volumes bound in 12, covering the period 1901-1906, $20; *Architectural Record,* 12 bound volumes, 1892-1902, $100; *Journal of the American Osteopathic Association,* 43 volumes (1901-1944), 30 bound in cloth and the remainder in their original paper wrappers, scarce, $200; *Journal of the Military Service Institution of the United States,* 15 volumes, 1896-1903, bound in three-fourths morocco, $75; *Magazine of American History,* eight volumes, 1877-1882, bound in three-fourths leather, $60; *Scientific American,* two volumes bound in one, July, 1878-June, 1879, $25, and *Western Journal,* one volume bound, 1849-1850, $7.50.

The *National Geographic Magazine* is almost in a class by itself. Some special and scarce issues bring excellent prices. One dealer offers 43 bound volumes for 1907-1931 for $200. Routine issues, however, are not particularly valuable. Those published prior to 1905 are worth more than most later issues.

The average — if one may use that adjective in this connection — popular or literary magazine of fairly recent date is not of great value, but early periodicals of this type which are becoming scarce are worth substantially more than their original cost. Here are just a few of this type to indicate some values:

American Museum, Volume 1, 1787, $35; *Analectic Magazine,* single issues for 1818, $2.50 each; *Burton's Gentleman's Magazine & American Monthly Review,* March, 1839, $3; *Graham's Magazine,* single volumes for various dates, $5 each; *Ladies Companion,* two volumes, 1835-1836, $10; *Ladies' Repository,* one volume, 1845, $10; *Ladies' Wreath,* two volumes bound in one, undated, $7.50; *Lady's Monthly,* one volume, 1795, $8.50; *New World,* two issues, 1841 and 1842, $35; *New York Magazine,* one

Comic magazine collecting is spreading rapidly around the country today. Here are covers of some of the magazines which are eagerly sought. (Photos through the courtesy of Jerry G. Bails, Warren, Michigan.)

volume, 1792, with title page lacking, $20; *New York Mirror* (a weekly periodical), single volumes from 1828 to 1837, $10 to $15 per volume; *New Yorker* (the weekly published by Horace Greeley), one volume, 1839-1840, $35; *North American Miscellany,* Volume I, 1851, $10; *Sartain's Union Magazine of Literature and Art,* two volumes bound in one, 1849, $10; *Scribner's Monthly,* one volume, 1875, $5, and *Weekly Visitor,* Volume I, 1802-1803 (very scarce), $75.

Generally speaking, agricultural and religious magazines are of rather small value unless they are early and scarce. Here are a few of those which fetch better prices than the average:

American Evangelist, Volume I, Number 1, September, 1827, $5; American farmer, Volume I, 1840, $25; *Evangelical Magazine & Gospel Advocate,* one volume, 1830, $20; *Horticulturist, and Journal of Rural Art and Rural Taste,* six volumes, 1846-1851, $50; *Illustrated Christian Weekly,* Volume I, 1871, $15; *American Agriculturist,* Volumes I through III, 1843-1844, $15; and *Christian Magazine of the South,* one issue, October, 1849, $1.

Note that several of the magazines listed above are Volume 1. Subsequent volumes are worth less. Here are the values of Volume I of certain other magazines:

Analectic Magazine, 1813, $15; *Atlantic Monthly,* 1857-1858, $10; *Beadle's Monthly,* 1856 (lacking back page), $12.50; *Family Magazine,* Volume I plus Volumes II and III, 1843, $10; *Magazine of Western History,* 1884-1885, $10; *Massachusetts Magazine,* 1789, $35; *New Mirror,* 1843, $35; *New York Military Magazine,* 1841, $25; *Parthenon & Academian's Magazine,* 1832-1833, $12.50; *Quarterly Anti-Slavery Magazine,* Volume I and Volume II, 1836-1837, $20; *Stephens Illustrated New Monthly,* 1856, $12.50; *Two Worlds,* Volumes I and II, 1925-1927 (containing material by James Joyce and Ezra Pound), $25; and *The Union,* Volume I, lacking one issue, 1867 (rare), $50.

As mentioned earlier, the work of many authors who became famous later in their careers was first published in magazines, and, of course, other authors contributed to magazines between writing books. If you collect magazines, by all means examine the tables of contents. Did you know, for example, that work by or about Thomas Wolfe was published in such magazines as *The New Republic, Press Time, Scribner's, North American Review, The Modern Quarterly,* and others?

Such magazines lacking the work of noted authors are now selling at 50 cents to $3 per issue, depending largely upon scarcity or other factors. There are a number of back-issue magazine companies around the country which stock back issues of a great variety of periodicals. Some issue regular priced lists of what they have to offer. To be eligible for top price the magazine

LES MODES PARISIENNES PETERSON'S MAGAZINE AUGUST, 1891.

Magazines such as *Peterson's,* from which this fashion print is taken, are collected because of their color prints. Another favorite in this field is *Godey's Lady's Book.*

must be in excellent condition with no pages missing or torn and with covers intact.

The collector who really wants to know American periodicals and their background will read a monumental work on the subject by Frank Luther Mott. It is entitled *A History of American Magazines.* Published in four volumes between 1930 and 1957 by Harvard University Press, it was the Pulitzer Prize winner for American history. This work will probably be found in the reference departments of most of the larger public libraries. Another work of interest in this field is *Some Magazines and Magazine Makers,* by Dean John E. Drewry of the University of Georgia School of Journalism, published in 1924.

A list of book dealers who buy and sell certain magazines will be found in *The AB Bookman's Yearbook,* published by *Antiquarian Bookman.*

Some individuals earn tidy sums annually by clipping articles on specific subjects or by certain authors and offering them for sale to researchers or others who collect author ephemera or need background material.

Magazines are discarded by the hundreds of thousands each year by subscribers or persons who purchase them on the newsstands. Hundreds of attics are undoubted filled with early periodicals, and many of their owners probably would be happy to have a few cents each for them.

In addition to those magazines of value already listed, a few others you might want to keep your eyes out for are *De Bow's Review, The Dial, Southern Literary Messenger, American Magazine and Historical Chronicle, Overland Monthly, American Magazine of Wonders and Marvelous Chronicle, Others, Columbian Magazine,* and *National Intelligencer.* Look out also for early magazines which contain exceptionally good engravings or other types of fine illustrations.

The first significant magazine published in the American Colonies, incidentally, was entitled *American Magazine and Historical Chronicle,* mentioned in the paragraph above. It lasted from 1743 to 1746. Two other pioneer periodicals were *American Magazine, or a Monthly View of the Political State of the British Colonies,* edited by Andrew Bradford, and *Historical Chronicle, for All British Plantations in America,* edited by Benjamin Franklin. Both were printed in Philadelphia.

Bear in mind that the great bulk of magazine back issues now available are worth between 25 cents and $3 — but don't let that deter you from searching for the more valuable ones.

21.
"Go West, Young Man" –
and Save Those Western Books

Drama galore was associated with the opening of the American West. In the popular imagination today the West conjures up images of wagon trains with their dauntless pioneers, the frantic, greedy and almost unbelievably fantastic rush for gold, and — perhaps above all — Indians.

One need only turn on his television set at almost any hour of day or night to confirm the grasp which the West has upon the imagination of present-day writers of television scripts and motion picture scenarios. There are as many Dead-Eye Dicks moving in and out of our televisions plays right now as there were moving about in the dime novels of 60 or 70 years ago; and fully as many Indians are still biting the dust.

The opening of the West did constitute a saga of momentous proportions, and first-hand accounts of its various aspects compose a dramatic part of the history of the United States. It is not so much fiction dealing with the opening of the West which is in demand today as it is factual accounts, and particularly published accounts written by eye-witnesses to the drama and by those who were part and parcel of it.

Robert G. Hayman, well-known dealer in antiquarian books, of Route 1, Carey, Ohio, says that enthusiasm for collecting books and pamphlets relating to the early history of the American West is undoubtedly at a high peak and that he thinks it will remain at a high level for years to come.

How can it be otherwise, he told the writer, in a field so broad and filled with so many fascinating topics — wild Indians, cattle drives, covered wagons, outlaws, fur trappers and mountain men? Can collectors be blamed for becoming excited?

It so happens, he added, that this unprecedented demand for good items in the field of Western Americana seems to have occurred at the same time that the

157

supply of many of the classic items in the field has been diminishing. This has resulted in the high-priced rarities which receive so much publicity today. That the true rarities will continue to go even higher seems inevitable because the demand is great and the supply is almost non-existent. Then, too, the situation is affected by the fact that much of the buying today is done by libraries, and once a book has gone to an institution, there is little likelihood of its appearing on the market again.

Speaking as a dealer, it is not unusual for us to receive a dozen or more orders for a single good item listed in our catalogue. Of course, we have only one copy and another one may not turn up for several years. Given such a situation, it is pretty obvious what will happen to prices. You may remember, for example, the Jacob Parkhurst narrative which we had in our Catalogue not long ago priced at $750. Here was a little pamphlet printed about 125 years ago, and our copy was only the second known copy. Such an item, (if it has good historical content, and this one does) is worth about whatever a dealer wants to ask and can get for it. In view of the number of orders we had for this one, if another copy (by some miracle) should turn up, we would price it even higher.

Remember, however, that it is the original editions and not the reprints which, in most cases, are of value. And don't jump to the conclusion that every early book about the West is valuable: The book must be important as well as early. If there is no demand for it, its value is little. If it is not in good condition with all pages intact, its value will be lessened sharply.

One might say that books about the West and books about Indians almost go hand-in-hand. Certainly, good books and important books about both are in high demand today, and the values of the rare ones in good condition are rising.

There are several book dealers around the country who specialize in books about the West and about Indians. Many of these are listed in the reference directory of antiquarian and specialist booksellers which is a regular feature of the annual *Antiquarian Bookman Bookman's Yearbook,* edited by Sol M. Malkin and Mary Ann O'Brien Malkin and published by *Antiquarian Bookman: The Specialist Book Trade Weekly* in Newark, New Jersey. These dealers know the values of the specialized books in which they deal; and if you wish to sell to them, you will have to price the books you have to offer at a level which will enable them to make a reasonable profit.

There are hundreds of books about Indians and the West which are valued at $25 and up. Some of them are worth hundreds of dollars. Perhaps the best way to ascertain values is to study the lists and catalogues issued by the specialist booksellers who deal in out-of-print material. Most of the lists and catalogues of the veteran dealers are thoughtfully prepared. Many contain a wealth of helpful information, and some are elaborately and beautifully printed. The majority of the lists and catalogues are offered without charge, but it isn't quite cricket to ask a dealer for copies of his catalogues unless you are seriously interested in buying books of the type he offers.

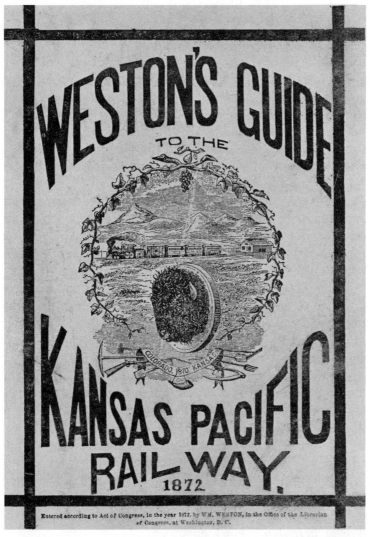

This is the front wrapper of an exceedingly rare item of Western Americana. Published in Kansas City, Missouri, in 1872, it is valued at about $500. (Illustration through the courtesy of Robert G. Hayman, Antiquarian Books, R.F.D. 1, Carey, Ohio.)

Let's check through some recent catalogues and take a look at the values of some of the more desirable books in the categories with which we are now concerned. A 40-volume set of Edward S. Curtis's *North American Indians,* published in an edition limited to 500 sets and financed by J. Pierpont Morgan, is offered by a dealer at the "bargain" price of $2,000, bound in buckram, or $2,750 with 20 volumes of text bound in morocco and the 20 accompanying volumes of prints bound in buckram. The complete set in buckram had been offered earlier for $2,500.

In 1803, those intrepid explorers Meriwether Lewis and William Clark led a pioneering expedition from Missouri to Oregon. From this emerged a fascinating and important account entitled, to use its short title, *History of the Expedition Under the Command of Captains Lewis and Clark,* published in two volumes in Philadelphia in 1814. This edition in the original boards in which it was issued is valued now at $1,000 or more. This was edited by Nicholas Biddle and Paul Allen. Subsequent editions by other editors are also of value.

A book ascribed by Joseph Sabin (author of a monumental study entitled *Bibliotheca Americana: A Dictionary of Books Relating to America, from its Discovery to the Present Time*) to Benjamin Franklin, *A Narrative of the Late Massacres in Lancaster County, Of a Number of Indians, Friends of the Province, By Persons Unknown,* is offered at $560. It was printed in 1764. Although Sabin is listed as the author of the study mentioned parenthetically above, he actually edited the first 14 volumes in the 29-volume set which composes his dictionary, and additional volumes were edited by Wilberforce Eames and Robert W. G. Vail. And before getting away from the name Sabin, it might be well to mention that Edwin L. Sabin, an Illinois novelist, wrote several well-known books relating to the West which are in the collectible category. These include, among others, *On the Plains with Custer* (1913); *Buffalo Bill and the Overland Trail* (1914); *Kit Carson Days* (1914); *Sam Houston in Texas* (1916); *On the Overland Stage* (1918); and *Wild Men of the Wild West* (1929). The values of most of these, in good condition, will range from around $7.50 to $15.

A well-known book by the artist Frederic Remington titled *Pony Tracks* (1895) is valued at about $85. Remington's *Crooked Trails* (1898) is valued at $65 to $75; his *Drawings* (1897) is worth now about $150, and his *The Way of an Indian* (1906), about $90.

Another widely-known Western artist, Charles M. Russell, illustrated a book by W. T. Hamilton entitled *My 60 Years on the Plains, Trapping, Trading and Indian Fighting.* It was published in 1905 and is valued at around $30.

Early Western atlases are highly desirable. *Atlas of the City and County of San Francisco,* compiled by Wm. P. Humphreys & Company and published in 1876, is advertised at $150.

An interesting and informative book which is a bibliography of books and pamphlets on Western outlaws and gunmen, *Six-Guns and Saddle Leather,* by Ramon F. Adams, is priced at about $20. It was first published in 1954 by the University of Oklahoma Press and will prove quite useful to the

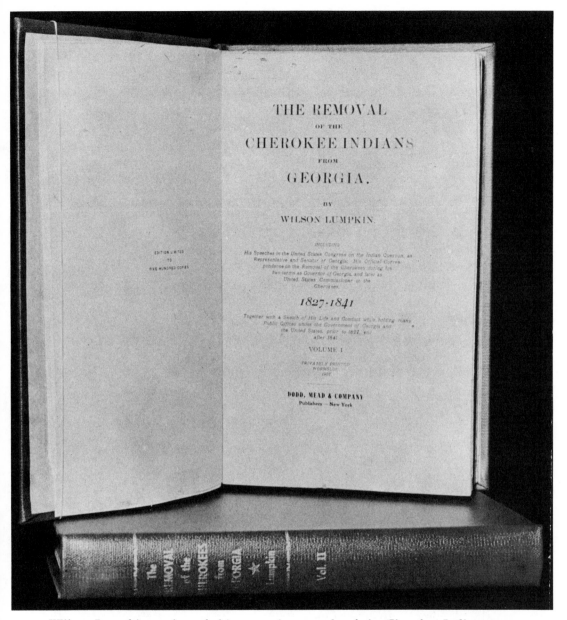

Wilson Lumpkin, author of this two-volume study of the Cherokee Indians, was an Indian agent and later Governor of Georgia. (From the author's collection.)

collector of Western material. Adams also is the author of other good books pertaining to the West, among them *Cowboy Lingo* (1936 — and worth about $15); *The Rampaging Herd*: *A Bibliography of Books and Pamphlets on Men and Events in the Cattle Industry* (1960); and *Western Words: A Dictionary of the Range, Cow, Camp and Trail* (1944).

Here are a few more books in the Indians and West category which are currently valued at $25 or more, listed by authors:

Alter, Cecil . *James Bridger: Trapper, Frontiersman, Scout, and Guide* (1925, limited to 1,000 copies). $47.50.

Clarke, Asa Bement. *Travels in New Mexico and California . . .* (1852). $250.

Cook, David J. *Hands Up; Or, Twenty Years of Detective Life in the Mountains and on the Plain* (1882). $150.

Tucker, Dr. J. C. *To the Golden Goal and Other Sketches* (1895), limited to 50 copies). $50.

Cox, James. *Historical and Biographical Record of the Cattle Industry and the Cattlemen of Texas and Adjacent Territory* (1895). $375. (This title was reprinted in a two-volume edition in 1959 and was limited to 500 sets. The reprint is now valued at $100 a set.)

Daly, James. *For Love and Bears* (1886). $100.

Bolton, Herbert Eugene. *Fray Juan Crespi. Missionary Explorer on the Pacific Coast* (1927). $35.

Brooks, Sarah Merriam. *Across the Isthmus to California in '52* (1894). $30.

Damon, Samuel C. *A Trip from the Sandwich Islands to Lower Oregon, and Upper California; or, Thirty Leaves Selected from Our "Log-Book"* (1849). $250. (This was originally published in instalments in a magazine and was bound with other issues of the same magazine and issued with the special title page given above.)

Hayden, F. V. *Geological and Geographical Atlas of Colorado and Portions of Adjacent Territory* (1881). $75.

Harlan, Jacob Wright. *California '46 to '88* (1888). $25.

Dodge, Grenville M. *Biographical Sketch of James Bridger, Mountaineer, Trapper, and Guide* (1905). $35.

Dyer, Mrs. D. B. *Fort Reno; Or, Picturesque Cheyenne and Arrapohoe Army Life before the Opening of Oklahoma* (1896). $37.50.

Hittell, John S. *History of the City of San Francisco and Incidentally, the State of California* (1895). $7.50.

Hall, James. *Legends of the West* (1832). $37.50.

Hunter, John Dunn. *Manners and Customs of Several Indian Tribes Located West of the Mississippi . . .* (1834). $37.50.

Keleher, William A. *The Fabulous Frontier . . .* (1945), limited to 500 copies). $37.50.

Manly, William L. *Death Valley in '49* (1894). $25.

McKenney, Thomas L. & Hall, James. *History of the Indian Tribes . . .* Three volumes (1865), bound in tooled morocco). $125.

Kroeber, A. L. *Handbook of the Indians of California* (1925). $25.

Mokler, Alfred James. *History of Natrona County, Wyoming, 1888-1922* (1923). $45.

Mooso, Josiah. *The Life and Travels of Josiah Mooso . . .* (1888). $75.

Parker, Amos A. *Trip to the West and Texas . . .* (1835). $45.

Pike, Albert. *Prose Sketches and Poems, Written in the Western Country* (1834). $275.

Ridings, Sam P. *The Chisholm Trail* (1936, limited edition). $30.

Swasey, William F. *The Early Days and Men of California* (1891). $50.

Thwaites, Reuben Gold. *Early Western Travels,* Thirty-two volumes (1907). $650.

Tuttle, J. H. *Wam-dus-ky* (1893), limited to 35 copies). $200.

Tyler, Daniel. *A Concise History of the Mormon Battalion . . .* (1881). $75.

Wilkes, Charles. *Western America, Including California & Oregon . . .* (1849, a rebound copy). $50.

Wren, Thomas. *A History of the State of Nevada; Its Resources and People* (1904). $50.

There are hundreds of other books relating to the West and to Indians which are worth $5 and up, and there are a great many more than those listed above worth $25 or more.

For a fine detailed study of Western books and pamphlets, one should consult Henry R. Wagner's *The Plains and the Rockies*: *A Bibliography of Original Narratives of Travel and Adventure, 1800-1865,* originally published in 1920 and subsequently revised and reissued with the revisions by C. L. Camp.

Mr. Wagner himself had a most extensive collection of Western Americana, which was acquired in 1922 by Henry E. Huntington, founder of the Henry E. Huntington Library and Art Gallery in San Marino, California. This library is world famous.

Many of the early accounts of the West were published in paper wrappers. If these wrappers are lacking or are badly damaged or if the book has been rebound without the wrappers, the value will be diminished. But many of them, even with wrapper missing or torn, are still of considerable value.

22.
Carder's Steuben Glass

Although a wide variety of art glass of the late nineteenth and the early twentieth century is currently in great demand, the glass created by the late Frederick Carder has captured the attention of serious glass collectors after a period of dormancy. So great is the demand for Carder's fine creations that items which a few years ago sold for less than $5 are now commanding prices which range into hundreds of dollars. Age seems to bear no relationship to price, but rarity and desirability are the dominating reasons for the price escalation of late.

History will record Frederick Carder as one of the truly great craftsmen of glassmaking of modern times. A member of a family of Staffordshire potters, he came to the United States in 1903, at the age of thirty-nine, and with the Willard Reeds incorporated his own business, the Steuben Glass Works, in Corning, New York. The business's major stockholder was T. G. Hawkes, Sr., already renowned for his cut glass, who probably exercised a greater influence on Carder's decision to launch his own enterprise than any other individual.

Carder operated the Steuben Glass Works and created masterpiece after masterpiece in glass. In 1918 his company became a subsidiary of the Corning Glass Works with Carder remaining as its head. He died in December, 1963 — a century and three months after his birth.

Carder began creating colored and parti-colored glass in the early days of the Steuben Glass Works, and he continued as a brilliant creative artist until he retired from active participation in the Corning Glass Company in 1934. Not only did he create new vistas in glass, but he also succeeded in reproducing virtually all, if indeed not all, of the fine glass techniques of many decades past, including the lost Roman art of Cire Perdue and Diatreta, in his laboratory.

At the age of seventeen, Carder had become a designer for the glassmaking firm of Stevens and Williams. His first activity at the Steuben Works was to supply crystal blanks for T. G. Hawke's company, while, at the same time, creating and producing wares under the Steuben name. Among the first of his own creations — and a type of glass eagerly sought today by collectors — was one he called Verre de Soie, a pearly, iridescent and slightly metallicized glass. This, together with Carder's Aurene, is generally accepted as among the finest iridescent glasswares made in this country. But Carder also created a great variety of colored crystal glass, producing more than 58 colors in several thousand shapes, according to Eric E. Ericson, fine arts dealer, historian, glass scholar and a friend of Mr. Carder, in his helpful and profusely-illustrated book, *A Guide to Colored Steuben Glass* 1903-1933 (Lithographic Press, Loveland, Colorado). This has gone through several printings and is available from the publisher, Stagecoach Stop, 1901 Kipling Street, Denver, Colorado, at $3.95.

Carder also mastered the Intarsia technique — a difficult and exacting procedure by which a solid glass object with a design trapped inside was produced. Only a small quantity of this type of glassware was made. This glass is personally signed "Fred'k Carder."

Another distinguished Carder creation was calcite, a cream-colored material of calcium derivation which, Mr. Ericson says, proved to be "an ideal material to apply the Aurene iridization to." Many thousands of light shades were made of this material, but numerous other shapes and designs also were produced, including some lined with gold or blue Aurene. The articles included vases, plates, bowls, compotes, salt dips, and a number of others. Still other calcite articles were lined with colored crystal, including blue, green, brown, gold-ruby, amethyst, and black. The great majority of calcite items were not signed. Carder's Ivrene was an outgrowth of calcite. Also a calcium derivative, it was a purer white and was used primarily for table articles, Mr. Ericson says.

We will not go into detail here about the technical details involved in the various types of glass Frederick Carder created for Steuben Glass Works. Those who want to pursue the subject at length will find helpful, in addition to Mr. Ericson's book already mentioned, a second volume by him, *A Guide to Colored Steuben Glass,* 1903-1933, *Book Two* (Lithographic Press, Printers; published by Stagecoach Stop at the same address mentioned earlier in this chapter, $5), which contains more than 200 additional photographs of half-page size and whose text covers some two dozen Steuben types heretofore reported unknown, including a panorama of the highly-prized Aurene and variants.

Also available and of major interest will be a profusely-illustrated booklet with photographs in color and an accompanying two-record, long-playing

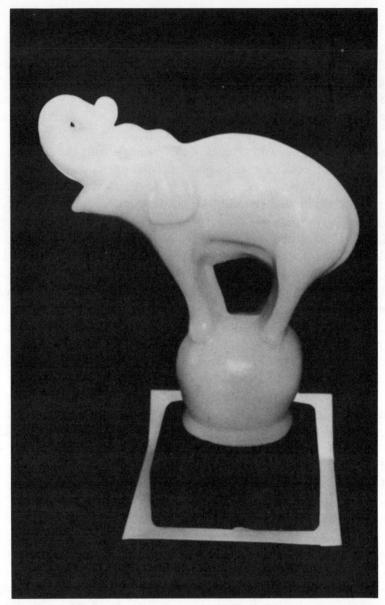

Ivory elephant and black glass base made at the Steuben Glass Works. (Photo through the courtesy of Eric E. Ericson, Denver, Colorado.)

album under the titles, *Creations by Carder of Steuben* and *Conversations with Carder on Steuben*. These were done by Cecily and Gerry Philpot, long-time collectors and scholars of art glass, and the booklet and album are available from The Fieldstone Porch, 46 Oakdale Road, Glenbrook, Connecticut, at $14.50 for both. The records present actual conversations with Mr. Carder about his glass shortly before his death.

Carder's Cire Perdue technique fish and crystal flower holder is shown here. This was a Steuben production item of the early 1930's. (Photo through the courtesy of Eric E. Ericson, Denver, Colorado.)

On the records, Mr. Philpot and Robert Rockwell questioned Mr. Carder regarding 20 different types of Steuben glass and on other subjects. The booklet pictures the types of glass discussed on the records, and the pictures are keyed to follow the records. There are 127 color photos, including 42 from Mr. Carder's own collection.

Among the Carder creations discussed by Mr. and Mrs. Philpot and Mr. Ericson, in addition to those already mentioned, are Jades, Rosaline, Ivory, and Alabaster, which are translucent glasses; acid cut back, which was called Cameo Etched in one of the Steuben catalogues and the production of which started in the 1920's; Cluthra, which was made both in shaded ware and solid color ware; Cintra, another type of exotic appearance; Bubbly Glass, and others.

Another book of interest in the field of Steuben glass is *Carder's Steuben Glass Index and Price Guide,* by John F. Hotchkiss (available direct from the author at 89 Sagamore Drive, Rochester 17, New York, at $5). This volume also reproduces, in reduced size, the 1932 Steuben catalogue with code price letters added to indicate the current price range. The price guide is applicable to the books mentioned earlier in this chapter by Mr. Ericson and Mr. and Mrs. Philpot and to still another book, *Iridescent Glass,* by Larry Freeman (available from American Life Foundation, Watkins Glen, New York, $6). Mr. Hotchkiss's reproduction of the fine Steuben catalogue will help collectors in learning classifications and establishing some guides to values. It also contains 40 small full-color photographs of various types of Carder's wares.

To find a piece of glass signed by Carder or bearing this impressed Steuben mark or the original label is a joy for the collector, because so many pieces are unmarked.

Fine pieces of Steuben glass have rarely been inexpensive of late, but a check of a number of dealers now handling this glass shows that values, and especially those of earlier productions, are continuing to soar. Against the advice of some of the experts in the Steuben glass field, many of whom don't like price guides, we present below some rough values to certain types of Steuben glass. These were values prevailing when this book went to press. Because of the mounting interest in Carder's glass, it is entirely possible, if indeed not probable, that a good many of these may have climbed by the time you read this chapter. Nevertheless, these prices may have some interest for the future collector at least — and particularly if he can still obtain the pieces at somewhere near the prices cited! At best, the prices serve as a very rough guide, because collectors consider price secondary to the desirability of the item itself — and desirability depends upon such factors as rarity, form, adornment, variation from the normal, and so on.

AURENE — Gold vase, about 11 inches tall, $125; blue bowl, 5 inches in diameter, $120; petticoat perfume bottle, $185; centerpiece bowl, 10 inches in diameter, $150; paperweight vase, 11¾ inches tall, $500; blue vase, 8 inches tall, $150.

CLUTHRA — shaded lamp base, 10½ inches tall, $375; green vase, 16 inches tall, $425; Spanish green vase, 10½ inches tall, $400.

This display of Frederick Carder's Steuben Glass is a part of the magnificent collection assembled by Bob Rockwell. This collection is now on display at The Rockwell Gallery in Corning, New York. (Photo through the courtesy of Mr. Rockwell.)

JADES — blue 6-inch-tall vase, $110; green flower pot, 5½ inches tall, alabaster threads around top edge, signed by Carder, $195; alabaster-footed dessert bowl, $65; champagne glass with alabaster stem and foot, $65; cup, saucer and matching plate, light green, alabaster handle on cup, $95; urn vase, 10 inches tall, M-shaped alabaster handle, $150; vase, 8 inches tall, green over alabaster, $350.

ROSALINE — green vase, 6 inches tall, $350; shrimp bowl with alabaster foot and small Rosaline glass inset for crushed ice, signed by Carder, $500; vase, rosaline over alabaster, 12 inches tall, $775; small bud vases, $225 a pair.

VERRE DE SOIE — vase, 11½ inches tall with 7-inch swirled rib bowl with rainbow iridescence, $150; perfume bottle, 7½ inches all, footed, teardrop-shaped stopper, $75; melon-ribbed cologne bottle with gold ruby stopper, $55.

MISCELLANEOUS CRYSTAL — bowl, amethyst edge, 11¾ inches in diameter, signed Steuben, $55; diamond quilted vase, green, 2½-inch white threading at top, 6½ inches tall, signed Steuben, $60; elephant paper weight, $110; champagne goblet, $55; light-green goblet, bell-shaped bowl and green disc foot, amber twist stem, $65; decorated bulbous vase, 5 inches tall, $55.

Those values are sufficient to give some indication of the wide variance in prices for different items, a great many of which originally sold for less than $5 each! They probably also will be sufficient to bring some yells of protest from some dealers!

One of the top if indeed not the top collector of Carder's Steuben glass is Robert Rockwell, director of Rockwell's Department Store in Corning, New York, and for some years a personal friend of Mr. Carder prior to the latter's death. His collection numbers well over 1,000 items and is housed in a gallery at his department store.

But other collectors are now striving to reach Mr. Rockwell's record. It will be a costly climb, but for most of them the magnificence of the glass itself will prove reward enough.

When you're visiting antique shops, especially the newer ones, it could pay you to examine the interesting pieces of glass carefully. No dealer knows everything there is to know about every type of glass, and it's conceivable that you could find a sleeper in the form of a piece of signed Steuben. A friend of ours who visited a group of small establishments in the South recently found a number of them that way. Unless you're an expert yourself, however, it would pay you to acquire your unmarked Steuben from an experienced dealer.

23.
Mary Gregory Glass:
It's Easy to Be Fooled

The transparent colored glassware with white or colored enamel designs painted on its exterior, which is known today as Mary Gregory glass, was named after a skilled employee of the decorating department of the Boston & Sandwich Glass Company, of Cape Cod, Massachusetts — the company whose guiding hand for years was that of Deming Jarves.

Today, Mary Gregory glass, though inferior to many of the fine art glassware and imitative of English Cameo glass, is attracting an increasing following. The prices are rising because the demand currently is running ahead of the available supply.

Mary A. Gregory, who did her work at the factory at Cape Cod during the 1870's and 1880's, specialized in painting or enameling children on the colored glassware. A spinster, she was reported to have had a great love for children, and boys and girls, charmingly depicted, featured many of the everyday scenes with which she decorated the wares entrusted to her. Often one will find a young boy on one side of a glass article decorated by her and a young girl on the other.

Mary Gregory decorated vases, water and lemonade sets, powder jars, drug and barber bottles, match holders, and similar items, most frequently in colored glass enameled in white. She was certainly not an immaculate artist but she was a skilled and understanding decorator, and the wistful charm of her work cannot be denied.

Mary Gregory herself was not the only decorator at the Boston & Sand- wich works who did this type of decoration; but whether the work was done by her or by some of her co-workers, it is now all lumped together under the name of Mary Gregory glass.

An example of Mary Gregory's work is this black kerosene lamp which shows purple when held to a strong light. (From the collection of Dr. Robert R. Bigelow, Oak Ridge, Tennessee.)

Unfortunately, a great deal of somewhat similar glass not produced at the Cape Cod works at all and much of it inferior to the Boston & Sandwich production also is being lumped with Mary Gregory, and this has created a dilemma for collectors. Because so much genuine Mary Gregory glass has been acquired by museums, the best way to familiarize yourself with the genuine article is to visit museums which have it on display or to talk with informed dealers who can tell the genuine from the imitation.

Very little has been written about this glass, but Robert W. Miller, erstwhile freelance writer turned antique buff, has done a good bit of research on the subject and has come up with an article entitled *Mary Gregory* (copyright 1965 by Robert W. Miller, 113 Albany Road, Oak Ridge, Tennessee), which will be most helpful to the collector and which is available directly from the author at $1 a copy. It is not an exhaustive study but it does emphasize certain distinguishing features by which Mary Gregory glass may be differentiated from enamel painted glassware turned out in Bohemia and elsewhere on the European Continent as well as in England.

Mr. Miller points out, for example, that much of the enamel on the Bohemian glass was over-tinted in various colors and that it "appears to be much more intricately designed and much more colorful" than the wares produced by the Boston & Sandwich Company but that, on the other hand, the white enameled figures of children done in Bohemia lacked the "certain skillful finesse" that Mary Gregory glass exhibits.

Mr. Miller also says that most experienced collectors do not include tinted pieces as an integral part of their Mary Gregory collections. Among the popular colors which Mary Gregory decorated, he adds, were ruby, amber, blue, emerald green, cranberry-red, and clear.

Reproductions of Mary Gregory glass are done in modern designs, writes Mr. Miller, and "the faces, hands and feet are crudely applied."

The author cites a number of other things to look for when searching for Mary Gregory, and the collector of this category of glassware will benefit by his sound advice.

Mr. Miller told the author that a collector in Texas had sent him a piece of "Mary Gregory" for appraisal. The Texan said he had paid $700 for it; but examination proved it to be a Bohemian glass of doubtful age and with a faked pontil! But it had taken the Tennessee expert a decade and a half of research to be able to tell the difference so easily.

Although genuine Mary Gregory glass is relatively scarce, glass of its type, made elsewhere and by others, is fairly abundant, so that approximate prices are difficult to judge by advertisements. Both collectors and some dealers are undoubtedly advertising as genuine Mary Gregory glass, wares made elsewhere — not by design or with malicious intent but because they don't know

Mary Gregory ruby-colored vase, inverted thumb print pattern, with white enameled figure. (From the collection of Robert W. Miller, Oak Ridge, Tennessee.)

the difference. During recent months advertisements for this type of glass have appeared with increasing frequency in collector periodicals. Here are some of the advertised prices for Mary Gregory:

Footed hinged box about 4¾ inches in diameter and 3¾ inches tall with a white enameled little girl with a bird on its lid, dark amethyst, $75; pair of footed wines in cranberry with a boy on one and a girl on the other, $65; tankard-type water pitcher, cobalt blue, 13½ inches tall, with applied handle and enameled painting of a woman watering flowers, $75; green bulbous water pitcher, 10 inches tall and 7 inches in diameter, enameled with a deer, $50; green tumblers, each with two enameled little boys and two girls, $27 a pair; cranberry bud case, 5 inches tall, enameled girl, $23.50; pair of sapphire blue vases with applied clear fan trim on each side from base to top, white enameled girl in foliage on one and boy on the other, $65.

Also, cranberry powder box, 4¾ inches in diameter, young lady enameled on cover, $27; pair of royal blue vases, decorated with boy and girl surrounded by hop blossoms, fruit and leaves, $120; tall hinged black box with enameled boy in white, plus foliage, $62; blue decanter, 12½ inches tall, with boy playing pipe, swan and foliage in white (small nick), $57; blue water pitcher, with Jack-and-the-Beanstalk decor in white enamel, about 12 inches tall, $49.50; and bud vase in amethyst, goblet-type base, figure of boy in white enamel, $36.50.

There also have been a good many advertisements recently for "Mary Gregory" glass with children with "tinted faces." Just remember Mr. Miller's warning in this respect. There is no reason for you not to collect glassware similar to Mary Gregory — but try not to buy it under the mistaken impression that it is actually Mary Gregory glass made at the Boston & Sandwich factory.

Incidentally, if you find a black piece of Mary Gregory-type glass, it will always show a deep purple color when held to the light if it is Sandwich glass. This glass is often referred to as black milk glass or as purple amethyst. Many of the black Mary Gregory pieces are gilded with a thin silver overlay. When a piece of this is found bearing a petite figure of a boy or girl, the owner has a real treasure. Pieces of this black glass showing a deep purple are as collectible as other types of Sandwich glass.

The best sources of Mary Gregory glass today are experienced dealers and experienced collectors who may wish to sell part or all of their collection. Buy it with the understanding or specific agreement that you may return it for a full refund should it turn out to be something else.

24.
Satin Glass May Be for You

Values of so many types of art glass produced in the late nineteenth century and in the first quarter of the current one are so high that they are inaccessible for the collector whose purse is not bulging. But Satin glass, produced in greater abundance than certain other types of art wares, is still available in numerous objects at prices which are not yet prohibitive for the average collector.

Satin art glass is an opaque ware with a satin-soft surface and, usually, a white lining. Mother-of-Pearl ware, sometimes called Pearlware and sometimes Pearl Satin ware, is cased or plated glass with a white lining and a surface finish that differs from plain Satin glass. The writer has recently seen Camphor glass on a few dealers' shelves labelled Satin glass. There is a great difference. Camphor glass is a cloudy glass whose surface somewhat resembles the appearance of gum camphor which has undergone a refining process. Inexperienced dealers who confuse it with Satin glass because the surface of both is soft to the touch do both themselves and their customers a disservice.

Several companies produced Satin are glass during the final two decades of the nineteenth century. Most of this ware had an opal white lining and its original glossy finish was transformed into a satiny finish as a result of a bath in hydrofluoric acid, a colorless, corrosive, volatile liquid.

Satin glass was made in the form of vases and rose bowls, baskets of various kinds, fruit and berry bowls, cracker jars, lamps, relish and pickle jars, and tableware. It was produced in painted and enameled colors and shadings, such as blue shading to white, pink shading to white, and yellow shading to white as well as solid white or cream, and, more rarely, purple, green, or brown.

In his authoritative book, *Nineteenth Century Glass: Its Genesis and Development* (Thomas Nelson & Sons, New York), Albert Christian Revi

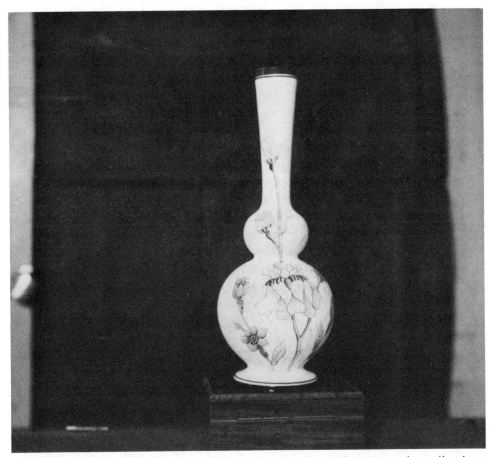

White decorated Satin Glass vase, signed Kimball-Durand. (From the collection of Ruth Pritchard, Denver, Colorado. Photo taken by author.)

reports that the first patented process describing the ware now known as Pearl Satin Ware was probably taken out by Benjamin Richardson, of England, in 1857. Mr. Revi describes several different methods used in the late nineteenth century to produce this type of ware. The Richardson method was to blow a gather of glass into a mold which carried the pattern in projected form with the result that it had surface indentations. The molten indented piece was then dipped in fluid metal which coated the outside surface; and the ornamentation was provided by the air traps between the indented molding and the glass skin.

Another method, Mr. Revi writes, "was to place the molded piece in a cup of glass blown to receive it, the worker then blowing and shaping the mass further into the article desired. The several layers in each case could be the same color or of different colors, according to the desired effect the worker wished to obtain."

Still another method, he reports, was to place either colored or crystal glass tubes in a heated mold and then to blow an inflated gather of glass into the mold.

"The hollow tubes adhered to the surface of the blow and the parison was rolled on the marver to firmly embed the tubes of glass into the surface of the mass. By deftly twisting the blow while it was still in a plastic state, the worker produced articles of glass with pearly swirled stripes on the outer surface."

Nineteenth Century Glass also describes, as follows, one type that did not depend for its pearly effects upon air traps.

"The outer skin of the triple-cased article was a thick layer of crystal glass that had been pattern-molded forming heavy bosses thereon. When acidized, these bosses presented a lovely pearly effect."

Pearl Satin ware, or Mother-of-Pearl Satin glass, was made in the United States by the Mt. Washington Glass Company, of New Bedford, Massachusetts, the Phoenix Glass Company, of Beaver County, Pennsylvania, Hobbs, Brockunier & Company, of Wheeling, West Virginia, and the New England Glass Company, of East Cambridge, Massachusetts, and in England by Thomas Webb & Sons, Ltd., of Stourbridge, and Stevens and Williams Company, of Brierley Hill in the Staffordshire district.

Mt. Washington Glass Company produced a type of Pearl Satin ware utilizing as its ornamentation a pattern of air traps within the glass walls based on a patent issued in 1881 to William B. Dean and Alphonse Peltier, of Brooklyn, New York. This method, Mr. Revi says, was almost indentical with that outlined by Benjamin Richardson earlier. Mt. Washington licensed Thomas Webb & Sons to produce this ware in 1886.

A very similar Pearl Satin ware was made by Mt. Washington under a patent issued in 1886 to Frederick S. Shirley, who also outlined two additional processes. These are reported by Mr. Revi as follows: "First, Shirley suggested that the pattern-molded body be covered with a sensitive metal, one that could be developed into different colors and shades of color by reheating certain portions of the articles in a furnace. Second, he suggested a lusterless surface for the articles, produced with the aid of an acid-roughing dip or by sandblasting, and all calculated to give the finished product a 'velvet-like finish or an appearance resembling the skin of a peach,' and a pearl-like appearance.' "

The Phoenix Glass Company's Joseph Webb in 1866 also patented a process for producing this type of ware, following closely the process originally outlined by Richardson. Two years later, according to Mr. Revi's research, he

Large blue mother-of-pearl Satin Glass jardiniere with a brass base and gold and enamel decoration. (From the collection of Albert Christian Revi, Dallas, Texas.)

patented another process making use of two molds. One of these molds was used to pattern the inner wall and the other was designed for use after the outer shell had been applied. "The finished product displayed a crisscrossed network of pearly indented lines in the surface of the article."

A process for producing this type of ware with cameo relief designs was patented by Thomas Webb & Sons in 1889. Some writers have contended that English-made Satin glass is heavier than the American Satin. Mr. Revi told this writer that he disagrees strongly with this statement. Many pieces of the Webb glass are extremely attractive and are eagerly sought by collectors.

A great deal of the Satin and Pearl Satin wares of the late nineteenth cen-turn emanated from glass houses in Bohemia and France, as Mr. Revi points out in his book. The Bohemian type was much cheaper than the finer types and hurt the sale of the latter.

We have quoted Mr. Revi at some length because numerous types of Satin glass are now being reproduced, and the collector should be able to distinguish them from the original wares. This type of ware now being turned out in Italy and Mexico is inferior in both quality and workmanship to the finer glass produced earlier in the United States and England.

However, the Japanese recently have been making a high-quality Satin glass. Its color is generally good, and the shapes are in the American taste rather than the Oriental. This glass is marked with paper labels which are easy to remove and which therefore places temptation in the way of the unscrupulous dealer. With the labels removed and a few marks of wear simulated, the Japanese product is not too difficult to confuse with the earlier articles.

If you are planning to collect Satin and Pearl Satin wares, you should buy from established dealers who know the field; otherwise, you may find yourself with reproductions for which you may have paid an excessive price.

Values of both Satin glass and Mother-of-Pearl Satin (often abbreviated "M.O.P.") depend upon the article itself, its quality, size, date of manufacture, its maker, scarcity, and condition. Most antique shops which handle glass usually have some Satin glass available, but often prices of almost identical articles will vary from shop to shop.

Veteran collectors, of course, seek the Mother-of-Pearl wares rather than the ordinary Satin glass, but beginning collectors will find much of the plain Satin interesting, fairly reasonably priced, and decoratively useful in the home.

Here are some recently-advertised prices of plain Satin glass:

Green ewer, 10 inches tall, with enameled white and mauve flowers, yellow leaves and an applied ribbon edge on a ruffled, turned-down top, $40; pale pink cracker jar with apple blossoms and buds and a silverplated rim, cover and handle, $25; dish with ruffled rim and camphor edging, 8½ inches in diameter, $45; blue rose bowl, $40; green ewer vase, 8½ inches tall, twisted Camphor glass handle, ruffled top, decorated with butterfly and flowers, $37; rose bowl, blue, 3½ inches tall and 4 inches in diameter, crimped top, $22; rose bowl, 4 inches tall, with tan and lavender floral decor, $35; red bowl with ruffled edge, 10½ inches in diameter, $30; butter dish, puffy red dome cover on silver-plated base and finial on cover, $28.50.

The more desirable Mother-of-Pearl comes higher. Here are some current values, which also will vary from area to area:

Mt. Washington Satin ovoid bowl, deep rose-colored airtraps on a Persian blue background, 4½ inches high, $275; pair of vases with swirled design,

A fine shaded rose-to-pink mother-of-pearl Satin Glass vase with a thorny frosted crystal handle. (From the collection of Albert Christian Revi, Dallas, Texas.)

dark apricot at top shading to light apricot at bottom, 11 inches tall and 5½ inches at base, $180; matching pair of lemon yellow herringbone vases, 6½ inches tall, crimped rims, $135; deep pink diamond quilted vase, 7 inches tall, $48; herringbone blue vase, 6½ inches tall, bulbous base, $85; pink diamond quilted vase, 12 inches tall, $135; tumbler, deep butterscotch shading to white, 3¾ inches tall and 2¾ inches in diameter, $48; basket, 5½ inches tall, herringbone pattern, rose color and camphor glass handle, $52.50; ruffled edge bowl, blue, 14 inches in diameter, enameling in bronze, gold, white and yellow, $85; and diamond quilted miniature pitcher, 6 inches tall, melon ribbed body, $75.

Some really fine pieces come a good bit higher. For example, a rainbow Mother-of-Pearl diamond quilted vase, 5½ inches tall, with a bell-shaped body and collared smooth rim top, white and yellow vertical stripes halfway down, in mint condition and old, is tendered at $575. A signed Webb M.O.P. light blue, square-topped pitcher whose sides taper up from 3 inches in diameter at the flat base to 6½ inches at the shoulder, and with an applied reeded camphor handle, is valued at $300.

The finest Satin glass items are beautiful to behold and lovely to touch. Although a great deal of Satin glass is advertised and sold by mail order, many collectors insist on buying it in person so they will know exactly what they are getting.

If you're entering the glass-collecting area for the first time, you'll find that it will pay you to examine and handle as much glass as you can before buying pieces. Talk with knowledgeable dealers about the glass and obtain as much background as you can.

Articles about Satin glass are published from time to time in the various collector publications. These are frequently illustrated, but unless the illustrations are in color, it is difficult to visualize the true beauty of the glass.

A good many books on glass in addition to the one by Mr. Revi also discuss Satin glass. Some of these are listed in the selected bibliography of this book.

Whenever you visit a museum featuring glass, take sufficient time to really examine the glass rather than merely to give it a glance. Note the shape, colors, and decorations and try to compare the quality of various items.

Once you have acquired a few pieces of fine glass, handle and clean them with the greatest care. Treat them as tenderly as you would a child. You may damage something you can replace only at great expense.

25.

Heisey Glass – Now's the Time to Buy It

Some of the best crystal glass produced in the United States during the closing years of the nineteenth and for some years into the twentieth century was made by A. H. Heisey & Company in Newark, Ohio. Fine examples of the earlier Heisey glass are now beginning to be collected, and "sleepers" are available for those who keep their eyes open. Some glass experts predict that the company's fine early productions may increase in value as more persons become aware of their existence, availability and attractiveness.

The company made wares for table and home decoration in pressed, blown, cut, etched, rock crystal and carved glass. It is of interest, too, that the mahogany models of the New England "Pineapple" pattern pressed glass originally made at the Sandwich factory at about the time of the Civil War were later acquired by A. H. Heisey & Company.

The Heisey firm was opened in 1895 by Major A. H. Heisey, a veteran of the Civil War who had fought valiantly with the Union forces at the Battle of Gettysburg and elsewhere and was wounded during Pickett's famous charge. As a result of his wounds, he was relieved from active duty.

According to Carl Gustkey, president of the Imperial Glass Corporation, Bellaire, Ohio, a friend of the Heisey family, Major Heisey went on a tour of New England with an Army friend while recuperating from his wounds. He visited a number of the glass houses in New England and developed an interest in glass and its production. Subsequently, he obtained employment as a salesman for King & Company, which for several years either owned outright or had an interest in several factories and also, later, sold the production of a number of other factories. After a while, Major Heisey was promoted to sales manager for King.

Heisey glass figures. These are reproductions made in the original Heisey molds which have been acquired by the Imperial Glass Corporation.

When the Duncan and Miller interests joined forces and built a factory in Washington, Pennsylvania, later known as the Duncan-Miller Glass Company, Major Heisey joined this firm. Subsequently, he married a member of the Duncan family.

Major Heisey then obtained financial backing in Newark, Ohio, and founded there his own company. His works emphasized quality production, and some of its most desirable creations were animals in crystal glass. These included a delightful array of such things as horses, ponies, and birds. Creation of these animals and birds undoubtedly stemmed from the fact that all of the members of the Heisey family were avid sportsmen, according to Mr. Gustkey. Among the most popular animals were a group of charmingly-fashioned horses, whimsical elephants and donkeys, and muscular buffaloes.

One of Heisey's most elaborate patterns was known as "Fandango" (also called Diamond Swag). This was produced in a full set of tableware in clear glass and is becoming highly collectible now.

Glass in Heisey's Greek Key pattern dating from about 1911 also is eagerly sought and its values are increasing. The original Greek Key molds have long since been destroyed. Other popular Heisey patterns included Provincial, Williamsburg Waverly, Colonial, Diamond Lace, Touraine, and Continental.

According to T. Clarence Heisey, who now lives in Newark, Ohio, the company's last president prior to its dissolution and a son of the founder, the Pineapple mahogany model referred to earlier in this chapter, together with a good bit of almost priceless old glass, were destroyed in a train wreck as they were en route between Seattle and Portland for use in a retail store display.

Carl Gustkey informs us that Major Heisey was the first person in the American glass industry to devise a magnetic separator — a belt conveyor onto which mixed batch is poured as it is moved into batch carts or otherwise into the actual melting units. By the utilization of such a device, all "tramp" metals are disposed of onto a magnetized belt and are scraped off of the bottom of the conveyor after the batch tiself has fallen off the device. This was undoubtedly the secret to the water-clear crystal glass produced by the Heisey company. Major Heisey failed to patent his invention, which has now become an essential facility for all except a very few American glass factories.

In 1958, the Imperial Glass Company, of Bellaire, bought the available A. H. Heisey & Company molds, tools, patents, trademarks, and virtually all of its production equipment. This was an especially interesting development in view of the fact that some years ago Imperial and Heisey were involved in litigation arising out of an alleged patent infringement.

Imperial today is producing the Heisey patterns in the latter's original molds, and many other molds are being held in reserve for possible use later. Imperial, founded more than 60 years ago, also is reissuing today's line of

Heisey glass in the Provincial pattern as reproduced in the original molds by the Imperial Glass Corporation.

iridescent glass items made in the original Imperial molds in which its "Carnival glass" was produced half a century ago. The company is identifying these items, as well as some of its reproductions, with the use of its registered "IG" hallmark impressed in the glass. This will help enable collectors to distinguish the reissues and reproductions from the originals. Glass collectors have long urged other glass companies making reissues and reproductions to use an impressed mark to identify them so they will not be mistaken for the original issues. Imperial registered its "IG" mark in 1950 and it is being used on the base of stemmed or footed wares and on the inside or bottom of bowls.

Even though some unscrupulous individuals and some shady dealers are reported to have ground off the hallmark and to have described the resulting scar as a punty mark, the Imperial action has been hailed by collectors and students of glass as a forward step in the industry. Some outstanding collectors have been seeking Congressional enactment of a law which will make mandatory the use of an impressed mark on all reissues and reproductions of old glass.

Imperial's reissues and reproductions are extremely attractive and are being widely bought by those who cannot afford to pay the high prices so much fine original glass brings today. Because glass is coming into even wider use in home decoration, there is no reason why individuals should not purchase reproductions as long as they know what they are buying and the glass is not misrepresented as original.

Heisey glass in the Waverly pattern, showing a crumpet bowl and matching candleholders as reproduced in the old Heisey molds by the Imperial Glass Corporation.

It is interesting to note, also, that Imperial has acquired all of the old Cambridge and Central Glass Company molds. The company has issued a booklet, *The Story of Hand-Made Glass*, which is available at 25 cents a copy and will prove of help and interest to those who wish to know about the processes and steps involved in the making of hand-made glass.

Early original Heisey glass is being offered now at widely varying prices. A Greek Key milk pitcher, 7 inches tall and 5 inches in diameter, is advertised at $10, and a Greek Key punch bowl and stand for $55. A covered butter dish, fluted, diamond pattern, is priced at $12, and a Flute pattern set consisting of a large dresser tray, powder jar, hair receiver and cologne bottle, dated 1901, at $21.

Here are some other advertised prices for various old Heisey items: water set with eight tumblers and pitcher, $34; powder jar with silver-plated lid, dated 1905, $10; pair of heavy candlesticks, 7½ inches tall, $12.50; cobalt blue vase, 9¼ inches tall, $12.50; diamond pattern knife rest, etched with leaf sprays, $6.75; cruet in clear glass with original stopper, $8.50; 7-inch-tall clear glass water pitcher, $8.50; pair of jelly compotes in ribbed pattern, $6.50; Comet pattern tumbler, $12.50; fluted tumbler, $19.50; punch bowl and base and 11 cups in Roman Key pattern, $80. and Colonial pattern footed ice cream dish with knob stem, $2.50.

It is not at all unlikely that the lower-priced items above will soon be selling at higher prices.

The Licking County Historical Society's Museum in Newark, Ohio, has an excellent collection of old Heisey ware.

Throughout the life of Heisey, incidentally, its greatest production was in lime crystal for pressed ware and lead crystal for blown stemware and some other blown items.

26.
They Smell Good Too:
Perfume Bottles

Bottle collecting rages over the land. Amateur collectors are buying bitters bottles, patent medicine bottles, food bottles, apothecary and barber bottles, whiskey bottles, beer bottles, wine bottles, cosmetics bottles, and, in fact, just about every type of bottle on which they can lay hands.

Even commonplace bottles produced less than a quarter of a century ago are changing hands for cash, and one suspects that some values are becoming increasingly distorted in the midst of a sort of mass hysteria over bottles. Many types of bottles are still so abundant that the field is wide open to anyone interested. In addition, several recent books have helped popularize the collecting of them. Anyone who plans to collect bottles should consult one or more of these books to learn something about the field before plunging into it.

Of special interest to the beginning collector (as well as to many advanced collectors) will be Albert Christian Revi's *American Pressed Glass & Figure Bottles* (Thomas Nelson and Sons, New York, $15) and Grace Kendrick's *The Antique Bottle Collector* (available from the author, 485 West Fourth Street, Fallon, Nevada 89406, at $2 a copy). Other good references include John C. Tibbitt's *1200 Bottles Priced* (available from the Little Glass Shack, 3161 — 56th Street, Sacramento, California, $4), and *Bottle and Glass Handbook*, edited by Don Maust (available from E. G. Warman Publishing Company, Uniontown, Pennsylvania, $4). In addition, Dr. Larry Freeman has written a rather long and interesting book on the subject, *Grand Old American Bottles* (Century House, Watkins Glen, New York, $20), for which a value guide is now available.

Collecting numerous types of bottles at random can be confusing and not nearly as much fun as specializing in one, or possibly two types. In the recent

The perfume bottles shown here are only a part of those in the collection of the Municipal Lightner Exposition, St. Augustine, Florida, which made this photograph available.

mad rush some of the most attractive bottles available seem to have been temporary forgotten. These are perfume and cologne, or scent bottles. A good many of them may be picked up now at relatively low prices — a situation which may not prevail too much longer. They are chiefly small so that a sizeable collection may be housed in a small area, and, for the most part, they are delightful to behold. Some of them, stoppered for years, still have a trace of their original aroma.

Thousands of highly collectible perfume bottles were made by some of this country's famous glass houses, including, among numerous others, the Whithall-Tatum works at Millville, New Jersey, Hagerty Brothers Glass Works, of Brooklyn, New York, and the Boston and Sandwich Glass Company, of Sandwich, Massachusetts. Thousands of others were imported from the famous factories at Nailsea, Baccarat, Clichy, Bristol, Venice, Bohemia, and elsewhere. They were made in pressed glass, engraved glass, cut glass; they were pressed, blown, blown molded, and pattern molded. In fact, every technique of glass making was used in their production, and the variety of their shapes and designs is astonishing. There are beautiful ones of overlay glass or with such embellishments as sulphide cameos or millefiori work. Some were produced with stoppers in miniature vase forms. Late nineteenth- and early twentieth-century purveyors frequently offered sets consisting of one or two cologne bottles plus a puff box, also of glass and often with a metal top. You are not likely to find too many of these sets intact today.

A great many of the cologne and perfume bottles of earlier years which are still available were brought into this country from France. Some American glass manufacturers also copied the French designs in profusion around the middle of the ninetenth century.

Collectible perfume and scent bottles are by no means limited to those made prior to 1850; thousands of intriguing ones were sold from that date to 1915 or thereabouts. A good many of them were originally sold empty to apothecary shops and druggists who filled them with essences of their own concoction; but others were purchased by manufacturers of essences and were sold under their brand names. Still others were offered empty to individual consumers at retail.

One distributing house offered "perfumizers" — bottles of cut glass with fine spray attachments — at prices ranging from $2.75 to $5.50 each in 1907. Some of these were beauties. Another establishment offered somewhat more ornate cut glass atomizers with burnished trimmings in a price range of $5.15 to $8 each. In 1887, the widely-circulated *The Youth's Companion* advertised a handsome set consisting of a plush odor case of wood lined with a bronze shade of satin and two white glass scent bottles with ground stoppers in exchange for one new subscription, 15 cents additional and 25 cents for postage and packing.

Perfumes and colognes were packaged under fancy brand names in the nineteenth century, just as they are today but without as much sensuous appeal. In 1895, Marshall Field & Company advertised Nirvana perfumes in 12 "exquisite odors" from Germany. The Crown Perfumery in London had a wide sale for its Crab-Apple Blossoms perfume and its Crown Lavender Salts in the United States. Another widely-known perfumery, Lundborg's, featured scents with such names as Goya Lily, Edenia, Nada Rose, Alpine Violet, and Swiss Lilac in 1894.

It would provide a challenge to collect, say, perfume and cologne bottles in colored glass, or in pattern glass, or in frosted glass. Also, a great many

Atomizers, "perfumizers," scent bottles, and perfume bottles such as these were favorites among the ladies in the late nineteenth century.

cologne bottles were produced in cut glass, and cut glass of various types appears to be coming back into popularity again. Fine cut glass of the type turned out by American glass works between 1880 and about 1905 will not be made again because of the high cost involved. Although the more inexpensive cut glass colognes usually are characterized by rather shallow cutting, better ones were deeply cut and in some quite intricate designs.

Scent bottles were designed to be toted around in milady's purse, so they were smaller generally than most perfume bottles and a good bit smaller than cologne bottles. These, as well as many perfume bottles, were produced in numerous novel shapes, including those of daisies, tulips, and other flowers, cannons, human figures, boots, lamp posts, and candlesticks, to mention a few of them.

Of special interest, also, are gemel bottles. These are twin or double bottles, and they were free blown in many forms during the first half of last century. Although a good many of the gemel bottles were in the category of novelties, some were designed to hold perfumes and other liquids. The two bottles were blown separately, then fused together and their necks customarily pointed in opposite directions, though not always. Some of the gemels were ornamented with various types of applied decoration and some were made in colored glass. The earlier gemel bottles are not inexpensive, but they will make a fascinating addition to any collection of perfume and scent bottles.

Some of the finer old perfume bottles are bringing fairly high prices today, but many others are selling at a fraction of what they may be fetching a decade or two hence unless fickle collectors suddenly abandon their wild scramble for bottles of all types and switch their allegiance to another area of collecting.

A 3-inch-all silver deposit bottle with a clear ball stopper was noted recently with a For Sale price of only $1.50. A perfume bottle of milk-white glass, 4½ inches high and an inch in diameter, is priced at $3, and at a time when the values of all milk-white glass are rising. A heart-shaped scent bottle with a stopper and dropper and described as "at least 100 years old" was advertised not long ago at $6. A Bohemian cologne bottle 9 inches tall was offered for $10.

Here are some other typical recently-advertised prices of perfume and scent bottles, although it should be borne in mind that these prices may be higher in the top-quality shops: satin glass bottle in eight-sided ivory-type holder, 4½ inches tall, $4.75; fan-shaped bottle in melon rib pattern with an opalescent marble-type stopper, of French manufacture, $3.75; French "Guerlain" bottle 2½ inches tall, $2.25; Sandwich glass bottle with diamond point and plain band, with stopper, $12.50; amethyst glass with Mary Gregory-type decoration, $30; Baccarat bottle 4¾ inches tall with matching stopper, $5.50;

and an elaborate cranberry bottle etched in gold and with a blue etched stopper, $25.

It seems downright unreasonable for folk to undertake a harum-scarum search for patent medicine bottles of recent vintage, canning jars and all manner of food bottles which have been in the discard only a few years when there are still so many truly attractive perfume and scent bottles to be had at low prices. But, after all, many collectors are unreasonable persons, and it's a good thing they are, because many of them are now salvaging items which, while they may be sneered at by thousands of fastidious individuals, are nevertheless going to be "hot" collectors' goods in a few years. And when that time arrives, they not only will find themselves loaded with items which have appreciated greatly in value but they can enjoy what must be an immense satisfaction in saying, "I told you so."

27.
For the "Iniquitous" Weed:
Tobacco Jars

Snuff bottles and boxes have beeen a focal point of interest for collectors for many years. Some collections of them represent tremendous financial investments. But a kindred field now open for the adventurous is that of nineteenth- and early twentieth-century tobacco jars of glass, pottery, porcelain, bisque, and metals.

An examination of old trade catalogues discloses that tobacco jars were produced in an almost astonishing variety of designs and shapes. Many were decorated whimsically, amusingly, or otherwise intriguingly. Jars which could be included in an interesting collection will now range in price roughly from 4 or 5 dollars to $60 or $70.

A collection of colored glass tobacco jars arranged in front of a window where the sunlight could filter through them will add to the decorative appeal of the living room, the kitchen, or the den. For the executive, a display of tobacco jars in the reception room will provide the visitor with an interesting way of whiling away the time before he gets in to see the boss.

Both pressed and cut glass tobacco jars were turned out late in the 1900's. Some were even produced in Carnival glass, and one of this type in the Purple Grape pattern was advertised for sale not long ago for the very neat sum of $75. The jars were originally sold by tobacconists, jewelry stores, hardware establishments, drug companies, and general stores. Most of the jars were designed to hold either cigars or tobacco, and, of course, they also could be used for cigarettes. In addition to the jars, most of which were cylindrical or square in shape, there also were tobacco boxes, many of the desirable ones being footed.

Some of the jars and boxes had ornaments attached or painted on or were

This array of tobacco jars in the shape of heads and figures is a part of the collections of the Municipal Lightner Exposition in St. Augustine, Florida, by whose courtesy it is reproduced.

embossed. Among the higher-priced ones were those made of sterling silver or silverplate. One in quadruple silverplate with scrolls embossed on its sides and the representation of a daschund standing in the center of the top was priced at $12.50 in a 1900 wholesaler's catalogue. It had a capacity of 50 cigars. This one had four paw feet.

A 1907 wholesaler's catalogue depicted a smoking set consisting of an oval jar for cigars with a lighted cigar pictured on the side, an oval match container, an ash tray, and a round tray to hold the set, all silverplated, for $8. The same catalogue showed a cigarette jar of cut glass with a silverplated lid for $3.35, and a glass jar with a satin finish and silverplated lid for $7. A beautiful porcelain tobacco jar with a hollow cover to house a sponge and with both cover and jar adorned with handpainted roses was advertised at $11.40.

A 1916 wholesale jeweler's catalogue listed a brass tobacco jar with a top with finial for only $2.50. An Egyptian scarabaeus was depicted on the top and the side of the jar. The same company offered a set in solid brass consisting of a tray with cigar holder, match holder, and ash tray for $2. These pieces also were decorated with the sacred beetles of the Egyptians.

A perfectly charming porcelain cigar jar with a depiction of an old fisherman smoking a pipe and with a silverplated lid is shown in a 1908 catalogue, priced at $7.50. It is 7½ inches tall and was advertised as a cigar or a cracker jar.

Many tobacco jars were used also as humidifiers, such as the one described above with the hollow top for a sponge. Earlier tobacco jars (they have been made for more than 200 years) were made of such metals as pewter and tin, but the more desirable of these are rather costly today, and there are enough interesting nineteenth- and early twentieth-century jars and boxes available to enable anyone to form an extensive and appealing collection without the necessity of investing a fortune. Besides, most jars designed specifically for cigars date from the mid-nineteenth century when the cigar and cigarette smoking habit began to take hold in earnest in the United States.

For the well-heeled collector, there are some beautifully-engraved cut glass tobacco jars, complete with cut glass stoppers, produced early in this century. Some of these are truly gems for either the cut glass or the cigar jar collector. Even in those days they were not cheap. One wholesaler advertised these in 1906 at prices from $18.35 to $33.35 each.

If one wishes to use these jars as well as to display them, they can be pressed into service to hold such objects as buttons, and such toilet items as lipsticks, and, of course, candy.

Because collecting the late nineteenth- and early twentieth-century jars and boxes is just coming into prominence, values have not as yet been well established. You can buy a beautiful Capodimonte jar for $65, or one of pressed glass with an imitation ruby set in the lid for $5.50. There are all kinds in between. Here are some of them, based on recent advertisements and prices asked by dealers:

Pressed glass with ivory lid, $10; Royal Bayreuth china "Pixie" jar, $18; majolica jar in the shape of a skeleton wearing a colored cap, $15; majolica, with water lily motif on three sides and a depiction of a man in full dress smoking a cigarette on the fourth side, with a pipe finial on the cover, $16.50; Deldare jar, $35; pottery jar with its body representing a bunch of cigars tied with a yellow ribbon and bow and its cover in the form of a bust of a bearded, red-haired man holding a cigar and drinking from a stein, $18.50; Doulton

Cigar and tobacco jars of glass, quadruple plate, and pottery from late nineteenth and beginning of twentieth century.

Lambeth jar with a verse of "America" and a flag showing 45 stars, $15; green and white bisque jar with a sphinx and dove finial, $15.

Also, majolica-type with the face of a "man in the moon" smoking a cigar on the cover, $11; bisque head of sailor with blue tassel on cap (made in France), $9.50; majolica-type with head of young girl and a rose-colored turban, $12.50; etched glass jar with copper top, $6.75; majolica-type, frog wearing green coat and cap with a pink tassel, $14; handled pottery jar with brown basket-weave base and a pipe resting on the side of its moss-green lid, $12; and majolica-type in pastel colors with a monkey with a pipe, cap and tassel, $12.

Other items in the same age group related to tobacco jars and worth collecting include plug tobacco cutters, cigar cutters, cigar and cigarette cases, and pocket match boxes.

The tobacco cutters of the counter type used by stores for cutting plug tobacco for customers in the days when having a "chaw" was a wide-spread custom can be used as doorstops. One favorite type made more than half a century ago was designated as the "Image." It bore astride the long cutter handle the figure of an imp wearing a pointed cap and thumbing its nose — an indelicate gesture today and certainly far more indelicate 50 years ago! Other popular tobacco cutters bore such names as "Little Giant," "Peter Schuyler," and "Improved Champion." A good many others were simply labeled with the names of their manufacturers or the processors of tobacco.

These cutters had long handles which were used to raise and lower the steel cutting blades housed in an iron frame. Handles were made in various shapes, and some were ornamented nicely. Around the turn of this century, store counter tobacco cutters were offered wholesale at prices from about $10 to $21 a dozen. Today, except for a few of the more elaborately-decorated ones, they will bring anywhere from 3 to 4 dollars to around $20 each.

In a similar category are cigar cutters used to trim the ends of cigars. Some of these, too, were elaborately fashioned. One, measuring 13 inches in height and made in conjunction with a Waterbury clock, was advertised about a year ago for $15. It was marked "King Alfred Cigars." An ornate cigar cutter in brass is offered for $8, a small scissors-type, gold-plated one for $4.50, and a cutter and lighter combined, dated 1889, for $9.50. Early in this century, the scissors-type cutters were wholesaling at prices ranging from $3.50 to $11 a dozen.

An excellent collection can be made of silver and silverplated cigar and cigarette cases and of match boxes. The better types of these were richly ornamented with embossed figures, flowers, and geometrical designs. In 1907, one company advertised quite attractive sterling silver match boxes in a price range from $2.85 to $8 each. Neatly embossed sterling silver cigarette

EXTRA QUALITY QUADRUPLE SILVER PLATED WARE.

SMOKING SETS AND ASH TRAYS.

Prices Each.

No. 2255. $3.50
Cigar Holder and Ash Tray, rococo border.
Chased leaves and bird.   Length 5½ inches.

No. 2256. $1.25
Ash Tray, square, with feet.
Gold lined.   Width 2½ inches.

No. 2257. $1.25
Ash Tray, raised rococo border.
Satin finish.   Diameter 4 inches.

No. 2258. $8.75
Smoking Set, raised rococo border, gold lined.
Fine hand burnished.   Cut is one-third size.

No. 2259. $6.50
Smoking Set, fancy embossed, gold lined
Cut is two-third size.

No. 2260. $5.60
Smoking Set, satin, bright engraved.
Gold lined.   Cut is one-third size.

No. 2261. $3.75
Smoking Set, satin, hand engraved.
Gold lined.   Cut is one-third size.

No. 2262. $4.00
Smoking Set, satin, hand engraved.
Beaded border.   Cut is one-third size.

No. 2263. $312.
Smoking Set, satin, hand engraved.
Beaded border, gold lined.
Cut is one-third size.

A page from the 1900 catalogue of Otto Young & Company, Chicago, picturing an array of smokers' sets.

STERLING SILVER AND QUADRUPLE SILVER PLATED WARE.

CIGAR, CIGARETTE AND TOBACCO CASES.

Prices Each.

No. 2247. $13.34
Cigarette Case, rich embossed.
Gold lined, cut is exact size.
Sterling silver.

No. 2248. CIGARETTE CASE. $8.00
Rich embossed, gold lined.
Cut is exact size
Sterling silver.

No. 2249. $9.00
Embossed Burnished Tobacco Box.
Satin, gold lined.
Sterling silver.

No. 2250. $5.00
Tobacco or Cigar Jar, rich embossed.
Chased letters, hand burnished.
Height 6 inches.
Quadruple silver plated.

No. 2251. $4.00
Cigar or Tobacco Jar, satin, bright cut.
Burnished top. Height 6¾ inches.
Quadruple silver plated.

No. 2252. $4.00
Cigar or Tobacco Jar, satin, bright cut.
Gold plated with burnished silver cap.
Cut is one-half size.

No. 2253. $12.50
Cigar Box, fancy embossed, to hold 50 cigars.
Cut is about one-third size.
Quadruple silver plated.

No. 2254. $10.50
Cigar Box, raised rococo ornaments, satin finish.
Cut is about one-third size.
Quadruple silver plated.

A page of silver and silverplated cigarette cases, tobacco jars, and boxes from the 1900 catalogue of Otto Young & Company of Chicago, showing prices then current.

cases were offered in 1900 by a wholesaler at prices ranging from $8 to $13.34 each. These would all bring a good bit more today but can still be picked up at reasonable prices — at least prices which are likely to seem quite reasonable a decade hence.

Tobacco processors could establish fascinating museums featuring such items as we have described in this chapter.

28.
To Cleanse Oneself:
The Washbowl and Pitcher

No. Virginia, we haven't always had running water. It wasn't too long ago, in fact, that hundreds of thousands of families pumped their water from wells or obtained it from springs — as indeed quite a number of rural families still do.

Last century, therefore, and even in the early years of the present one in some areas, washbowl and pitcher sets were not luxuries but necessities. Most respectable homes wouldn't have been caught without a set for each bedroom in the home and without a particularly well-decorated one for the guest room.

A great many tin or so-called graniteware pitchers and basins were used for hasty morning ablutions, but most families preferred the more attractive sets of pottery or, more rarely, of porcelain. Porcelain sets were much higher-priced and were easily broken, which meant money down the drain — if there was a drain.

Many toilet sets were made that consisted of a large pitcher (most of them were a foot or more in height), a large washbowl, a flat or an oval soap dish, a toothbrush holder, a shaving dish, a mug and a covered commode. Most frequently these were placed on or housed in washstands, the more desirable of which had marble tops and a bottom compartment in which the commode could be kept out of sight but not out of mind on cold winter nights.

Although some of these sets were plain white, the majority were decorated with flowers, scrolls, fruit, or various scenes or designs. Some of the porcelain sets which are found today were made in the famous French pottery center of Limoges and are decorated in three colors and embossed with gold.

During the latter part of the nineteenth century toilet sets could be had for as little as $2.50 to $3.00 Some companies even offered them as premiums for selling specified quantities of their goods or subscriptions to magazines.

These reproductions of old wash bowls and pitchers were made early in the twentieth century. Top, left to right, are reproductions of Mason's ironstone, Old Willow, and Wedgewood. Bottom, left to right, Spode's "Butterfly" pattern, Spode's "Pheasant," and Spode's "Rose."

Even though most of the pieces in these sets were heavy, they were susceptible to breakage, and thousands of pieces have been broken through the years so that many fine old sets now survive only in part. Perhaps the only pieces left are the washbowl and the pitcher.

Because the handsome washbowls and pitchers can be so easily adapted to use as planters for the sun room, living room, and elsewhere in the house, and because they make really attractive decorations, they are coming into considerable popularity, not only among collectors but also among homemakers who like to do their own decorating. The better old washstands also are being bought in quantity, although some dealers report a recent decline in popularity of the marble-top furniture pieces.

The stands, with or without the marble tops, can be pressed into service as both utilitarian and decorative pieces if they contain, as most of them do, a

The Hindoo Remedies Company, of New York City, offered this decorated toilet set, in 1904, to persons who sold six bottles of its patent medicine pellets at 25 cents a box and remitted the $1.50.

drawer and storage space at the bottom. These washstands were made in various woods, but principally pine, oak, and walnut. Many of the old stands were made with attractive spool-turned legs. As refinishing goes, the refinishing of one of these pieces is a relatively simple matter as compared with, say, a carved chair.

Moreover, the stands can now be obtained for not more — and in many cases less — than the cost of a washbowl and pitcher set. Softwood stands can be picked up at country establishments for around $15 to $35. A good many antique shops also handle them now. Refinished stands will bring from $20 to $60, depending upon their construction and their wood.

Matching washbowls and pitchers are still abundant, and hundreds of these two-piece sets will be found at prices ranging from $12 to $50. However, the lower-priced sets have started moving up in value within the past year. In addition to the porcelain sets made in Limoges, many nicely-decorated porcelain bowls and pitchers were produced in England and some in Germany, and thousands upon thousands of glazed earthenware, as well as porcelain, sets were turned out by potteries all over the the United States during the last half of the nineteenth century.

A simple white ironstone bowl and pitcher with scroll designs on the pitcher handle are listed for only $12. A five-piece porcelain toilet set decorated in pink and yellow flowers with flecks of gold is offered at $30. Many similar sets of two to five pieces are advertised currently at $15 to $35.

Washbowls or pitchers alone can be bought much more cheaply than can matching pieces. Good sets with the maker's mark on them usually bring a premium over comparable unmarked sets.

Although some more venturesome persons are using the commodes (sometimes referred to rather uncouthly as "slop jars" and sometimes more quaintly as "potties") as planters, such use will be undoubtedly limited.

To be of maximum value, washbowls, pitchers and other pieces should be in perfect condition with the decorations bright. Chips, cracks, and age lines invariably detract from value. Although these sets are still plentiful and can be found in scores of antique shops (particularly those which handle the recently-arrived collectibles), they are now coming into such widespread use that demand may soon overtake supply.

In addition to antique shops and country establishments, these pieces will frequently be found in second-hand furniture stores, and they often appear at auction sales. Many of them, as has been noted, are still in use for their original purposes in home ouside the cities, and their owners may often be induced to part with them — for a price.

If you're interested, it will pay you to look around for sets made by the better-known potters, such as Spode's, while they may still be found. These are the pieces that are most likely to show the greatest appreciation in value in the coming years.

29.
The Fascinating World
of Miniaturia

Quite some years ago the movie star Colleen Moore began exhibiting around the country a fabulous castle containing 11 rooms, a large entrance hall, and an extensive garden. Each room was equipped with fine furniture and accessories and the garden was a world of beauty.

How could she exhibit it in various areas of the United States? Because it measured roughly only nine feet square. This remarkable example of the art of miniature perhaps did more than any other thing to create a widespread interest among youngsters and adults alike in the fascinating realm of miniaturia. Of course, Miss Moore was not the pioneer in this field. Miniatures (a word which originally referred only to small portraits and other paintings) had been collected for some years before her exhibit in the form of replicas of a wide array of articles made on a very small scale. But today, more persons than ever before are participating in the collecting and fabricating of miniaturia, and other fabulous collections have been assembled during the past few years.

Miniatures are not recent. They were known in ancient Egypt. Miniature items, which existed prior to the birth of Christianity, are now housed in museums, including the Metropolitan Museum of Art in New York City. Archaeologists and explorers have uncovered tiny toys, vases, jars, and other miniature items made centuries ago from clay, metals, bone, and other substances.

The name of one early artisan who worked in miniature is known throughout the world of art. It is Benvenuto Cellini, the almost legendary sculptor, goldsmith, jeweler, braggart, and adventurer of the sixteenth century. Through the years other famous artisans also have fashioned miniatures in a wide variety of shapes and designs.

Miniature trunk, silk upholstered parlor set, boy's toy set, toy house set and kitchen set from the 1890's.

It is American-made miniatures with which we are primarily concerned here. Many of the choicest miniature articles made by craftsmen in this country have been acquired by private collectors. Nevertheless, there still remain many miniature collectibles to be ferreted out. These include sculpture, etchings, books, silhouettes, wax figures, and miscellany of almost every imaginable type — pitchers and vases made of a number of substances, tools, shoes, animals, wearing apparel, furniture, table service, military implements, musical instruments, pencil sharpeners, boxes, telephones, coffee mills, paperweights, and a host of others.

Among the articles most widely collected are miniature scale models of full-sized objects. There also are "microscopic" miniatures, so tiny that they are impossible to see completely without the aid of magnifying lenses.

A delightful and informative book on the subject is Georgene O'Donnell's *Miniaturia, The World of Tiny Things* (Lightner Publishing Corporation, Chicago). The author describes a bottle in one collection which is only 19/10,000th of an inch in its outside diameter and 4/10,000th of an inch on its inside diameter.

Active in the field of miniaturia is the Circus Model Builders, an organization founded in 1936 to bring together persons who build or own miniature models of circus equipment and paraphernalia. Actually, there are relatively few complete model circuses in existence, but many persons have single units of circuses in miniature. Headquarters of this organization is maintained in Torrington, Connecticut.

John M. Blauer, a collector and dealer from San Francisco, put together 20 miniature rooms housing more than 200 pieces of furniture and thousands of smaller objects scaled 1 inch to the foot. One room is a Louis XVI salon which contains, among other eighteenth-century appoinments, five pieces of Battersea enamel furniture, a 100-year-old ivory chess table complete with chessmen, an ivory sewing table with a drawer containing scissors and a tiny ivory thimble. The miniature china cabinet houses Staffordshire china with scenes painted on each piece. The wall panels and ceiling are painted in oils, a task that required many hours of exacting labor. This salon is lighted by two ornamented gold crystal candelabra, each of which holds three tiny electric lights.

Mr. and Mrs. William (Bill) Hanks, of Columbus, Kansas, have created a miniature farm covering 100 square feet and containing several thousand miniatures ranging from farm buildings and cattle to fences and electric lights. They specialize in animated miniatures.

Near Dublin, Ireland, Sir Nevile Wilkinson worked from 1907 to 1922 to create an astonishing miniature palace which was first publicly shown on July 26, 1922, and was immediately acclaimed as a true work of art. How the imagination of Sir Nevile's three-year-old daughter led him to this accomplishment is related in an interesting article in the September, 1958, issue of *Hobbies*. Incidentally, there is so much interest in miniaturia that *Hobbies* has a regular feature devoted to this subject in each issue. It is currently being conducted by the Rev. Stuart A. Parvin, an authority on the world of miniatures.

There are numerous miniature doll houses, some of these, too, in the "fabulous" category. *The Spinning Wheel,* in its March, 1954, issue, published an informative article on miniature doll houses by Flora Gill Jacobs, herself a collector of them.

In addition to castles and doll houses, there have been created in miniature such things as church chapels, railroads, saloons, armies, fleets of ships, map

A fully-equipped miniature dollhouse, built and furnished to scale by Mrs. Frank K. Toney, Atlanta, Georgia.

rooms, shops and stores, art galleries, inns, and groups of such items as china, sewing machines, kitchenwares, silver table service, books, "people," fans, automobiles, farm implements, sporting goods, and others too numerous to mention.

Many specialized shops have been established to cater to the collector of miniaturia. Some of these feature toys, others doll furniture, musical instruments, animals, and so on. Miniatures are made of such substances as wood, ivory, paper, metals, ceramics, glass, cloth, precious stones, and plastics. Some firms will make miniature items to order.

Miniatures also come in a wide price range, depending upon the article, the material of which it is made, and the workmanship. A spinet piano with an ebony finish is advertised at $12.95, a cobbler's bench at $2.50, and tiny hinges at eight for $1. A miniature Sandwich glass lamp is advertised at $45 and miniature soldiers made in England at 50 cents each. A miniature doll house with a walnut bedroom set of 11 pieces, including marble tops, was advertised some time ago for $21, and an Empire style love seat with purple silk upholstery for $9. One ingenious individual carved two tiny books of wood and put them on the market for $4.50 for the pair.

Collectible miniaturia of 1891: a French doll and a miniature trunk filled with accessories.

Other recent prices for miscellany include these: vases with flower arrangements, 1 to 2 inches in height, 15 cents; desk sets with blotter, notebook, inkwell, and pencil, $1; miniature tools, six for 60 cents (and they actually operate); candle holder, 1¾ inches high, 50 cents; leather boots, $1.50 a pair; dressmaking dummy, 5½ inches tall, $6; wine set with brown glass goblets and a pitcher, $5; Honeycomb and Tulip pattern punch bowl, $25; Sawtooth pattern spooner and pitcher, $6.50; mercury glass wigstand, $23; hand-braided rug, $2.50; ivory elephants mounted on the head of a pin under a glass dome, $2; Victorian photo album containing four photos and measuring ⅞ x 15/16th of an inch, $12.50.

Naturally, early and scarce miniature items will come considerably higher, if they are really desirable, than the newly-made ones.

Among the "wants" of collectors in addition to the commonplace things are harps, gardens and patios, music stands, tool boxes, paperweights, tape measures, pergolas, spice boxes, kerosene lamps, fireplace and hearth accessories, and vegetables.

Not only is it fun collecting miniaturia; it is fun making the replicas if one has the patience. "How-to" books on the subject are available and are advertised from time to time in the collector publications. One of the most interesting of these is by Elizabeth Andrews Fisher and is entitled *Miniature Stuff* (available from the author, 2112 Middlefield Street, Middletown, Connecticut, $5). Mrs. Fisher, who also publishes *The Toy Trader,* has put together here an informative book about miniaturia, illustrated with photographs and drawings. There are chapters contributed by Betsy Baldinger on dollhouses, Eunice P. Tuttle on her model house, Eloise Kruger on a dollhouse within a dollhouse, and others on various aspects of model fabrication. These instructions will be quite helpful to those who want to build their own miniatures.

Typical of those who are fascinated by the collecting of miniaturia are Mr. and Mrs. Frank Toney, of Atlanta, Georgia. They have constructed a miniature replica of a large two-story house and have equipped it with furnishings to scale. These range from beds and chairs to tableware, and Mrs. Toney has collected these items over a period of many years from all parts of the United States. Although the Toneys have a home filled with beautiful antiques, Mrs. Toney's pride and joy is her miniature house.

30.
Strike up the Band:
Collecting Sheet Music

Although early sheet music and scores by noted composers have been collected for many years, sheet music published during the period from the middle of the nineteenth century through the 1920's has been making "addicts" of hundreds of collectors during the past year or two.

Locating copies of early American songs in their original editions — and especially collecting songs with lithographed covers — is such an inexpensive hobby, compared with some others, that it can be pursued with diligence by almost anyone. Needless to say, it also can provide a tremendous amount of pleasure.

A good many years ago, Josiah Kirby Lilly, a native of Greencastle, Indiana, began collecting material by and about Stephen Foster, the prolific song writer, Lilly established memorials to Foster in Indianapolis and Pittsburgh. Mr. Lilly, who was president of the Eli Lilly Company, of Indianapolis, from 1898 to 1932, helped stimulate an interest not only in Stephen Foster but in the collecting of the songs of other nineteenth-century song writers and composers.

Some years ago, Harry Dichter and Elliott Shapiro wrote a rather monumental study entitled *Early American Sheet Music* (R. R. Bowker & Company, New York), which describes more than 600 important pieces of early music and includes a wealth of biographical details. It embraces such helpful data as a list of the names and addresses of sheet-music publishers and of sheet-music lithographers up to 1870.

This work stimulated many persons to start collecting early American sheet music and awakened an interest in the lithographed covers, many of them done by noted lithographing firms of the nineteenth century. Actually, al-

Remarkable woodcut title page of the quintus score of a musical composition by M. Praetorius, published in 1611. (From the collection of The Folger Shakespeare Library, Washington, D.C., with whose permission it is reproduced. Photograph through the courtesy of Mr. Sidney Hamer, proprietor, Leamington Book Shop, Washington, D.C.)

though the front and back pages of such music are ordinarily referred to as the "covers," in many cases they are not literally covers, because the music itself so frequently is begun on the inside of the front cover. Nevertheless, for the sake of simplicity, we shall refer to them here as covers, even though use of this term is technically incorrect.

Collecting American sheet music of past years represents the collecting of true Americana in its best sense, since so much of this music actually reflects the fads, fancies, fashions, and follies of earlier years in this country.

Mr. and Mrs. Bly Corning, of Flint, Michigan, are owners of a large outstanding collection of sheet music. A part of their worldwide collection has been donated to the University of Michigan at Ann Arbor. European music is housed in the School of Music library, and American music relating to historical events in this nation is on display at the William L. Clements (early American) Library, also in Ann Arbor. With the addition of this Corning Music Collection to its present holdings, the University of Michigan's music collection will undoubtedly be recognized as among the finest in the United States.

Mr. and Mrs. Corning's private collection has been sorted into categories and is exceptionally interesting since it relates to so many subjects.

The music of Stephen Foster, incidentally, seems of special interest to many collectors. In addition to Foster Hall, which was established by Joseph K. Lilly at the University of Pittsburgh, as mentioned earlier, and which is the outstanding repository of Foster first editions, manuscripts, and other memorabilia, the Stephen Foster Memorial in White Springs, Florida, has

A music publisher's advertisement of 1891, featuring a popular composition of that day.

This museum at the Stephen Foster Memorial in White Springs, Florida, houses a number of the famous composer's first editions and other mementoes.

many of this composer's original editions on display in its excellent museum. It also seems fitting that the museum at White Springs, along the bank of the Suwannee River of which the composer wrote, should also have the desk upon which Foster completed his lyrics for *Suwannee River* (also known as *Old Folks at Home*). The museum houses nine dioramas depicting the talented musician's most popular songs, and other dioramas are in the 200-foot-tall Stephen Foster Carillon Tower there, which presents concerts daily. The memorial is the state of Florida's tribute to the composer.

Why do folk collect sheet music? Clarence H. Hogue, of Covina, California, president of the National Sheet Music Society, Incorporated, attributes the hobby to memories or associations.

"A song or a melody," he told this writer, "sometimes recalls people or events in one's past life or has an association with a pleasant incident or episode of the past. One hears an old song which he associates with a cherished memory — and he goes out and buys it. Then he buys another piece of music; and he has started down the road of collecting. I think you will find that most collectors start with these 'memory-chest' songs — these numbers that stir memories of people and places and events."

No one knows exactly how many sheet-music collectors there are. This is largely because the hobby is a "quiet" one and has been little publicized. But the chances are that someone in your neighborhood collects sheet music, and there are literally thousands of collectors around the United States.

Just as is the case with collectors in the majority of other fields, most collectors of sheet music specialize. Some collect only original or first editions. Others collect lithographed covers or seek only ragtime music or early jazz or the works of specific composers or songs about such things as wars and catastrophes. Clarence Hogue says he knows an individual who collects only numbers with depictions of roses on their title page. Others shun everything except sheet music which bears a likeness of their favorite screen or television personality. And there are some persons who specialize in songs relating to modes of transportation, such as the automobile, the train, or the airplane.

Sheet music actually offers a vast choice to the specialist because songs mirror and reflect virtually every facet of life.

Where does one find old sheet music? Favorite hunting grounds are the salvage stores and institutions such as the Goodwill Industries and the Salvation Army, shops handling used books and manuscripts, dealers in second-hand merchandise, and, of course, a good many antique shops. There is an increasing number of dealers in old music who advertise in the collector periodicals, and you may also find some of these listed in the yellow pages of your telephone directory. If you're interested, try placing a want ad in your home-town newspaper. You might be surprised at the response from persons who have sheet music lying around in their attics or basements. Another opportunity lies in corresponding with other collectors who sometimes have duplicates for sale or trade.

Prices for sheet music are not yet very well established. The price often will depend upon how much one desires a specific item and how reluctant its owner may be to sell it. One collector will shell out $5 for an item on which another wouldn't be willing to spend more than a dime. Condition of the music also affects price. A piece in fine condition is virtually always worth more than one whose pages have been trimmed down or torn or soiled. In most cases (though not all) a first edition is worth more than a subsequent edition.

Numerous items of known scarcity, high desirability, age, and by famous composers are highly valued. For example, there are only nine known copies of the *Star Spangled Banner*. In 1958, one copy sold at auction for $3,500. Some collectors say the price was cheap. A catalogue by a specialist in music lists items ranging in price from $2.50 to $750.

Actually, right now there is no standardization of prices in the field of sheet music. Nevertheless, here are some recently advertised prices of various types picked at random from dealer advertisements which will serve only to indicate some asking prices and may not be typical but may be of interest notwithstanding:

My Old Kentucky Home, Stephen Foster's Plantation Melodies No. 20, first edition (1853), $20; *Grand Centennial March*, dedicated to the Mayor of Boston by Ch. Zeuner, with lithographed cover by Pendleton of "State House from the Mall" (1830), $7.50; bound volume of 28 pieces of sheet music in original editions and printed in various places between 1901 and 1909, $25; *The Vacant Chair*, by Geo. F. Root, six pages, with lithographed vignettes of Civil War and home scenes (1863), $10; *Flag of the Free*, by H. Millard, six pages, with engraving of eagle crouching over American flag in colors on cover (1863, twentieth edition), $6; *Marching Through Georgia*, by Henry C. Work, five pages (1865), $7.50.

Also, *My Poor Heart Is Sad with its Dreaming*, by Brigham Bishop, lithographed cover of young lady by fireplace (copyrighted 1877), $4; *Genl. Joseph E. Johnston Manassas Quick March*, by Adolphus Brown, six pages, lithographed cover featuring bust portrait of General Johnston, published in New Orleans in 1861 (note that this is a Confederate imprint), $35; *Thou Art the Queen of My Song*, by Stephen Foster, five pages, 1859, first edition, $25.

Also, *I Want to Be a Soldier*, by "Johnson & Company Song Store," issued during the Civil War and actually in the form of a broadside, $2.50; *The Live Oak Polka*, by J. H. Kalbfleisch, lithographed cover in colors by Endicott & Company, 1860, featuring the earliest known baseball print, $200; 25 lithographed covers published between 1900 and 1925, 35 cents each; *Will the New Year Come To-night, Mama?*, by Cora Eager and James Perry, 14 pages, 1864, lithographed cover depicting dying child in crib with mother beside him, $10; lot of 45 pieces of sheet music, all with pictorial covers showing American troops or individual officers or soldiers, plus 20 pictorial covers alone without the music, published chiefly in the 1840's and 1850's and nearly all "quick steps," $200; *The Rock Beside the Sea*, by Charlie C. Converse, six pages, lithographed cover of cloaked damsel on rock beside the sea, copyrighted 1857, $5.

Lithographed cover of sheet music by Stephen C. Foster copyrighted in 1889. This is from the collection of Mr. and Mrs. Bly Corning, of Flint, Michigan, by whose courtesy it is reproduced.

During 1964, Dean Snyder, a long-time collector of sheet music, of Los Angeles, California, compiled a list of songs published between 1890 and 1960 which were considered "hits" in their day. The list was published in *Western Collector* magazine.

Outstanding private music collectors in this country include Lester Levy, of Baltimore, James Fuld, of New York City, W. H. N. Harding, of Chicago, and Mrs. Josephine L. Hughes, of Charleston. Institutions with large and important collections include Yale University, Brown University, the New York Public Library, the Grosvenor Library (Buffalo and Erie County Public Library), of Buffalo, New York, the Henry Huntington Library, of San Marino, California, Free Library of Philadelphia, Cornell University, and the Library of Congress.

Clarence Hogue has this advice for beginning collectors:

"I recommend 'memory-chest' songs for the beginner — songs we associated with persons, places and events in our personal lives and whose words and melodies will bring back long-forgotten memories. A little reminiscing will bring many of these to mind. Make a list of the titles and then start hunting. I think these 'memory-chest' songs will become the most highly prized in the entire collection.

"Don't collect blindly, for songs and tunes are like people: There are all kinds of them — good, bad, indifferent, famous and obscure. Try to learn something about America's songs and the country's individual composers. They compose an intensely absorbing story. Visit your public library and make use of its facilities. Consult with the reference librarian and find out about the extensive bibliography on the subject. Seek out the story behind the song. You will be amazed at the abundance of material that is at your disposal, and the more you learn about the music you collect, the more fascinating your hobby will become."

Torn sheet music can be mended, Mr. Hogue points out, but two cardinal rules must be borne in mind: (1) Never use ordinary cellophane or gummed paper tape, and (2) always mend from the inside unless impossible to do so. He recommends the use of "Magic Mending Tape" or a similar thin colorless gummed tape of 1-inch width, which is available at most stationery stores. He also urges home-menders to avoid trimming down the margins of the music. Wrinkled sheets can be ironed smooth if one sets about this carefully and watches the temperature of the iron, which must not be too hot and must not be allowed to scorch the paper.

"Hunting for and acquiring sheet music," Mr. Hogue told the author, "are only half the thrill of collecting. The other half lies in searching out the facts, records, and anecdotes relating to the music that is collected. Playing detective by running down clues and tabulating evidence about pieces of sheet music is both exciting and rewarding. So if you want to derive the greatest measure of satisfaction from this hobby, don't be content merely to acquire and file away."

One way in which collectors can learn a great deal more about music collecting is by subscribing to *Musicgram, The Journal of Musical History,"* published by the National Sheet Music Society, Incorporated, 5010 Reeder Avenue, Covina, California 91723.

As Mr. Hogue adds, "Music collecting need not be just something to do with one's spare time. It can be an absorbing, intensely interesting pursuit that can broaden one's knowledge and understanding not only of America's music but of America's people and of its history. Each bit of knowledge gained opens the door to new vistas of inquiry and new areas of pleasurable exploration. And with added knowledge comes a deeper appreciation of those sheets of music we have gathered and filed away."

31.
Mechanical Musical Instruments:
What Ingenious Men!

Add the juke box to the list of remarkable things that are becoming antiques in their own time.

Actually the forerunner of today's juke boxes dates back to the nineteenth century, but numerous mechanical playing instruments made in the present century already are in the possession of collectors, and more are moving into their hands daily.

There apparently has been a recent revival of interest in the player piano. A number of dealers report that sales are headed upward, and piano rolls are selling at a rapid clip.

Of course, the more intricate of the juke boxes of yesterday are now of substantial value, and one doesn't pick them up for a few dollars. This naturally limits the collecting potential; but devotees of the nineteenth- and early twentieth-century mechanical players are a determined lot, and some of them will forego food and raiment if this proves necessary to the acquisition of a choice machine.

This is not the place for a history of the development of the player piano and its various outcroppings. That would require a book in itself. But let's hit a few of the high spots in the development of these instruments with the help of Arthur H. Sanders, who operates the truly fascinating Musical Museum in Deansboro, New York, and who knows their history intimately. For those who want to delve further into history, there is available *The Player Piano Treasury* (Vestal Press, Vestal, New York), compiled by Harvey Roehl, an outstanding collector. He also is the author of *The Player Piano, an Historical Scrapbook* (Century House, Watkins Glen, New York).

Authorities are not in complete agreement as to the exact origin of the

222

This early nickelodeon was made by Engelhardt, of St. Johnsville, New York, about 1909. (From the collection of The Musical Museum, Deansboro, New York, by whose courtesy it is reproduced.)

player piano, but Alfred Dolge in his work, *Pianos and Their Makers* (Covina Publishing Company, Covina, California), attributes the first successful effort to play a keyboard instrument with a mechanical device to Justinian Morse, of England, in 1731. Other developments followed, and nearly a century ago one John McTammany, a Scottish immigrant and a machinist by trade, built a mechanism that would permit the automatic playing of organs.

By 1874, McTammany had constructed his first three Automatic Air Organs while employed in St. Louis, Missouri. Writing in *Hobbies* in August, 1951, Mr. Sanders revealed that McTammany shortly thereafter took over the Munroe Reed Organ Company, of Worcester, Massachusetts, on a claim of infringement of his patent rights, and in that plant he developed the player piano.

M. Debani, of Paris, France, invented a piano in 1877 with a second set of hammers operated from above by the movement of a board with extruding pegs across the hammers. Six years later, the English firm of Bishop & Downe obtained a patent for a keyboard attachment for musical instruments, but a crank had to be turned to set the mechanism in motion.

A high spot in the player piano's development was the perfection by G. B. Kelly, in 1886, of a wind motor with slide valves which opened and closed ports to pneumatic motors. Later this type of device was almost universally adopted. About 1892, or shortly thereafter, a player mechanism called the Angelus Piano Player was manufactured by Wilcox and White Company, of Meriden, Connecticut, on the basis of a patent granted to William D. Parker for a combination piano that could be operated either manually or automatically. It possessed a pneumatic operating mechanism which was controlled by a sheet of perforated music, the forerunner of the extremely popular player piano roll.

E. S. Votey developed the Pianola in 1897. This consisted of a unit which could be used to convert any piano into an automatic player and it utilized a perforated music roll which moved across the tracker bar to actuate pneumatic devices. These devices pushed down levers which pressed the piano keys. About the same time, Theodore P. Brown, of Worcester, Massachusetts, perfected an interior player mechanism. Subsequently, his patents were acquired by the Aeolian Company, of Massachusetts, which marketed a cabinet player.

Many other developments followed and by around 1900 just about all piano makers began equipping their instruments with player mechanisms hidden from view inside the cabinets. In 1901, Melville Clark had perfected a player called the Apollo with an 88-note tracker bar (as contrasted with the earlier 65-note tracker bar), and this type also was adopted by nearly all manufacturers. The best-known of all the early players was the Pianola, manufactured by the Aeolian Company, of New York City.

The coin-operated player piano was in full swing by 1906, and various developments were added to these machines in succeeding years. Their mechanisms were activated by the insertion of a nickel in a slot; and the name nickelodeon derives from this. (Another popular one was called Coinola.)

The more advanced coin-operated contrivances featured multiple instruments, including piano, xylophone, mandolin, violin, castanets, triangle, marimba, trumpet, snare and bass drums and so on. One of the most popular as well as the best of the early coin machines was the Rudolph Wurlitzer Pianino. It had only 44 keys, taken from about the middle of a standard upright piano. Its dimensions were about 5 feet high, 3 feet wide and 2 feet deep. Its perforated roll traveled from top to bottom. The Pianino was produced from the early part of this century until around 1910.

Popularity of the juke boxes reached its zenith in the years following World War I. By 1912, the J. P. Seeburg Piano Company and Western Electric Company had perfected a machine that not only would play the piano but several other instruments. In addition, Seeburg made a smaller machine with only a mandolin and piano effect. The Englehardt Company had perfected a machine with a xylophone, which became extremely popular, and other companies followed suit.

More complicated machines were perfected as the years passed. For example, the Coinola Company made a machine which boasted a piano, mandolin effect, brass drum, tympan drum with two beaters, cymbal, snare drum roll effect, snare drum single beat, tambourine shaker, Indian block, castanets, triangle, set of violin pipes, set of flute pipes played with the right-hand section of the keyboard, and a xylophone. It seems astonishing that all of these instruments could be played from the music roll, but it was achieved by an ingenious switching arrangement and various couplings of rubber tubes. The entire affair operated with an air pump which was started by the insertion of a coin. Air operated the organ pipes, and vacuum operated the various instruments.

Also developed were machines which played solo banjo, or a dulcimer, or a concert style harp, or a small pipe organ. Coin-operated phonographs also were developed during the cylinder phonograph era.

The reproducing piano, introduced about 1907 by the German Welte company, enabled the player piano to become an instrument of great artistry. It reproduced the touch and temperament of the recording artist, in many cases the geniuses of the keyboard, a great many of whom are now dead. By a system of valves, the exact touch or pressure with which Paderewski,

Coinola, made by the Coinola Company, is a fabulous machine which plays many instruments. (From the collection at The Musical Museum, Deansboro, New York, by whose courtesy it is reporduced.)

Top section of Seeburg KT Special showing bass drum, cymbal, triangle, tambourine, Indian block, and snare drum. The extra two beaters on the bass drum are for tympani effect. The piano soundboard can be seen behind all this equipment. (From the collection of The Musical Museum, Deansboro, New York, by whose courtesy it is reproduced.)

for example, pressed each key is reproduced so that, in effect, these reproducing pianos were the "hi-fi" instruments of their day.

Early in this century, Edwin Welte and Carl Bookisch, his associate, began the creation of a library of music by the outstanding artists of the day to accompany the Welte reproducing pianos. The Welte factory was destroyed in World War II. The Welte as built in Germany was never sold in the United States, but some American companies were licensed under the Welte patent and produced instruments bearing the Welte name. However, these instruments differed from the genuine Welte machines. One such license was issued to the Auto Pneumatic Action Company. Foremost among the other American companies making reproducing pianos were the American Piano Company (Ampico), the Aeolian Company (Duo-Art), and the Welte Artistic Player Piano Company.

Other names associated with the early Nickelodeons included the Peerless Player Piano Company, with a factory at St. Johnsville, New York; Nelson-Wiggin Piano Company, of Chicago; Link Piano Company, of Binghamton, New York; National, of Grand Rapids, Michigan; Artizan, of North Tonowanda, New York; Mills Novelty Company, of Chicago; the Operators Piano Company, of Chicago; and the Regina Company, of Rahway, New Jersey.

Among the makers of the early player pianos and mechanisms for private use in addition to those already named were The Maestro Company, of Elbridge, New York; Regal Piano Player Company, New York City; Behr Bros. & Company, New York City; the Melville Clark Piano Company, Chicago; Hasbrouck Piano Company, New York City; Lauter Company, Newark, New Jersey; American Player Piano Company, New York City; Standard Pneumatic Action Company, New York City; Story and Clark Piano Company, Chicago; the Autopiano Company, New York City and elsewhere; Gulbransen-Dickenson Company, Chicago; Peerless Pneumatic Action Company, New York City; Christman Piano Company, New York City; Steger & Sons, Chicago; Marquette Piano Company, Chicago; Automatic Musical Company, Binghamton, New York, and a number of others.

The most fantastic of all early juke boxes was the Mills Violano-Virtuoso, an electro-mechanical violin and piano. Here is how Mr. Sanders describes its operation:

After a coin is deposited, the first action that takes place is that of rosining the bows — four wheels which rub the strings when pushed down on them. The electric meter which spins these bows has variable speed to simulate the action of bowing.

Electromagnets operate levers which press the proper bow onto a string; other electromagnets move levers which finger the strings much as the violinist does with his left hand, and still other electromagnets operate the vibrato effect. Weights hang at the left end of the violin to keep the strings in proper tension and the violin in tune.

A 44-note piano of unusual oval shape with the bass strings in the center and treble notes on either side also operates by electromagnets.

There is a Violano Virtuoso Society, established in memory of Henry K. Sandell, the inventor, with Mills Dean, 5804 Karlson Street, McLean, Virginia, as supervising director. There also is the Reproducing Player Owners Society, with headquarters at The Musical Museum, at Deansboro.

The fabulous Musical Museum, incidentally, features a Violano Virtuoso exhibit, plus exhibits of numerous other fascinating musical devices of past years, including a sixteenth-century harpsichord, a magnificent pipe organ made about 1835, nineteenth-century melodeons, a rare 1835 harmonium, an 1830 lap organ, small crank organs, a Mississippi steamboat organ, numerous fascinating music boxes, a Wurlitzer Fair Organ, a Tel-Ektra Player,

The Aeolian Orchestrelle, a fine reproducing player piano of 1906.

a Regina Hexaphone, all types of early phonographs and other instruments. The Museum's collection of fully-restored nickelodeons is perhaps the largest in the world.

There are other collections of musical instruments also open to the public. Among these are the Wicasset Musical Wonder House at Wicasset, Maine; Svoboda's Nickelodeon Tavern in Chicago Heights, Illinois; Cliff House, San Francisco; Gay Nineties Village, Sikeston, Missouri; Horn's Cars of Yester-year, Sarasota, Florida; Chuck Wagon Cafe, Atoka, Oklahoma; and the Henry Ford Museum, Dearborn, Michigan. In addition, there are literally dozens of magnificent private collections.

Of course, there is a considerable demand today for player piano rolls,

A group of player pianos as advertised in the opening years of the twentieth century. From left to right, top row: Metrostyle Pianola and Apollo. Second row: Autopiano and Angelus. Third row: Aeolian Orchestelle, Pianotist, and Rex. Bottom row: Simplex and Pianola.

just as there is for early phonograph records and discs and for music box discs. A number of companies made piano rolls earlier in this century, among them United States Music Company, Chicago; American Piano Company, New York City; the Vocalstyle Music Company, Cincinnati; Republic Player Roll Corporation, New York City; Perforated Music Roll Company, New York City; Connorized Music Company, New York City; the QRS Company, Chicago; Rhythmodik Music Corporation, Belleville, New Jersey; the Aeolian Company, mentioned earlier; Imperial Player Roll Company, Chicago, and others. The QRS (Quality Roll Service) rolls are still being made by the Imperial Industrial Company, New York City. Melodee Music Rolls are again being manufactured by Larry Givens, Wexford, Pennsylvania. Aeolian Music Rolls are still available from that company in New York City.

What are the early player pianos and juke boxes worth? It's difficult to say because values are changing rapidly as the machines become scarcer. Prices have soared, however, in recent years. Here are some typical recently-asked prices for certain instruments. These will serve only as a rough guide and may vary widely around the country:

Coin-operated Link piano with xylophone, $995; Seeburg, Mascott, $750; Cremona piano with mandolin and xylophone, $1,100; National roll changer piano and mandolin, $1,750; Weber Duo-Art electric reproducing piano, $1,200; Mills Violano with 10 rolls, restrung and action rebuilt but needing a reassembly of the violin, $550; Nelson-Wiggen style 4X, playing mandolin, piano, xylophone, snare drum and triangle, in unrestored condition, $675; Seeburg Style L Nickelodeon, restored, plays mandolin and piano, $875; Weber Duo-Art grand, unrestored, with 20 rolls, $575.

Also, Link, with mandolin and pipes, $500; Apollo player, restored, $350; small Wurlitzer 105 Band Organ, restored, $875; Wurlitzer 146A Band Organ, mint condition, $2,500; Aeolian piano player, $100; Seeburg B piano-mandolin, perfect condition, $750; Mills Violano Virtuoso, 1927 model, rebuilt and restored, with four rolls, $850; Coinola in good condition, $650; Wurlitzer Pianino, $650; automatic Regina, $750; Wurlitzer 103 Band Organ, $600; Coinola Reproduco Piano-Organ, fully restored, with a collection of rolls, $1,150.

The rolls also vary in price, ranging from about $1 to $50, depending upon their type and rarity.

There are relatively few persons today qualified to repair and restore the more intricate of the old mechanical instruments. The job requires expert knowledge and tedious work. So remember that if you purchase a machine in need of repairs, the cost of putting it in playing condition may add substantially to your investment.

32.
Victorian Furniture –
No? Yes? Maybe?

Victoria, Queen of the United Kingdom and Empress of India, reigned from 1837 until her death on January 22, 1901 — a total of 63 years, seven months and two days, or longer than anybody.

Much furniture produced in England and copies of it produced in America during her reign are alluded to broadly as Victorian furniture, which seems perfectly natural. Until relatively recent years Victorian furniture (and furnishings) were castigated almost *in toto* by those with sufficient funds to buy Chippendale, Hepplewhite, or Sheraton. They made little if any distinction among early, middle, and late Victorian furniture, probably because they didn't want to think about it at all if they could help it. And because they didn't want to think about it, or look at it, or investigate it, they passed by some attractive pieces which today are beginning to fetch rather handsome prices.

It is true that a great deal of Victorian furniture is rather horrible. Some of it is uncomfortable. But some long-collected Tudor furniture and Queen Ann furniture and furniture of other periods also is distressingly bad; and if you sit in some of the chairs for more than a few minutes, you will get a backache and perhaps a headache as well. On the other hand, some Victorian furniture is quite comfortable because it was made to live with and in and some of it is also quite interesting and not nearly as horrendous as we had been led to believe. Note the use of the qualifying word "some." Within the last few years experts have even written books about the desirability of certain items of Victorian furniture and about its design and construction.

One of the easiest-to-read of these books is *The New Antiques: Knowing and Buying Victorian Furniture* (Doubleday and Company, Garden City,

A corner of a typical Victorian room might feature these items. This is part of a Victorian room in the Municipal Lightner Exposition, St. Augustine, Florida, which made this photograph available.

New York), by George Grotz, who discusses the Victorian furniture available in this country, its characteristics and its auction values. The author also tells how to refinish pieces. Illustrated with drawings, this volume will prove of great assistance to those now seeking the good American Victorian pieces — a group which we would not be surprised to see include some of the folk who turned up their noses at all Victorian pieces just a few years ago.

Another excellent reference for the collector is Thomas H. Ormsbee's *Field Guide to American Victorian Furniture* (Boston, Little, Brown and Company). This volume also is illustrated with dozens of drawings. It describes characteristics of numerous pieces and gives approximate values.

If you already have read and digested these two books, there won't be much point in your reading further in this chapter, because, armed with the knowledge imparted by the Messrs. Grotz and Ormsbee, you can sally forth and collect Victorian with the best of them. If you haven't read them, you may want to complete this chapter and then read them.

Values of Victorian pieces vary from region to region. Some woods which are popular in certain areas are unpopular in others. Certain pieces considered desirable in Maine will be undesirable in Mississippi. As Mr. Grotz points out, early Victoran furniture was made chiefly of mahogany; walnut was widely used in the middle Victorian period; and late Victorian was altogether of oak.

To further round out the picture, Mr. Grotz includes in the category of early Victorian all styles classed under the French influence; in middle Victorian, the Gothic, Renaissance, and Eastlake styles, and in late Victorian, the Mission and Golden Oak furniture. He minces no words about his own preferences. The following paragraph is from his book referred to above:

For a long time now the seventeenth century has been known as the Golden Age of Furniture Design. It was the era of Chippendale, Sheraton, Hepplewhite, the Adam Brothers, Duncan Phyfe. And what did they produce? Rickety, ostentatious furniture that had nothing to do with the nature of the material it was made of or the use to which it was to be put. And they call that the Golden Age of Furniture Design? When grown-up men were making chairs no intelligent person would take a chance on sitting on? Give me a big roomy, comfortable Victorian chair any day. (Please understand that I am talking about the later Victorian furniture — of the second half of the era — when we had gotten over imitating European styles, and true American Victorian had emerged.)

Those words are tantamount to slapping a lot of connoisseurs in the face with a wet fish. And of course a great many persons won't agree with Mr. Grotz. But he does make a point. It is simply stupid to continue going on ignoring all the furniture produced during Victoria's long and impressive reign. A great many collectors already have realized that, including some "investors" who are getting rich, and more are going to within the next few years.

Carved chairs with gargoyles and sundry grotesqueries were popular in the late Victorian era. This one, of mahogany, features a carved gargoyle on the back and a curved seat. (From the author's collection.)

What types of Victorian furniture are being bought and sold today? Here are some of the items of furniture and accessories in demand: Round Golden Oak tables of the pedestal type; spool beds and stands; colored glass lamps and shades of various types; chandeliers; fancy chairs, upholstered chairs, and rockers; the better washstands and dry sinks; tables of cherry (especially) and of pine; chests of drawers with simple lines; upholstered sofas; small-size roll-top desks; all types of art glass as well as colored vases; and étagères. Other items also are being bought, but this list includes pieces which are apparently being sought out in the nicer examples with a bit of increasing fervor. Marble-top tables and stands were red-hot for a while, but the fever is now cooling a little. Victorian adaptations of étagères are simply called whatnots. Etagères come in the large economy sizes replete with mirror, or mirrors. The ordinary whatnot is usually smaller, and it has a diverse arrangement of open shelves, frequently with little railings, for the display of numerous articles, ranging from china to knick-knacks and gimcracks. Many whatnots were designed as corner pieces but others were round or rectangular. Those with spool-turned supports for the selves are particularly desirable. A great many of them taper in size toward the top.

Whatnots were highly favored articles in the nineteenth century. After World War I, most persons wouldn't touch them with pool sticks. Now they're back in favor again, and a large part of the credit for this must be given the astonishing variety of little gimcracks folk are currently collecting. They need shelves on which to display these, and what can better serve the purpose than a whatnot? If you have an answer to that please keep it to yourself because it looks as if folk are determined to go right on buying whatnots.

Elaborate nineteenth-century étagères are selling now at prices ranging generally from $60 to $150. The average whatnot is cheaper. The better ones are made of walnut or mahogany and some are done in oak. Values depend on size, quality, and whether or not they need refinishing.

One of walnut with five shelves and with scroll work above the shelves in back is offered at $47.50. It stands 50 inches tall. Another in walnut with five shelves and spool turnings is priced at $39. One with six shelves and a mirror is tendered at $65. Most others of this type and which do not need refinishing are in a similar price range.

Smaller (and later) whatnots made to hang on the wall are cheaper. These will be found at prices from around $15 to $25.

An early twentieth-century adaptation of the whatnot was called a parlor cabinet. These are stands, usually with two or three shelves and a mirror at the top, and sometimes a mirror at the rear of the center as well. They range from aroound 52 to 60 inches in height, and their shelf widths will vary from around 20 to 30 inches. They were made primarily of mahogany. If you simply must have a conversation piece, you can buy one of these. You may not like the conversation, but the parlor cabinets are still available in about the same price range as whatnots.

George Grotz cites auction values of Victoriana in his *The New Antiques,* but you may be interested in a recent sampling of dealer prices for miscellaneous Victorian era furniture. Here are some:

Late Victorian high chest with six long drawers and a small top one, walnut, $50; walnut poster bed, $21; walnut tilt top table, $25; four cane seat chairs, $56; walnut round marble-top candle stand, 29 inches high and 10½ inches across the top, $20; walnut, decorated upholstered rockers, $40; walnut finger-carved sofa, $75; six walnut side chairs, $105; mahogany, two-drawer sewing stand with basket drawer base, $35; walnut marble-top sideboard, brass pulls, mirror needing resilvering, 43½ inches wide and 39 inches high, $75; set of four finger-carved side chairs, upholstered seats

The whatnot was a great favorite with Victorian families. It was used, as is this one, to display a variety of treasures — or miscellaneous showpieces. (From the collection of the Municipal Lightner Exposition, St. Augustine, Florida, by whose courtesy it is reproduced.)

This parlor, from the Robert J. Milligan House, Sarasota Springs, New York, which is now in The Brooklyn Museum Collection, Brooklyn, New York, dates in the period 1854-1856. Note the interesting upholstered Victorian chairs, the table, and the Victorian period mantel decorative accessories. (Courtesy of the Brooklyn Museum.)

showing wear and some repairs needed on two backs, $110; walnut marble-top buffet, $125; Golden Oak secretary, 56 inches high, 19½ inches wide, and 12 inches deep, slant front and three drawers below with serpentine front, $37.50; and two finger-carved early Victotian chairs covered in red velvet, $100.

When it comes to Victorian, you should be your own judge. Buy what pleases you. Remember, too, that earlier antiques are drying up, and that their rising prices undoubtedly will eventually force the prices of Victorian up. That doesn't mean *all* Victorian pieces, but it does mean the choicer ones.

You'll find Victorian these days in the majority of antiques shops around the country, and you'll still find a lot of it in homes. Even the shopkeepers with upturned noses are lowering them, and grudgingly taking on a few pieces.

33.
Primitive Collectibles
of Rural America

We hear a lot about "primitives" these days. The word has been used in so broad a sense that a whole book could be written about collectible primitives.

Some authorities class as primitives early country furniture, early tools and implements, a vast array of early household articles (including kitchenwares), amateur paintings and drawings, all types of early implements and accessories for the fireplace and hearth, and so on.

We won't attempt to cover the field in this chapter; but we will discuss some of the primitives which are being sought more eagerly right now than ever before in our history. This fact is a tribute not only to the pioneers who made and used these items but also to the astute collectors who are now seeking to preserve these intriguing "relics" of an America in the days before assembly line production, the forty-hour work week, Social Security taxes and topless bathing suits.

We won't include here a discussion of paintings, because some of the primitive paintings of yesterday are going to be accepted as the classic paintings of tomorrow and, on the other hand, some of the paintings being classified right now as collectible primitives were done by amateurs who actually weren't qualified to do a competent job of painting the side of a barn. Worse than that, some of the "primitive paintings" you come across may have been done by skilled artists just yesterday. One dealer advertised in a widely-circulated publication some months ago to this effect:

"American primitive paintings painted to your specifications. On stretched canvas, already framed with dust backing. x x x Each is hand painted & antiqued so that it really looks old. x x x You name subject and colors. We'll even work from your sketches. x x x Dealers only please."

The interior of Miner Grant's General Store at Old Sturbridge Village, Sturbridge, Massachusetts. Shown here are pewter mugs, cow bells, clay pipes, pottery jugs, baskets, and all types of early containers. The store dates back to the late eighteenth century. (Photo through the courtesy of Old Sturbridge Village.)

Needless to say, too, some rare and high-priced primitive furniture has been faked in the past and undoubtedly will be faked again by unscruplous persons eager for a quick buck. They do not advertise frankly and openly, as in the case of the "primitive paintings" above, that their work represents reproductions or reconstructions, so that those not familiar with the tell-tale marks of reproductions may be taken in. Incidentally, for those interested in ways in which fakes may be detected several good books are available. One of them is *Fakes, A Handbook for Collectors and Students,* by Otto Kurz, published in 1948 by the Yale University Press. Another is *Antique Fakes &*

Vertical.

Figure 1.

Figure 2.

The stones are genuine French Burr. Steel spindle running in anti-friction metal bearings, with steel seat at end of spindle to receive the pressure when grinding. The frame is composed of hardwood and iron, with adjustable bridge-tree, so as to place stone in proper position for dressing, as shown in figure 2, which can be done by removing cap from end of bearing.
    This mill can be driven direct from engine or line shaft, and requires no extra counter shaft or hangers to run it. It will grind either wheat or corn, making good meal or flour. Can readily be adjusted to grind either coarse or fine when desired.

Nineteenth-century grinding mills once used on farms. These illustrations are from an early catalogue of Belknap Hardware and Manufacturing Company.

Reproductions, by the late Ruth Webb Lee, published by Lee Publications in Wellesley Hills, Massachusetts.

We will not concern ourselves here with those rare primitive items which are tempting to the faker, but with the less expensive ones available in greater abundance.

Some items often lumped into the primitive category already have been discussed in other chapters in this book. These include early signs and certain fireplace and hearth implements and accessories. Some of the things we want to talk about here were produced in limited quantities, often by home craftsmen, were used predominantly in rural America, and have now been displaced by machine-made goods turned out on assembly lines.

Early hand-made tools and implements, including farm implements, certainly would be included, but many of these were discussed in the author's earlier book, *Treasure at Home.* Early examples of tools used to help build the nation certainly are worthy of preservation, and they are being preserved in several museums.

Would you class illicit whiskey stills as primitives? At least one dealer does, and he offers a copper still for only $22.50!

A number of pieces of hand-made furniture fashioned by amateur craftsmen who were nevertheless possessed of a certain skill and taste may be classed

A "primitive" washing machine offered by Belknap Hardware and Manufacturing Company in the late 1800's.

as primitives. One of these, a pine cupboard with wooden hinges, made in Texas about 1850, is advertised at $100. Many cradles of earlier days were put together by the man of the household when the new baby arrived and may be designated as primitives. A farm-crafted child's wagon seat from the horse-and-buggy days was advertised not long ago at $7.50. Some dealers also suggest that hand-made wooden egg crates are collectible primitives. These are currently valued at $2 to $3 each. Early egg baskets of cane are worth $1.50 to $3.

Numerous iron household implements made by the erstwhile village blacksmith and other craftsmen are now viewed as primitives. These are beginning to attract large numbers of collectors. Here are recently-advertised prices for some of these:

Iron ladles, $5; strainers, $5; forks, $4; hand-made toaster with iron

STOVE HOLLOWWARE

FLAT BOTTOM KETTLES

STRAIGHT KETTLES

PLAIN, GROUND AND TRIUMPH—ENAMELED FINISH.

No.		7	8	9	No.		6	7	8
Capacity, quarts		6	8	11	ROUND BOTTOM Height, inches		7	7½	8½
Diameter, inches		9	9¼	10	Diameter bottom, inches		8½	9½	10½
Weight each, pounds		6	7	8	Weight each, pounds		5	6	7
Each		$0 65	70	85	Each		$0 55	65	70

TEA KETTLES

HAM BOILERS

PLAIN AND TRIUMPH—ENAMELED FINISH.

No.		6	7	8	No.		6	7	8
Height, inches		6½	7	7¾	Top, inches		18½x10¾	20x11½	22½x12½
Diameter top, inches		5½	5½	6	Height, inches		8	9	10
Weight each, pounds		8½	9½	11½	Weight each, lbs.		14	15	23
Each		$0 75	80	90	Each		$1 40	1 90	2 25

COUNTRY HOLLOWWARE

SKILLETS AND LIDS

SHALLOW OVENS AND LIDS

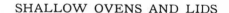

No.	0	1	2	3	4	No.	0	1	2	3	4
Depth, inches	2	2	2	2	2	Depth, inches	2½	2½	2½	2½	2½
Diameter, inches	13	12	11	10	9	Diameter, inches	13	12	11	10	9
Weight each, lbs.	18	14	13	11	9	Weight each, lbs	17	15	12	11	8
Per pound	$6 50	6 50	6 50	6 50	6 50	Per pound	$6 50	6 50	6 50	6 50	6 50

Much holloware of this type is moving into the category of "primitive" collectibles.

handle, $18; small wooden kraut cutter with iron blade, $2; large kraut cutter with dovetailed wooden box, $10; bear trap, $12.50; hand-wrought iron tongs hammered together from three pieces, $7; ladle for molding bullets, 22 inches long, $8; hand-wrought hinges and door latch, $10; foot scraper, 9½ inches high, $4; early three-legged pots, $5 to $15 (depending on size); kettles with bail handles, $3 to $20, (depending on size and workmanship); pie lifter with maple handle, $8.50; cake turner with wooden handle and brass ferrule, $5.50, and early handles for chest, $1.50 each.

Many other hand-wrought iron items can be added to that list.

There also are dozens of wooden primitives, many of them made in the home or on the farm. Here are some of them:

Boot jacks, $2.50 to $5; lard press, $4; knife box, $3.50; peck measure, $4; dough trays, $5 to $30 (dough boxes on legs will often bring $35 to $150; bowls, $5 to $15; quilting frame, $10; well buckets, $5 to $10; sugar scoops, $2.50 to $5; darning eggs, $1 to $2.50; salt boxes, $5 to $25 (depending on type and workmanship); rolling pins, $3 to $6; wagon seats, $15 to $30 depending on size and quality); rocking horses, $12.50 to $35; crude cutting boards, $2 to $5; and ox yokes, $15 to $20 (those with bows are usually a bit higher).

A good many early tin items also are collectible primitives. A tin sugar shaker is tendered at $3; a yarn dispenser at $3; and bread boxes are valued at about $3 and up, depending upon the quality of their workmanship. Such things as early candle holders and lighting devices come in a wide range of prices, their values being governed by scarcity and demand.

One may stretch the word primitive to include a host of other things. An early wagon jack is advertised at $6; a hand-made bullet pouch with a few hand-made pieces of shot still inside, at $2.50; a clay pipe at $2.75; and iron keys at $1 to $7.50.

Also worth watching for and preserving are grindstones, tinder boxes, mortars and pestles, carpet beaters, wooden scoops, sap buckets, all types of measures, early barrels, food molds, decoys, apple driers, tin wash basins, examples of needlework, grease and oil cans and fillers, wire baskets and containers, churns, hand-whittled items, home-made toys, skillets, stencilled wares, trunks and blanket chests, Bible boxes, hooked rugs, shoe lasts, weathervanes, pottery flower pots, and desk boxes, to mention only a few of the scores of primitive-type articles still available, and, in most instances, widely and at reasonable prices.

A large part of the fun in collecting primitives lies in identifying some of the curious devices you are likely to come across. Durng the past year and a half, scores of outlets have opened which deal almost wholly in primitives. Prices are likely to vary widely from area to area so that once again you

DOUBLE PLOW STOCKS

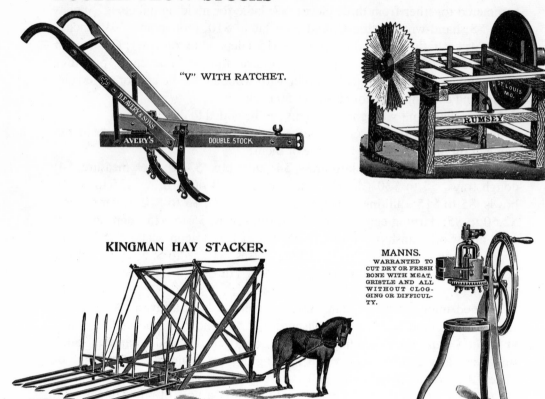

"V" WITH RATCHET.

KINGMAN HAY STACKER.

MANNS.
WARRANTED TO
CUT DRY OR FRESH
BONE WITH MEAT,
GRISTLE AND ALL
WITHOUT CLOG-
GING OR DIFFICUL-
TY.

ANIMAL POKES

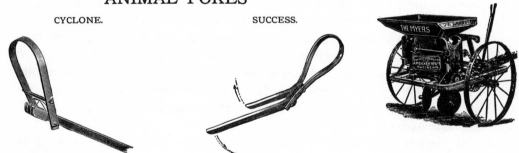

CYCLONE.   SUCCESS.

These agricultural implements of a bygone era are now considered "primitive"
by collectors.

should use those listed in this chapter as merely a rough guide.

Genuine country auctions often turn up numerous articles of the types mentioned in this chapter. You also are apt to find many of them in older farm houses and farm outbuildings.

34.
How to Buy and Sell
Antiques by Mail

If you've been bitten by the bug, the chances are that sooner or later — probably sooner — you are going to do some shopping by mail.

And if you've been bitten severely enough, you are likely to accumulate — and sooner than you think — so many collectibles that your house will overflow with them and you will be stuffing them in the corners of drawers and cupboards and under the bed and in the attic until your spouse screams bloody murder at you. And then you are going to start thinking about the possibility of selling those which you decide you can part with so that you can make room for more and your spouse can start screaming all over again.

Of course, the chances are that you will find a great many collectibles you want to buy right in your own community, or at least nearby. Moreover, if you are an addict (the probability is that you wouldn't be reading this book if you weren't), you likely will spend a good part of your out-of-town vacation shopping around for collectibles of the type in which you are interested.

Of course, you may find establishments in your own community which will take some of the excess of your collection off your hands at a price which will enable them to resell at a profit. But sooner or later you may run out of nearby outlets at which to buy or in which to sell, and then you are going to start reading more closely those tempting advertisements with which the various collector publications are filled. If you haven't already subscribed to one or more of these publications, you eventually will. After all, doesn't everybody?

Buying collectors' items by mail is often a satisfying and rewarding experience. You order, say a Weller vase from an advertiser located in Klopstock, Michigan, and when it arrives, carefully packed so that it will not be damaged in transit, and you unwrap it tenderly, you discover that it is even more beautiful than you had anticipated and that you really have a whale of a bargain on your hands. You are so thrilled that you rush out into the kitchen and prepare a sumptuous dinner for your husband that night and give him an extra scoop of ice cream on his pie, and you not only kiss him when he arrives home, but you kiss him again before he goes to bed. You don't have to tell your husband that you have acquired a beautiful new vase: The kisses and the extra dessert tell him that, so that maybe he doesn't mind your having spent a few more dollars of his hard-earned cash. If you don't have a husband, the chances are that you'll prepare the special dinner just for yourself and kiss the cat.

It often works out just that way. But sometimes it doesn't. You read a glowing description in an advertisement of a set of glass tumblers you have always wanted. You order the set and when it arrives, you unpack the box and find two of the tumblers have been broken in transit or that three of them have rim chips or that the whole set is cloudy; and your day is ruined. When your husband comes home from work, worn out from toil and anxious to be cheered up by a loving wife, you bawl him out for something he forgot to do last month or kick him on the shins and give him leftover stew for his dinner. He doesn't have to ask you what the trouble is. He knows that you have bought a set of tumblers and that two of them were broken in shipment or that some of them had rim chips or that the whole set was cloudy.

Buying by mail can be a precarious pursuit. It doesn't necessarily have to be but it can be, especially if you're buying from a housewife like yourself who doesn't know how to pack a box properly so that its fragile contents won't be damaged when left to the mercies of the Post Office Department.

There are certain rules that must be followed to sell successfully by mail and there are rules that should be followed in buying by mail. This is not a treatise on salesmanship or a dissertation on advertising. All we intend to do here is to make some pertinent suggestions that will help you buy antiques satisfactorily by mail or that will help you sell articles by mail which will not be immediately returned to you by an irate purchaser.

Needless to say, there are certain things you will have to do by yourself, such as checking into your city, county, or state regulations which may pertain to going into business, and there are certain records you will have to keep, if you sell, to satisfy Uncle Sam. If you'd rather not check into these, you'd better not go into business.

A large percentage of individuals who advertise their wares in collector periodicals are primarily collectors. Some of them are selling their duplicates and others are trying to sell their collectibles which they desire the least in order to derive revenue to buy those which they desire more. Other advertisers are individuals or companies which engage exclusively in selling by mail; and still others are firms which sell both by mail and directly to customers who call at their shops. The majority of established companies get along all right. It's the individual inexperienced in selling who gets into trouble.

Let's tackle the business of selling by mail first.

When you advertise, describe what you have to sell adequately and accurately. List any defects. Give dates when you can. Advertising books can be particularly troublesome when dates of publication are not listed. For example, a first edition of Joel Chandler Harris's *Daddy Jake the Runaway,* published in 1889, is worth $40 to $75 in first-class condition. Subsequent editions are worth only a very few dollars. But a first edition in poor condition is worth considerably less than $50.

If you advertise books for sale, state whether they are in poor, fair, good, very good, or fine condition and give the date of publication (usually listed on the title page but sometimes on its verso).

If you advertise glass or china, include, wherever possible, such details as the pattern name, manufacturer and date, or approximate date of production. Of course, dates and manufacturers in this area are often difficult to pin down. Also, give dimensions of such items as plates, platters, compotes, and vases.

State whether the price includes postage and insurance or whether these charges are additional.

Know the value of what you offer for sale and advertise it at a realistic price. Here again, in the realm of books in particular, ignorance of values is a pitfall which can mean the difference between a sale and having the book remain on your shelf. Don't guess at what an item may be worth. In the case of books, there are price guides available to help you. Among them are the following:

The Bookman's Bible: A Coded Guide to the Pricing of Antiquarian Books, compiled by Philip M. Roskie and available in two volumes from Roskie & Wallace Bookstore in Oakland, California.

The Used Book Price Guide, available in three parts from Price Guide Publishers, Kenmore, Washington.

American Book-Prices Current, an annual publication containing a record of literary properties sold at auction in the United States and in London, edited by Edward Lazare and published by American Book-Prices Current, New York City.

Gold in Your Attic and *More Gold in Your Attic,* both by Van Allen Bradley, published by Fleet Publishing Corporation, New York City.

Bookman's Guide to Americana, compiled by J. Norman Heard, published by The Scarecrow Press, Inc., New York City.

Books Relating to the Civil War: A Priced Check List, by John Mebane, published by Thomas Yoseloff, New York City.

Johnson's Civil War Book Prices, by Lucetta A. Johnson, available in four parts from the publisher, William T. Johnson, Box 68, Allegan, Michigan.

Second Value Guide to Old Books, by E. G. Warman, published by E. G. Warman Publishing Company, Uniontown, Pennsylvania.

There also are others, and you can check the reference department of your public library to determine which ones may be available there. In addition, some books in specialized literary fields, such as Ralph D. Gardner's *Horatio Alger; or The American Hero Era,* published by The Wayside Press, Mendota, Illinois, list values of books by specified authors.

Numerous value guides to antiques of all types also are available. Hundreds of values are listed in the book *Treasure at Home* by the author of the book you are now reading, published by A. S. Barnes and Company, Inc., New York City. Another price guide is *8th Antiques and Their Current Prices,* by E. G. Warman, published by E. G. Warman Publishing Company, whose address also is listed above. Mr. Warman and T. T. Foley have compiled price guide books to milk-white glass and prints.

In the field of historical glass, there is available *Historical Glass Price Guide,* by Mrs. Vernon W. Smith, available from the author at 8111 Chadbourne Road, Dallas, Texas, 75209. Mrs. Smith also is the compiler of *Greentown Pressed Glass Guide,* which will be helpful to the increasing number of collectors of Greentown glass.

A fine guide for pressed glass buyers and sellers is *Early American Pattern Glass,* by Alice Hulett Metz (published by the author, 2004 West 102nd Street, Chicago).

The late Ruth Webb Lee compiled guides to values of certain types of glass, and these are published by Lee Publications in Wellesley Hills, Massachusetts. Values of bottles are given in *1200 Bottles Priced,* by John C. Tibbitts, published by The Little Glass Shack in Sacramento, California. Marion T. Hartung, author of several books on Carnival glass, has compiled a *Price Guide on Carnival Glass,* available direct from the author in Emporia, Kansas. Another reference in this field is *Carnival and Iridescent Price Guide,* by Mrs. Rose M. Presznick, available from the author, Route 1, Lodi, Ohio. John F. Hotchkiss lists prices of Steuben glass in his *Carder's Steuben Glass,* available from the author, Rochester, N. Y. Postcard prices are listed in Walter E. Corson's *Know Your Cards and Their Value,* available from Moe Luff, Spring Valley, New York. *American Card Catalogue,* by J. R. Burdick, available from The Card Collectors' Company, New York City, lists values of advertising and other cards.

A good many other value guide books also are on the market. Some are advertised frequently in the collector periodicals, and some undoubtedly will be found in your public library.

The point is that when you don't know the approximate value of what you want to sell, energy devoted to looking it up in a price guide or in checking prices at antique shops or in advertisements will be well spent. Generally speaking, collectors are informed individuals when it comes to their particular field or fields of collecting. They know when a price is too high; they also know when a bargain is being offered.

Inexperienced collectors are forgetful, so it will be to your advantage in your advertisements to request that a stamped envelope or at least a stamp accompany all orders so that checks may be returned if the item ordered has been previously sold. When checks are received for items which already have been sold, return them promptly to the persons who ordered too late.

Good will is vital for successful selling by mail. If you receive a request for information or for one of your lists, accompanied by a stamped envelope, reply as promptly and as accurately as possible. If you let your mail pile up unanswered for weeks, you won't be in business long.

When transportation costs are extra and a customer sends more than is required for the actual transportation charges, refund the excess amount immediately. You aren't entitled to it; it belongs to the customer who was unable to estimate precisely the amount that would be required.

Pack fragile articles carefully, using sufficient paper or similar material to prevent fragile articles from being damaged in transit, and be sure to mark the package itself FRAGILE — HANDLE WITH CARE.

Insure any articles of value. If they are lost or damaged through fault of postal employees, you won't stand to lose. The Post Office Department pays promptly when a substantiated claim of loss on articles it insures is tendered.

Remember that it may cost a bit more to send a package by express than by parcel post. Investigate to determine the difference in charges for various methods of shipping; and if a package is to be sent collect, choose the cheapest method.

If a customer requests an article on approval and is willing to pay transportation costs both ways, oblige him unless you are certain of selling that article promptly and on a firm basis to another customer. The majority of potential customers who order items on approval retain them — and particularly if the items live up to their advertising!

If you think you are going to be in the business of selling by mail for a while, try to accumulate some reference books about the antiques in which you will deal. It is embarrassing not to be able to answer customer's questions about items you offer for sale. Besides, don't you yourself want to know?

If you handle a great many items, it may be advantageous for you to prepare your own mimeographed (or printed) lists to send out to prospective
customers. Some dealers send lists free; others make a small charge to cover
their printing costs and postage. You can advertise the availability of these
lists in the collector periodicals. Most collectors are fascinated by catalogues
and lists. Some even collect them.

Whether or not you ever intend to sell any of the collectibles you acquire,
you should keep a written record of what you pay for every item you buy and
from whom you bought it as well as the date you purchased it. If you do
decide to sell articles later, you'll know whether you're making a profit or
sustaining a loss. If you don't sell, you can refer to the list in later years and
can sit back with smug satisfaction if you find that your collection has increased substantially in value since you originally acquired it.

If you can bring yourself to do so, refrain in your advertising from using
such descriptive adjectives as "darling," "lovely," and "sweet." The items
will speak for themselves, and extra words in advertising cost money.

Keep a list of the names and addresses of all the customers to whom you
sell and what they bought. After a period of time, you may have a valuable
mailing list on hand.

Check the advertisements in as many collector publications as you can as
carefully as you have the time to; this is one excellent way to keep abreast of
values.

If you're in the mail order business on a large scale, you may want to have
letterheads and billheads printed with your name and address on them. If
you plan to sell only a few items, this isn't necessary. You can use plain
paper for bills, invoices, and correspondence. After all, you need to watch
your costs.

It has been said frequently that the customer is always right. That isn't
necessarily so. Give the customer the benefit of any doubt; but if you lay
hold of a really cantankerous one who keeps coming back to give you more
of the same, you'd do well to drop him — or her. It's hard enough to get
along with your neighbors these days. So don't coddle obstreperous customers
too long. Let them take their business elsewhere and irritate your competitors
instead.

Now for the elementary lesson on buying by mail.

The first rule of buying is to enclose a self-addressed, stamped envelope
with your order. This will enable the dealer to return your check if the item
you want has already been sold without having to spend her own money on
postage. The same rule applies when you write a dealer to ask a question.
A few dealers advertise that they will not return such checks when an addressed, stamped envelope is not enclosed. This is an understandable if im-

proper attitude. Even if they have to send you a postcard to ask for an addressed, stamped envelope in which to return your check, it now costs them four cents — and with the way postage has been going up in recent years, it may cost more than that by the time you read this book.

Unless the article you order is advertised as prepaid, be sure to enclose a sum sufficient to cover parcel post charges for mailing it. If you aren't certain what the exact amount should be, don't worry about sending along too much. Nearly all dealers are honest and will refund any overcharge.

Read the descriptions of merchandise in the advertisement carefully, noting whether any defects are listed. Unless they are, you have a right to expect any item you order to arrive in good condition and without defects. If defects which are not listed appear on items you receive, you have a right to send them back and ask for a refund of your money. Reliable dealers will make such a refund — and most reliable dealers also will take pains to describe any defect.

Because advertisements cost money, the majority of dealers do not describe in great detail the items they advertise. If you are not certain that an advertised item is specifically what you want, write the dealer and ask for a fuller description, remembering to enclose that stamped, self-addressed envelope. Of course, someone may have purchased the item in the meantime. If you wish, you may describe in detail the item you want and ask the dealer to hold it for you if it fits your description. If the dealer replies in the affirmative, send your firm order and check for the article promptly.

Most dealers insist that payment accompany an order unless the order happens to come from a well-known and faithful customer. This is only proper, because there are some deadbeats who collect. Just ask the dealer who has trusted one of them. Other potential purchasers may hold an order sent on approval for weeks and then return it. Chances are the dealer could have sold it elsewhere in the meantime. So don't be offended if the dealer declines to send you an article on approval unless you send her a check in payment with the approval order. If the article isn't what you want, the dealer will return your payment when you send the item back.

If you do return an article which you did not request on approval, write the dealer before you mail it and state that it is being returned and why. And if you do return something you have ordered, return it as promptly as possible. Pack it carefully and insure it for its full value.

Generally speaking, dealers will not ship articles on a collect-on-delivery basis. It is time-consuming and costly, so don't request them to do this. Express-collect is a different matter, but naturally you will be expected to pay the express charges. However, you'll find that most dealers prefer to have payment for both the article and the transportation charges in hand before shipping, except for bulky items which must be shipped by express or methods other than parcel post.

Remember that even the most conscientious and careful dealer is likely to make an error once in a while. That's everybody's right. So if a mistake has been made in your order, don't berate the dealer. You'll achieve results more quickly by writing a pleasant letter about the error. Nobody likes a sourpuss.

Some small-scale dealers issue typewritten lists (making carbon copies of them) to a few customers and often request the return of the list when a potential customer has finished with it. In such cases, the dealer should enclose a stamp or a stamped envelope for the list's return. When she does this, you should return the list as soon as you can. Every seller can't be a big business operator and issue printed or even mimeographed lists.

Some dealers ask a small payment for their lists. It is costly to prepare, print, or mimeograph such lists and mail them out, especially when many of them are mailed to individuals who don't buy from them. So don't feel antagonistic toward a dealer who asks a few cents for a copy of her latest list.

When you buy on the basis of advertisements in periodicals, read the advertisements thoroughly throughout the publication before placing an order. You may often find two or more dealers advertising the article you want at different prices.

When you order as a result of a periodical advertisement, name the periodical in which the advertisement appeared when placing your order. Dealers frequently advertise in more than one publication, and it helps them to learn which periodical brings the best response.

Periodicals do not accept advertisements from dealers who misrepresent their offerings if they know about them. If you buy from a dealer or individual who misrepresents what he is selling, and you have reason to believe that it is deliberately misrepresented, tell the magazine about it. This will be a favor to the periodical and to other collectors.

There are liars and cheats in the business of selling antiques, but there aren't many of them — certainly no larger a percentage than you will find in the business of selling groceries or insurance or salvation.

So if you want to order by mail, go right ahead. The chances are that although your pocketbook will be flatter, you'll be happy. And the fellows who say you can't take it with you will be correct.

35.
You Owe It to Yourself
to Visit a Museum

There is no better way to familiarize yourself with the American past than to visit museums which preserve mementoes of it. And there is no better way to learn to distinguish original items of Americana from reproductions than to visit such museums and examine these items on a face-to-face basis.

The United States doesn't have the oldest museums in the world, but among those it has are some of the finest to be found anywhere. If you travel in the vicinity of a museum on your vacation or on a business trip, drive out of your way a little if necessary and visit it. In fact, have you given consideration to a vacation devoted to visiting the museums within a radius of a few hundred miles from your home? The experience would be a most rewarding one.

Almost every geographical section of the country has a variety of museums within its boundaries. Many of these provide guided tours. Some make a small charge for admission; others are open to the public without charge. This chapter is merely a brief introduction to some of the typically fine museums in this country. You can locate others yourself. In fact, a book which has recently been published tells you about dozens of them. It is *Museums, U.S.A.: A History and Guide,* by Herbert and Marjorie Katz (Doubleday & Company, Garden City, New York).

Among the distinguished regional museums of the United States is the Shelburne Museum, Incorporated, located in the community of Shelburne, Vermont, just a few miles south of Burlington. Founded in 1947 by Mr. and Mrs. J. Watson Webb, it now covers 40 acres, and its buildings and exhibits compose a fascinating and faithful portrait of early life in New England.

Many of the fine old buildings have been moved to Shelburne as was the 168-foot covered bridge which leads off the highway to the museum property.

The property includes the Charlotte Meeting House, furnished with an altar, pews, stoves, and prayer books from the early Miltonboro Church; a furnished early schoolhouse; Stagecoach Inn, originally built in 1783 as a tavern; and numerous other buildings, including a horseshoe barn, blacksmith shop, country store, stencil house, lighthouse, the early Shelburne depot, and others.

These buildings were moved from their original locations and reassembled timber by timber and brick by brick on the Museum grounds. They all contain intriguing displays, among the outstanding of which are collections of American folk art, dolls and doll houses, toys, relics of horse-and-buggy days, farm implements and tools, early household utensils, decoys, a vertical beam passenger and freight steamer, a ten-wheel steam locomotive engine and cars, weaving machinery (Jacquard and other looms), hat boxes, bandboxes, quilts and coverlets, pewter, glass, ceramics, Toby jugs, lustre wares, stamp-work embroideries, patterns for brass and bronze castings, furniture and furnishings.

Ralph Nading Hill and Lilian Baker Carlisle have told the story of this fabulous museum in a beautiful book, *The Story of The Shelburne Museum*, published by the Museum in 1960. Mrs. J. Watson Webb is president of the Museum corporation, and Sterling D. Emerson is director.

In Boston, The Society for the Preservation of New England Antiquities, founded in 1910 by William Sumner Appleton, not only operates a New England Museum but owns 45 historic houses and some other properties in Boston and its vicinity. These properties range in date from the 1650's to the 1830's and include a gristmill and cooperage shop, a meeting house and family burying grounds.

The houses have been furnished with gifts and materials which have been loaned to the Society. Some of the properties are partially supported by endowments. The majority of these properties are open to the public at specified times during the year. A small admission charge or voluntary contribution is requested for inspection of most of them. These historic houses are described in a "Visitor's Guide," published by the Society, which maintains its headquarters at 141 Cambridge Street, Boston 14. In addition, the Society maintains an outstanding library with fine collections of architectural photographs, measured drawings, and historical views of all types.

All members of the Society receive its illustrated quarterly magazine, *Old-Time New England*, issues of which are rich in historical material relating to early New England. Bertram K. Little is director for the Society.

Not as large as some other museums but crammed with a magnificent collection of early New England material is the Middleborough Historical Museum, operated by the Middleborough Historical Association, Incorporated, in Middleboro (now spelled without the final "ugh"), Massachusetts.

The museum building was opened in 1962 and the physical structure is

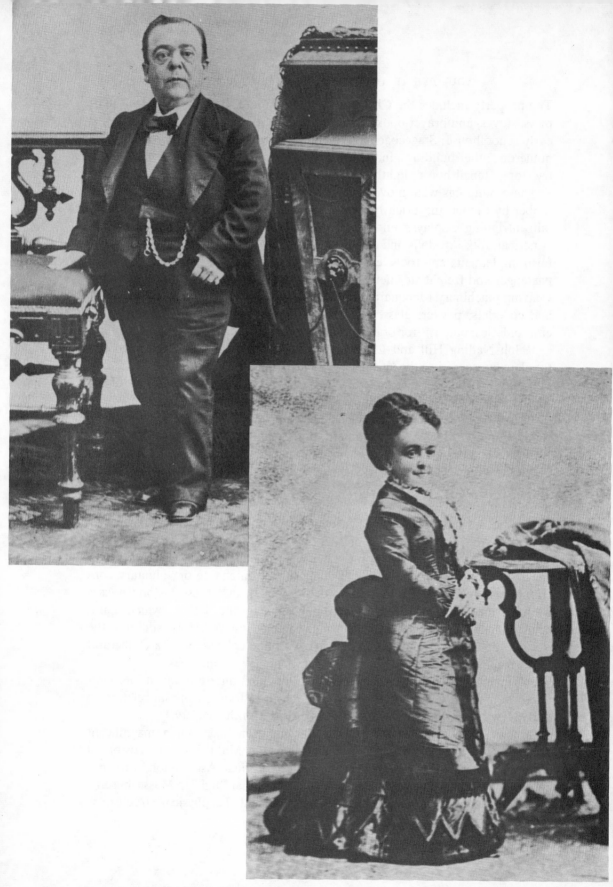

General and Mrs. Tom Thumb. (Photos through the courtesy of The Middleborough Museum, Middleboro, Massachusetts.)

composed of two mill houses built around 1820. Its most popular exhibit is its Tom Thumb collections — hundreds of the possessions of the midget made famous by the great showman, P. T. Barnum. General Tom Thumb married Lavinia Bump, of Middleboro. There also is a replica of a country store of the nineteenth century. It features even the original counters, bins, barrels, and merchandise of a store operated in that community by Colonel Peter H. Peirce. The replica of the store is stocked with everything from tinware and tobacco to paisley shawls.

Other displays include a blacksmith shop, a textile room, early tools and implements manufactured in Middleboro, carpenter's shop and cobbler's shop, early kitchens, agricultural and farming memorabilia, firearms, coins, and even the original outhouse of the old Sproat Tavern!

Among the outstanding exhibits also is a splendid model of Judge Peter Oliver's nineteenth-century shovel works done by Ted Eayrs, of Middleboro, when he was a senior in high school.

Model of Judge Peter Oliver's nineteenth-century shovel works shown here was created by Ted Eayrs and is among the exhibits in the Middleborough Museum, Middleboro, Massachusetts.

The Middleborough Historical Association publishes *The Middleborough Antiquarian,* devoted to interesting articles about the community's early history. This publication is edited by Lawrence B. Romaine, one of the moving spirits behind the museum's organization and its curator, and the author of *A Guide to American Trade Catalogues* 1744-1900 and other books. The museum is open to the public from July through September and by appointment.

Hobbyists and collectors from all over the world have visited the Municipal Lightner Exposition in St. Augustine, Florida. This fabulous collection of thousands of objects which were components of American life in the past was founded by the late Otto C. Lightner, who also founded the Lightner Publishing Corporation and *Hobbies* magazine.

Now owned in trust by the city of St. Augustine with Cecil Zinkan as its director and general manager, this museum houses everything from a quilt made by Mrs. Abraham Lincoln to fine Dresden china. It would be impossible to list everything the museum contains in the short space of this chapter, but you name it and it's probably there. It boasts fine collections of art glass, shaving mugs, tobacco jars, cut glass, buttons, stamps and coins, dolls, musical instruments, furniture, agricultural implements, early household goods, Carnival glass, toys, and scores of other categories.

The Americana collection there is one of the finest anywhere, and many of the museum's exhibits were associated with famous Americans of the past. As one example, it has an Edison phonograph which was originally presented by Thomas A. Edison to William Howard Taft.

The museum is housed in the palatial structure which formerly was the Alcazar Hotel, one of the projects of Henry M. Flagler in his expansive development of the east coast of Florida. Mr. Lightner deeded the building and its collections to the City of St. Augustine in trust, and the museum was formally opened there on January 1, 1948.

Mr. Lightner himself probably knew as many outstanding collectors as anyone in the country prior to his death in 1950, and he had a vital interest in the preservation of virtually every worthwhile item of Americana. As the editors of the magazine he founded say of him on this publication's "Americana Page," his "enthusiasm in spreading the cause of collecting and the cultural arts pertaining thereto left us all a legacy of real beauty," and "by providing the means of bringing persons together under the mutual bond of collecting, he enriched thousands of lives with the formation of new and enduring friendships."

Back again to New England, Old Sturbridge Village is one of America's prime historic attractions. The Village is a re-created New England farm community of the early nineteenth century. Its rolling acres consist of a village green with numerous early structures including a Meeting House, district school house, pottery, printing office, general country store, blacksmith and other artisan shops, taverns, bank, residences, and barns.

This magnificent attraction had its beginnings in the 1920's with the collecting activities of Albert B. and J. Cheney Wells, of Southbridge, Massachusetts. By 1936, they had amassed such a tremendous collection of Americana that they decided to provide the proper historic setting for it and bought the town of Sturbridge which was spread over a tract of 250 acres.

There were only two buildings on the property at the time, but the Messrs. Wells began their own building program, and the Village was opened to the public in 1946. Today, it is a private, nonprofit educational institution which has been chartered by the state of Massachusetts. There are now more than 38 major buildings arranged in a typical New England village plan. Last year it required a staff of about 275 persons to handle the thousands of visitors and to demonstrate numerous New England crafts. These demonstrations, carried out in the settings in which they were originally performed, provide an education in themselves. Many of the Village's buildings were originally constructed in the eighteenth and early nineteenth centuries.

Visiting Old Sturbridge Village is truly taking a step into the American past — an America in which there were no television sets, no telephones, no automobiles and little of the frenzied bustle which characterizes so much of the life of today. Although officials of the Village corporation say that it requires a minimum of three hours to see the attractions there, most visitors will want to spend at least a full day —and probably more.

Old Sturbridge Village is located at the junction of routes 15 and 20 and the Massachusetts Turnpike, 60 miles from Boston and 45 miles from Hartford. It is accessible by car or bus.

Those interested in colonial American furniture will find the largest and choicest collection of it at the Henry Francis du Pont Winterthur Museum near Wilmington, Delaware. Here, in a great country house built in 1839 by James Antoine Bidermann and his wife, Eveline Gabrielle du Pont, one may see more than 125 rooms, plus numerous halls, passages and alcoves, furnished with the most exacting attention to minute details.

When Henry Francis du Pont, a great-nephew of Mrs. Bidermann, endowed an educational foundation and deeded this magnificent house to it, his desire was to show the public how Americans have lived through the years. This house-museum, which was opened to the public in November, 1951, has achieved this goal admirably.

One will find in these rooms not only abundant groups of fine furniture but metalwork, textiles, ceramics, and paintings, all related intimately to the rooms in which they are housed. The interior architecture was brought from

Flatbed press at the Isaiah Thomas Printing Office at Old Sturbridge Village, Sturbridge, Massachusetts, dates from the 1760's. (Photo through the courtesy of Old Sturbridge Village.)

The Montmorenci Stair Hall at The Henry Francis du Pont Winterthur Museum, near Wilmington, Delaware. The Stair Hall came from a house built near Warrenton, North Carolina, in 1882. (Photo through the courtesy of The Henry Francis du Pont Winterthur Museum.)

many old houses around the nation and was installed as close as possible to its original form.

A selection of the most important rooms in the museum is presented in text and photographs in the booklet *Great Winterthur Rooms,* by John A. Sweeney, Curator, and published by the museum in 1964.

In his selection of the furnishings and in the putting together of the rooms, Henry Francis du Pont exercised great skill and extraordinarily good judgment and taste, and many of the objects one will find there have prime historical associations. New pieces are being constantly added by purchase and gift with a view to extending the museum's scope.

So that the visitor may enjoy the Winterthur collections to the fullest, during most of the year the guest list is limited to 60 visitors a day so that reservations are necessary well in advance. No reservations are needed, however, to see ten rooms in the Museum's south wing. Also, for five weeks each spring, a special museum garden tour is held at Winterthur when the public is admitted without the customary advance reservation. A tour of this museum has been described as similar to visiting a house whose owners have left only a short time before.

In 1929, the late Henry Ford founded in Dearborn, Michigan, what today has become one of the world's truly great museums — a general museum of American history. Founded as the Edison Institute but more popularly known as Henry Ford's Greenfield Village, this project consists actually of three divisions — the Henry Ford Museum, its outdoors extension, Greenfield Village, and an outdoors museum of American buildings, Greenfield Village Schools.

The Museum houses a vast array of exhibits which represent a virtual panorama of American decorative and mechanical arts and industrial progress. In the adjacent Greenfield Village, some 100 historic buildings have been transplanted from various parts of the nation to display the Americana in authentic settings.

Both the Museum and Greenfield Village are open seven days a week the year around except for Christmas and New Year's Day. The executive director of all operations is Dr. Donald A. Shelley.

An accurate way to describe the Museum would be to say that it is fantastic. Replicas of Independence Hall, Congress Hall, and the old Philadelphia City Hall are connected by corridors with the Mechanical Arts Hall. The collections of Americana are featured in an American Decorative Arts Gallery, a Street of Early American Shops and the Mechanical Arts Hall. A special collection of mementoes relating to the life of Henry Ford is housed in seven rooms dedicated to his memory.

What makes the Museum of special interest to the average collector and, in fact, the average person, is that it displays not just prime examples of the unusual or exceptional facets of the American past but numerous "everyday" or more commonplace objects which are of interest to us all.

The exhibit cases in the Decorative Arts Galleries are devoted to individual subjects developed in chronological succession. For example, the development of American furniture and decoration is arranged from the Pilgrim era to the twentieth century, period by period and style by style.

Preserved in the Street of Early American Shops are the tools and handi-

A replica of Independence Hall was chosen by Henry Ford for the entrance to his museum of American history. Historic Greenfield Village and Henry Ford Museum trace three centuries of American life in the development of our arts and skills. (Photo by courtesy of Henry Ford Museum, Dearborn, Michigan.)

work of the pre-industrial crafts as well as the later industries and trades, and many of these shops are in operation daily. The Mechanical Arts Hall houses in its eight-acre space exhibits which relate to industrial machinery, agriculture, steam and electric power, crafts, communications, lighting, and transportation. The Village itself occupies 260 acres.

So farflung are the attractions of the Henry Ford Museum and Greenfield Village that only a personal visit will enable one to visualize accurately their scope.

The museums mentioned in this chapter represent only a fraction of those now in operation in this country and open to the public, but each is outstanding and unique. Their common objective has been to preserve the American past so that this and future generations may become more intimately acquainted with our history than is possible through a study of books.

Selected Bibliography

(The books listed below by no means represent an inclusive bibliography of published material relating to the subjects discussed in this book but are suggested for additional reading. Some of them are out of print but may be found in your public library or in the stocks of out-of-print book dealers.)

Advertising Cards

Hornung, Clarence P. *Handbook of Early Advertising Art*. New York: Dover Publications, Inc.

(Laundauer, Della C.) *Early American Trade Cards from the Collection of Della C. Laundauer*. Notes by Adele Jenny. New York: William E. Rudge.

Towne, Morgan. *Treasures in Truck and Trash*. Garden City, New York: Doubleday & Company, Inc.

Broadsides, Posters and Handbills

Crawford, James Lindsay. *Catalogue of English Broadsides* (Volume V of *Bibliothece Lindesiana*). New York: Burt Franklin, Publisher.

Towne, Morgan. *Treasures in Truck and Trash*. Garden City, New York: Doubleday & Company, Inc.

Winslow, O. E. *American Broadside Verse*. New Haven: Yale University Press.

Spice Boxes and Thread Cabinets

Gould, Mary Earle. *Antique Tin & Tole Ware. Its History and Romance*. Rutland, Vermont: Charles E. Tuttle Company.

Jenkins, Dorothy. *A Fortune in the Junk Pile*. New York: Crown Publishers.

Powers, Beatrice Farnsworth, and Olive Floyd. *Early American Decorated Tinware*. New York: Hastings House, Publishers.

Williams, H. Lionel. *Country Furniture of Early America*. New York: A. S. Barnes and Company, Inc.

Telephones and Radio

Archer, G. L. *Big Business and Radio.* New York: The American Historical Company.

Casson, Herbert N. *The History of the Telephone.* Chicago: A. C. McClurg Company.

DeSoto, Clinton B: *Two Hundred Meters and Down. The Story of Amateur Radio.* Newington, Connecticut: The American Radio Relay League.

Greenwood, Harold S. *A Pictorial Album of Wireless and Radio, 1905-1928.* Los Angeles: Floyd Clymer.

Page, Arthur W. *The Bell Telephone System.* New York: Harper & Brothers.

Political Mementoes

Lindsey, Bessie M. *Lore of Our Land Pictured in Glass.* Two volumes. Forsyth, Illinois: Published by the author.

Marsh, Tracy H. *The American Story Recorded in Glass.* Paynesville, Minnesota: Published by the author.

Weitenkampf, Frank. *Political Caricature in the United States in Separately Published Cartoons.* New York: The New York Public Library.

John Rogers Groups

Drepperd, Carl W. *Victorian, the Cinderella of Antiques.* Garden City, New York: Doubleday & Company, Inc.

Smith, Mr. and Mrs. Chestwood. *Rogers Groups.* Boston: Goodspeed's Book Shop, Inc.

Dedham Pottery

Barber, Edwin Atlee. *The Pottery and Porcelain of the United States.* New York: G. P. Putnam's Sons.

Boxes

Bedford, John. *All Kinds of Small Boxes.* London: Cassell.

Carlisle, Lilian B. *Hatboxes and Bandboxes at Shelburne Museum.* Shelburne, Vermont: Shelburne Museum.

Jenkins, Dorothy. *A Fortune in the Junk Pile.* New York: Crown Publishers.

Robacher, Earl F. *Pennsylvania Dutch Stuff.* Philadelphia: University of Pennsylvania Press.

Door Knockers

Burgess, Fred W. *Chats on Old Copper and Brass.* Edited and Revised by C. G. E. Bunt. New York: A. A. Wyn, Inc.

Ormsbee, Thomas H. *Know Your Heirlooms,* New York: The McBride Company.

Shackleton, Robert and Elizabeth. *The Quest of the Colonial.* New York: The Century Company.

Maps

Bagrow, Leo. *History of Cartography.* Revised and Enlarged by R. A. Skelton. Cambridge: Harvard University Press.

Brown, Lloyd A. *Early Maps of the Ohio Valley.* Pittsburgh: University of Pittsburgh Press.

— *Map Making: The Art That Became a Science.* Boston: Little, Brown and Company.

Child, Heather. *Decorative Maps.* Boston: Boston Book & Art Shop, Inc.

Crone, R. C. *Maps and Their Makers.* New York: Hillary House Publishers.

Cumming, William P. *The Southeast in Early Maps.* Chapel Hill, North Carolina: University of North Carolina Press.

Goodman, Marie C. (Ed.). *Map Collections in the U.S. and Canada: A Directory.* New York: Special Libraries Association.

Tooley, R. V. *Maps and Map-Makers.* New York: Bonanza Books.

Signs and Signboards

Endell, Fritz. *Old Tavern Signs. An Excursion in the Story of Hospitality.* Boston: Houghton Mifflin Company.

Larwood, Jacob, and J. C. Totten. *English Inn Signs.* New York: Humanities Press, Inc.

Tin Cans

Can Manufacturers Institute, Inc. *The Metal Can: Its Past, Present and Future.* Washington, D.C.: Can Manufacturers Institute, Inc.

McKie, James W. *Tin Cans and Tin Plates.* Cambridge: Harvard University Press.

Fireplace Accessories

Carrick, Alice Van Leer. *Collector's Luck.* Boston: The Atlantic Monthly Press.

Drepperd, Carl W., and Marjorie Matthews Smith. *Handbook of Tomorrow's Antiques*. New York: Thomas Y. Crowell Company.

Gould, Mary Earle. *The American House*. Revised edition. Rutland, Vermont: Charles E. Tuttle Company.

Winchester, Alice. *How to Know American Antiques*. New York: Dodd, Mead & Company. (Also available in a paperback edition from The New American Library of World Literature as a Signet Book, New York.)

Mustache Cups

Jenkins, Dorothy. *A Fortune in the Junk Pile*. New York: Crown, Publishers.

Wilson, Everett B. *Vanishing Americana*. New York: A. S. Barnes and Company, Inc.

Military Mementoes

Barnes, R. M. *Military Uniforms of Britain and the Empire*. New York: British Book Centre, Inc.

Brown, Dorothy Foster. *Button Parade*. Chicago: Lightner Publishing Corp.

Johnson, David F. *Military Uniform Buttons*. Two volumes. Watkins Glen, New York: Century House.

Kerrigan, Evans E. *American War Medals and Decorations*. New York: Viking Press.

Magazines

Ellison, Rhoda Coleman. *Early Alabama Publications*. University, Alabama: University of Alabama Press.

Flanders, Bertram H. *Early Georgia Magazines*. Athens, Georgia: University of Georgia Press.

Gilmer, Gertrude C. *Checklist of Southern Periodicals to 1861*. Boston: F. W. Faxon Co., Inc.

Gohdes, Clarence *Periodicals of American Transcendentalism*. Durham, North Carolina: Duke University Press.

Goldwater, Walter. *Radical Periodicals in America, 1890-1950*. New York: University Place Book Shop.

Lewis, Benjamin M. *Guide to Engravings in American Magazines, 1741-1810*. New York: New York Public Library.

— *Register of Editors, Printers and Publishers of American Magazines, 1741-1810*. New York: New York Public Library.

Lutrelle, Estelle. *Newspapers and Periodicals of Arizona*. Tucson: University of Arizona Press.

Peterson, Theodore. M*agazines in the Twentieth Century*. Urbana, Illinois: University of Illinois Press.

Smyth, Albert H. *The Philadelphia Magazines and Their Contributors, 1741-1850*. Philadelphia. (1892.)

Whittemore, Reed. *Little Magazines*. Minneapolis: University of Minnesota Press.

Woodward, Helen. *The Lady Persuaders*. New York: Ivan Obolensky.

Books About the West and Indians

Adams, Ramon F. *Rampaging Herd: A Bibliography of Books and Pamphlets on Men and Events in the Cattle Industry*. Norman, Oklahoma: University of Oklahoma Press.

Decker, P. C. (Comp.). *George W. Soliday Collection of Western Americana*. New York: Antiquarian Press.

Eberstadt, Edward & Sons. *Americana Catalogue*. Four volumes. New York: New York Public Library.

Newberry Library. *Narratives of Captivity Among the Indians of North America: A List of Books & Manuscripts . . . in the Edward E. Ayer Collection*. Chicago: Newberry Library.

Withington, Mary C. (Comp.). *Catalogue of Manuscripts in the Collection of Western Americana Founded by William Robertson Coe, Yale University Library*. New Haven: Yale University Press.

Yale University. *Catalogue of the Yale Collection of Western Americana*. Four volumes. Boston: G. K. Hall and Company.

Steuben Glass

Barret, Richard Carter. *Identification of American Art Glass*. Manchester, Vermont: Forward's Color Productions.

Freeman, Larry. *Iridescent Glass*. Watkins Glen, New York: Century House.

Lagerberg, Ted and Vi. *A Color Picture Guide to Over* 100 *Types of Collectible Glass*. New Port Richey, Florida: Modern Photographers.

McKearin, Helen and George S. *Two Hundred Years of American Blown Glass*. New York: Crown Publishers.

Mary Gregory Glass

Revi, Albert Christian. *Nineteenth Century Glass: Its Genesis and Development*. New York: Thomas Nelson & Sons.

Satin Glass

Lee, Ruth Webb. *Nineteenth-Century Art Glass.* New York: M. Barrows and Company.

McKearin, Helen and George S. *Two Hundred Years of American Blown Glass.* New York: Crown Publishers.

Revi, Albert Christian. *Nineteenth Century Glass: Its Genesis and Development.* New York: Thomas Nelson & Sons.

Heisey Glass

Revi, Albert Christian. *American Pressed Glass and Figure Bottles.* New York: Thomas Nelson & Sons.

Perfume and Scent Bottles

Drepperd, Carl W., and Marjorie Matthews Smith. *Handbook of Tomorrow's Antiques.* New York: Thomas Y. Crowell Company.

Maust, Don (Ed.). *Bottle and Glass Handbook.* Uniontown, Pennsylvania: E. G. Warman Publishing Company.

Tibbitts, John C. 1200 *Bottles Priced.* Sacramento, California: The Little Glass Shack.

Tobacco Jars

Pinto, Edward H. *Wooden Bygones of Smoking and Snuff Taking.* Newton Centre, Massachusetts: Charles T. Branford Company.

Miniaturia

Arnold, Arnold. *Arnold Arnold Book of Toy Soldiers.* New York: Random House, Inc.

Baldet, Marcel. *Lead Soldiers and Figures.* New York: Crown Publishers, Inc.

Benson, A. C., and Sir Lawrence Weaver. (Eds.) *Books of the Queen's Dolls' House.* New York: Frederick A. Stokes Company.

— & — . *Everybody's Book of the Queen's Dolls' House.* London: Methuen.

Gee, Kenneth F. *Make Your Own Dolls' House Furniture.* Newton Centre, Massachusetts: Charles T. Branford Company.

Jacobs, Flora G. *A History of Dolls' Houses.* London: Cassell.

Mercer, Eileen. *Let's Make Doll Furniture.* New York: Harper & Row, Publishers, Inc.

Worrell, Estelle Ansley. *The Dollhouse Book.* New York: D. Van Nostrand Company.

Sheet Music

Backus, Edythe N. *Catalogue of Music in the Huntington Library Printed Before* 1801. San Marino, California: Huntington Library.

Berkowitz, Freda P. *Popular Titles and Subtitles of Musical Compositions.* New York: Scarecrow Press, Inc.

Dichter, Harry (Ed.). *Handbook of American Sheet Music. (Series I and II.) Illustrated Price Guides to Collectible Music.* Philadelphia: Albert Saifer.

Ewen, David. *Panorama of Popular American Music.* New York: Prentice-Hall, Inc.

— *History of Popular Music.* New York: Barnes & Noble, Inc.

— *The Life and Death of Tin Pan Alley.* New York: Funk and Wagnalls Company, Inc.

Fuld, James J. *American Popular Music,* 1875-1950. Philadelphia: Musical Americana.

— *A Pictorial Bibliography of the First Editions of Stephen C. Foster.* Philadelphia: Musical Americana.

Goldberg, Isaac. *Tin Pan Alley.* New York: Frederick Unger Publishing Company.

Harwell, Richard B. *Confederate Music.* Chapel Hill, North Carolina: University of North Carolina Press.

Marcuse, Maxwell F. *Tin Pan Alley in Gaslight.* Watkins Glen, New York: Century House.

Meyer, Hazel. *Gold in Tin Pan Alley.* Philadelphia: J. B. Lippincott Company.

Sonneck, Oscar George Theodore, and William Treat Upton. *A Bibliography of Early American Secular Music.* New York: Da Capo Press.

Spaeth, Sigmund. *History of Popular Music.* New York: Random House, Inc.

Ulanov, Barry. *History of Jazz in America.* New York: Viking Press.

Wolfe, Richard J. *Secular Music in America,* 1801-1825. Three volumes. New York: New York Public Library.

Player Pianos and Juke Boxes

Bowers, Q. David. *Put Another Nickel In.* Vestal, New York: Vestal Press.

Buchner, Alexander. *Mechanical Musical Instruments.* New York: Tudor Publishing Company.

Givens, Larry. *Rebuilding the Player Piano.* Vestal, New York: Vestal Press.

Grew, S. *The Art of the Player Piano.* New York: E. P. Dutton & Company.

Roehl, Harvey. *The Player Piano Scrapbook*. Watkins Glen, New York: Century House.

White, William B. *Piano Playing Mechanisms*. Vestal, New York: Vestal Press.

— *The Player-Piano up to Date*. New York: L. Bill.

Victorian Furniture

Drepperd, Carl W. *Victorian, the Cinderella of Antiques*. Garden City, New York: Doubleday & Company, Inc.

Gloag, John. *Victorian Comfort*. London: Adam and Charles Black. (Distributed in the United States by The Macmillan Company.)

Lichten, Frances. *Decorative Art of Victoria's Era*. New York: Charles Scribner's Sons.

Ormsbee, Thomas H. *Know Your Heirlooms*. New York: The McBride Company.

Otto, Celia Jackson. *American Furniture of the Nineteenth Century*. New York: The Viking Press.

Pevsner, Nikolaus. *High Victorian Design*. London: Architectural Press.

Roe, F. Gordon. *Victorian Furniture*. New York: Roy Publishers.

Symonds, R. W., and B. B. Whineray. *Victorian Furniture*. London: Country Life, Limited.

Primitives

Bowles, Ella Shannon. *About Antiques*. Philadelphia: J. B. Lippincott Company.

Drepperd, Carl W. *Handbook of Tomorrow's Antiques*. New York: Thomas Y. Crowell Company.

Lazeare, J. *Primitive Pine Furniture*. Watkins Glen, New York: Century House.

Sloane, Eric. *A Museum of Early American Tools*. New York: Wilfred Funk, Inc.

Wilson, Everett B. *Vanishing Americana*. New York: A. S. Barnes and Company, Inc.

Buying and Selling by Mail

Alexander, Ken. *How to Start Your Mail Order Business*. New York: Stravon Educational Press.

Arco Editorial Board. *How to Win Success in the Mail Order Business*. New York: Arco Publishing Company.

Chapel, Charles Edward. *The Gun Collectors' Handbook of Values.* New York: Coward-McCann, Inc.

Ferrara, V. Peter (Ed.). *Complete Course in Mail Order Business.* Chicago: Nelson-Hall Company.

Freeman, Larry. *How to Price Antiques.* Watkins Glen, New York: Century House.

Graham, Irwin. *How to Sell Through Mail Order.* New York: McGraw-Hill Book Company, Inc.

Howard, James E. *How to Use Mail Order for Profit.* New York: Grosset & Dunlap.

Lee, Ruth Webb. *Current Values of Antique Glass.* Wellesley Hills, Massachusetts: Lee Publications.

— *Price Guide to Pattern Glass.* New York: M. Barrows & Company.

Metz, Alice Hulett. *Reproductions. Pitfall Patterns.* Chicago: Published by the Author.

Ormston, Frank. *Antiques for Profit.* New York: Greenberg: Publisher.

Simon, Julian L. *How to Start and Operate a Mail Order Business.* New York: McGraw-Hill Book Company.

Yates, Raymond. *The Antique Collector's Manual.* New York: Harper & Brothers Publishers.

Museums

Alexander, Edward P. *Museums: A Living Book of History.* Detroit: Wayne State University Press.

Antiques Magazine, and Alice Winchester (Eds.). *Antiques Treasury of Furniture and Other Decorative Arts.* New York: E. P. Dutton and Company.

Faison, S. Lane, Jr. *Guide to the Art Museums of New England.* New York: Harcourt, Brace & World, Inc.

Spaeth, Eloise. *American Art Museums and Galleries.* New York: Harper & Row, Publishers, Inc.

Webster, Polly. *Antique Collectors' Guide to New England.* New York: Grosset & Dunlap, Inc.

Index

AB Bookman's Yearbook, 156, 158
Academy of Comic Book Fans and
  Collectors, 151
acid cut back glass, 168
Adam brothers, 134
Adams, Ramon F., 160, 161
advertising cards, 21-28, 251
—— novelties, 26-27
Aeolian Co., 224, 225, 227, 231
—— Orchestrelle, 229
Alabaster glass, 168
Albany Institute of History and Art, 67
Alcazar Hotel, 260
Allen, Paul, 150
——, Frederick W., 82, 84
Allison, C. F., 76
Alter, Cecil J., 162
Ameche, Don, 45
American Agriculturalist, 154
American Antiquarian Society, 27
American Book-Prices Current, 250
American Card Catalogue, 22, 24, 26, 251
American Evangelist, 154
American Journal of the Medical Sciences,
  151
American Magazine and Historical
  Chronicle, 156
American Magazine of Wonders and
  Marvelous Chronicle, 156
American Magazine, or a Monthly View
  of the Political State of the British
  Colonies, 156
American Museum, 151
American Ornithology, 151
American Piano Co., 227, 231
—— Player Piano Co., 228
—— Political Item Collectors, 61
American Pressed Glass & Figure Bottles,
  189
American Radio Relay League, 52
—— Revolution, 33
—— Society of Military Insignia
  Collectors, 144
Ampico, 227
Analectic Magazine, 151, 154
andirons, 132, 137
Angelus Piano Player, 224
Antiquarian Bookman, 156, 158 (also see
  AB Bookman's Yearbook)
Antique Bottle Collector, The, 189
Antique Fakes and Reproductions, 241
Antique Radio Guild of America, 51
—— Wireless Association, 52
Antiques (magazine), 82, 84
antiques, buying and selling by mail,
  248-255
Antiques Journal, The, 56, 70, 88, 97
Apollo piano, 224
Appert, Nicolas, 120
Apple pottery, 85
Apple Blossom pottery, 79
Appleton, William Sumner, 257
Architectural Record, 151
Arnold, Benjamin W., 67
Arrowsmith, Aaron, 105

art glass, 164-182, 235
Artizan Piano Co., 228
Atlantic Monthly, 154
Atlas of the City and County of
  San Francisco, 160
atlases, 105, 160
atomizers, 191
auctions, 19, 247
Aurelian pottery, 70
Aurene glass, 165, 168
Auroral pottery, 70
Auto Pneumatic Action Co., 227
Automatic Air Organs, 224
—— Musical Co., 228
Autopiano Co., 228
A. W. & H. C. Robertson, 82
Azalea pottery, 85

Baccarat, 190, 193
badges (political), 53, 57, 59
Bails, Jerry, 151, 152
Baldinger, Betsy, 212
Baldwin pottery, 71
ballots (political), 53
Baneda pottery, 79
banners (political), 53
Barber, Edwin Atlee, 84
barber poles, 109-110
Barcelona pottery, 71
Barck, Dorothy C., 62, 63
Barnum, P. T., 259
Baseball Gum Card Check List, 24
Baston, Prescott W., 66
Bavarian china, 141
Beadle Dime Novels, 148
Beadle's Monthly, 154
Behr Bros. & Co., 228
Belknap Hardware and Manufacturing
  Co., 39, 130, 132, 134, 136, 137, 242
Bell, Alexander Graham, 45
Bennett, George, 140
Bessemer, Henry, 123
Bibliotheca Americana . . ., 160
Biddle, Nicholas, 160
Bidermann, Eveline Gabrielle du Pont,
  261
—— James Antoine, 261
Big Cap Factory, 59
Bigelow, Dr. Robert R., 172
Binneman, W., 107
Biographical Sketch of James Bridger . . .,
  162
Bird in Orange Tree pottery, 85
Bishop & Downe, 224
Blackberry pottery, 79
Blauer, John M., 209
Blue Drapery ware, 71
—— Ware pottery, 71
Bohemia, 173, 191
bolt cases, 44
Bolton, Herbert Eugene, 162
Bonaparte, Napoleon, 120
Bonito pottery, 71
Bookisch, Carl, 227
Bookman's Bible, The, 250
—— *Guide to Americana,* 250

book selling, 250-251
books, Indian, 157-163
Books Relating to the Civil War, 251
books, Western, 157-163
—— (also see value guide books)
Boston and Sandwich Glass Co., 171,
  173, 183, 190
—— Museum of Fine Arts School, 85
Bottle and Glass Handbook, 189
bottle values, 251
bottles (see perfume bottles, gemel bottles
  and scent bottles)
Boulle, Andre-Charles, 17
boxes, 86-92
——, Spice (see spice cabinets)
Bradford, Andrew, 156
—— T.G., 100
Bradley, Van Allen, 250
Bray, Charles R., 24
Brazenose College, 97
Bristol, 191
British Museum, 28
broadsides, 29-37
Brooklyn Museum, 238
Brooks, Sarah Merriam, 162
Brown & Williamson Tobacco Corp., 115
Brown, D. Russell, 59
——, Theodore P., 224
Brown University, 220
"Brownies," 150
Bryan, William Jennings, 59
Bryant, William Cullen, 150
Bubbly glass, 168
Buffalo and Erie County Public Library
  (see Grosvenor Library of Buffalo),
Buffalo Bill and the Overland Trail, 160
Bump, Lavinia, 259
Burdick, J. R., 24, 27, 251
Burford & Sons, 21, 22
Burgess, Fred W., 97
Burroughs, John, 150
Burton's Gentleman's Magazine &
  American Monthly Review, 151
Butterfly pottery, 85
buttons (political), 53, 54, 55, 57, 59, 60
buying and selling antiques by mail (see
  antiques, buying and selling by mail)

calcite glass, 165
California '46 to '88, 162
Cambridge Glass Co., 188
cameo etched glass, 168, 171
Cameo pottery, 71
Camp, C.L., 163
camphor glass, 176
Can Manufacturers Institute, 121, 122, 124,
  126, 127, 128
canes (political), 53
cans (tin), 120-128
caps (political), 53, 59
Carder, Frederick, 164-170
Carder's Steuben Glass Index and Price
  Guide, 168, 251
cards (values), 251
Carlisle, Lilian Baker, 257

276

Carlsbad china, 141
Carnelian pottery, 79
Carnival and Iridescent Price Guide, 251
Carnival glass (values), 251
Carron Co., 133
cartography, 105
cartoons (political), 53
Cellini, Benvenuto, 207
Central Glass Co., 188
Century (magazine), 150
Champion, Richard, 17
Chapel, Charles Edward, 145
Charleton, T.U.P., 37
Chattanooga Roofing & Foundry Co., 134, 135
Chats on Old Copper and Brass, 97
Chelsea Keramic Art Works, 82
Chelsea Keramic Art Works Robertson and Sons, 82
Chelsea pottery, U.S.A., 84
Chengtu pottery, 71
Cherry Blossom pottery, 79
Chicago World's Fair, 69
Chicken pottery, 85
Chisholm Trail, The, 163
Christian Magazine of the South, 154
Christman Piano Co., 228
Chuck Wagon Cafe, 229
cigar cases, 199
—— cutters, 199
—— jars (see tobacco jars)
Cigar Store Indians in American Folk Art, 110, 112
cigarette cases, 199
Cintra glass, 168
Cire Perdue, 164
Circus Model Builders, 209
Civil War Centennial, 29, 144
—— maps, 106, 107
—— prints, 150
Clark, Melville, 224
——, William, 160
—— Stoneware Co., 76
Clarke, Asa Bement, 162
Classic pottery, 71
Clements, William L. Library, 215
Clichy, 191
Cliff House, 229
clothes brushes (political), 53
Clover pottery, 85
Cluthra glass, 168
Coal hods, 129-131
—— Vases, 129-131, 134
Coinola Co., 225, 226
cologne bottles (see perfume bottles)
Colonial furniture, 260
—— pattern glass, 185, 188
Columbian Magazine, 156
combs (political), 53
Comet patternglass, 188
comic magazines, 150, 152-153
commodes, 205, 206
Concise History of the Mormon Battalion . . . A, 163
Congress Hall, 264
Connorized Music Co., 231
Contempo, 150
Continental pattern glass, 185
Conversations with Carder on Steuben 166
Cook, David J., 162
Corinthian pottery, 78
Cornell University, 220
Corning, Mr. and Mrs. Bly, 215, 219
—— Glass Works, 164
Cornish pottery, 71
Corson, Walter E., 251
counter display cards, 24
Cowboy Lingo, 161
Cox, James, 162
—— Palmer, 150
Crab pottery, 85
Crackle ware, 84, 85
Cradles, 243
Cranes, iron, 136
Creations by Carder of Steuben, 166
Cremona piano, 231
—— pottery, 79
Crooked Trails, 160
Crown Perfumery, 191

Currier & Ives, 21, 22, 26, 53, 62
Curtis, Edward S., 159

Daddy Jake the Runaway, 250
Daly, James, 162
Damon, Samuel C., 162
Dean, Mills, 228
—— William B., 178
Dearborn, Mrs. Ella, 116
Death Valley in '49, 162
Debani, M., 224
DeBow's Review, 156
Debs, Eugene V., 59
Dedham Historical Society, 83
Dedham pottery, 82-85
Della Robbia pottery, 78
Demuth, Christopher, 112
Dial, The, 156
Diamond Lace pattern glass, 185
—— Swag pattern glass, 185
Diatreta, 164
Dichter, Harry, 213
Dickens, Charles, 70, 97
Dickensware, 70, 73
Directory of the J.R. Burdick Collection . . . in the Metropolitan Museum of Art, 27
Disraeli, 53
Dodge, Grenville M., 162
Dogwood pottery, 79
Dolge, Alfred, 224
Dolphin pottery, 85
Donaldson & Co., 143
Donatello ware, 78, 79
door bells, 93, 99
—— buzzers, 93, 99
—— knockers, 93-99, 100
—— stops, 19, 100-103
Dorland pottery, 71
Dorr, Thomas Wilson, 33
Dorr's Rebellion, 33
Douglas, Mrs. Damon G., 56
Dow, George Francis, 27
Drawings (Frederick Remington), 160
Drewry, John E., 155
Duck pottery, 85
Duncan, Ira L., 144
Duncan-Miller Glass Co., 185
Duo-Art, 227
du Pont, Henry Francis, 261, 263
Durand, Peter, 120, 123
Durham Cathedral, 97
Dyer, Mrs. D.B., 162

Eames, Wilberforce, 160
Early American Pattern Glass, 251
Early American Sheet Music, 213
Early American Trade Cards, 27
Early American Wooden Ware, 89
Early Days and Men of California, The, 163
Early Western Travels, 163
earrings (political), 53, 59
Eastlake style, 234
Eayrs, Ted, 259
Edison Institute, 264
——, Thomas A., 45, 260
effigies, 109-119
Egg crates, 243
8th Antiques and Their Current Prices, 251
Elephant pottery, 85
Eli Lilly Co., 213
Emerson, Sterling D., 257
Encyclopedia of Firearms, 145
Endell, Fritz, 119
Englehardt Co., 223, 225
Eosian pottery, 70, 73
Ericson, Eric E., 165, 166, 167, 168
Essex Institute, 27, 64
etageres, 235-236
Evangelical Magazine & Gospel Advocate, 154
Evans, Henry, 123

Fabulous Frontier, The, 162
Fairfield pottery, 71
Fakes, a Handbook for Collectors and Students, 241
F.D.R. Collectors' Association, 57

Family Magazine, 154
Famous Funnies, 150
Fandango pattern glass, 185
Farmer, John, 107
fashion prints, 148, 155
Faulkner, William, 150
Ferella pottery, 79
Ferrell, Frank, 79
Field Guide to American Victorian Furniture, 234
fire bellows, 136
—— cranes, 136
—— dog irons, 132, 133
—— fenders, 132, 133
—— grates, 131, 133, 134
—— fronts, 133, 134
—— tools, 132, 136
firearms, 144, 145
firebacks, 134
fireplace forks, 136
fireplaces, 129-138
firescreens, 136
firesets, 132
Fisher, Elizabeth Andrews, 211
Flagler, Henry M., 260
flags (political), 53, 59
"flea markets," 19
Flemish pottery, 71
Floral pottery, 71
Florentine pottery, 79
Flute pattern glass, 188
Foley, T.T., 251
Folger Shakespeare Library, 214
For Love and Bears, 162
Ford, Henry, 264 (also see Henry Ford Museum and Henry Ford's Greenfield Village)
Forest pottery, 71
Fort Reno . . ., 162
Foster Hall, 215
——, Stephen, 213, 215, 219
Foster, Stephen, Memorial, 215, 216
Franklin, Benjamin, 156, 160
Fray, Juan Crespi . . ., 162
Free Library of Philadelphia, 220
Freeman, Larry, 168, 189
French, Daniel Chester, 63
Frost, A.B., 150
Fugiyama, 78
Fuld, James, 220
furniture (See Victorian furniture and Colonial furniture)

Gardenia pottery, 79
Gardner, Ralph D., 251
Garfield, James A., 59
Gay Nineties Village, 229
Geological and Geographical Atlas of Colorado . . ., 162
gemel bottles, 193
George III, King, 120
Gibson, Charles Dana, 150
Gillingham, Harold E., 27
Givens, Larry, 231
glass (see: art glass; Carnival glass; cologne bottles; historical glass (values); perfume bottles; pressed glass (values), and also individual patterns, types and makers)
Gloria pottery, 71
Godey, Louis A., 148
Godey's Lady's Book, 148, 155
Gold in your Attic, 250
Golden Oak furniture, 234, 235
Gothic style, 234
Gould, Mary Earle, 86, 88, 89, 90
Graham, C.B., 107
——, J.R., 107
Graham's Magazine, 151
Grand Old American Bottles, 189
Grant, Ulysses S., 59, 63
Grape pottery, 85
Great Winterthur Rooms, 263
Greek Key pattern glass, 185, 188
Greeley, Horace, 154
Greenaway, Kate, 150
Greenfield Village (see Henry Ford's Greenfield Village)
—— —— Schools, 264

Greentown Pressed Glass Guide, 251
Gregory, Mary A., 171
——, —— glass (see Mary Gregory glass)
Grosvenor Library of Buffalo, 220
Grotz, George, 234, 236
Guide to American Trade Catalogues 1744-1900, A, 260
Guide to Colored Steuben Glass 1903-1933, A, 165

——, Book Two, 165
Gulbransen-Dickinson Co., 228
Gun Collector's Handbook of Values, The, 145
Gustkey, Carl, 183, 185

Hagerty Brothers Glass Works, 190
Hale, Sarah J., 148
Hall, James, 162
Hamer, Sidney, 214
Hamilton, W.T., 160
handbills, 29-37
Handbook of Ornament, 94
Handbook of the Indians of California, 163
Hands Up . . ., 162
handkerchiefs (political), 53, 59
Hanks, Mr. and Mrs. William, 209
Harding, W.H.N., 220
Harlan, Jacob Wright, 162
Harper's (magazine), 150
Harris, Joel Chandler, 250
Harrison, Benjamin, 58
——, William Henry, 56, 57, 59
Hartung, Marion T., 251
Harvard University, 63
Hasbrouck Piano Co., 228
hats (political), 53, 59
Haviland, Mustache cup, 141
Hawkes, T.G., Sr., 164, 165
Hawthorne, Nathaniel, 150
Hayden, F.V., 162
Hayman, Robert G., 157-158, 159
Heard, J. Norman, 250
Heisey, A.H. & Co., 183-188
—— glass, 183-188
——, Major A.H., 183, 185
——, T. Clarence, 185
Hemingway, Ernest, 150
Henry E. Huntington Library and Art Gallery, 163, 221
Henry Ford Museum, 95, 229, 264-266
Henry Ford's Greenfield Village, 264-266
Henry Francis du Pont Winterthur Museum, 261, 263-264
Herold, John J., 78
Hill, Ralph Nading, 257
Historical and Bibliographical Record of the Cattle Industry . . ., 162
Historical Chronicle, for All British Plantations in America, 156
historical glass (values), 251
Historical Glass Price Guide, 251
History of American Magazines, A, 155
History of the City of San Francisco . . ., 162
History of the Expedition under the Command of Captains Lewis and Clark, 160
History of the Indian Tribes . . ., 163
History of Natrona County, Wyoming, 163
History of the State of Nevada . . . A, 163
History of Signboards, The, 119
Hittell, John S., 162
Hobbies (magazine), 66, 82, 85, 128, 209, 224, 260
Hobbs, Brockunier & Co., 178
Hogue, Clarence H., 216, 217, 220
Hondius, 108
Horatio Alger; or The American Hero Era, 251
Horn's Cars of Yesteryear, 229
Horse Chestnut pottery, 85
Horticulturist, and Journal of Rural Art and Rural Taste, 154
Hotchkiss, John F., 168, 251

Hotten, John Camden, 119
Hudson pottery, 71
Hughes, Mrs. Josephine L., 220
Humphreys, Wm. P. & Co., 160
Hunter, John Dunn, 162
Hunting Indians in a Taxi-Cab, 115
Huntington, Henry E., 163
Huntley and Palmers, 125

Illustrated Christian Weekly, 154
Imperial Glass Corp., 183, 184, 186, 187, 188
—— Industrial Co., 231
—— Player Roll Co., 231
—— pottery, 78, 79
Independence Hall, 264, 265
Indians, books about, 157-163
——, wooden, 109-115
Intarsia technique, 165
Iridescent Glass, 168
Iris pottery, 85
Iron and Brass Implements of the English and American Home, 138
iron household implements, 243
Ivoris pottery, 71
Ivory glass, 168
—— pottery, 71
Ivrene glass, 165

Jackson, Andrew, 58, 61
——, "Stonewall," 30
Jacobs, Flora Gill, 209
Jade glass, 168, 170
James Bridger . . ., 162
Jarves, Deming, 171
Johnson, Lucella A., 251
Johnson's Civil War Book Prices, 251
Jordan, March & Co., 59
Journal of the American Osteopathic Association, 151
Journal of the Military Service Institution of the United States, 151
Joyce, James, 154
juke boxes, 222, 231

Katz, Herbert, 256
——, Marjorie, 256
Keleher, William A., 162
Kelley, Bruce, 52
Kelly, G.B., 224
——, William, 123
Kendrick, Grace, 189
Kennedy, President (John F.), 57
Kensett, Thomas, 123, 125
Kimball-Durand glass, 177
Kimmerle, F., 145
King & Co., 183
Kit Carson Days, 160
kitchen implements, 245
Klemesrud, Judy, 150
Knifewood pottery, 71
Know Your Cards and Their Values, 251
Krober, A.L., 163
Kruger, Eloise, 212
Kurz, Otto, 241

Ladies Companion, 151
Ladies National Magazine, 148
Ladies' Wreath, 151
Lady's Monthly, 151
Lamar pottery, 71
Landauer, Mrs. Bella C., 27
lanterns (political), 53
LaPoe, Wayne G., 54, 58, 60, 61
L'Arte de Conserver . . ., 120
La Rose pottery, 79
LaSa pottery, 71
Lasell pottery, 71
Laurel pottery, 79
Lauter Co., 228
Lazare, Edward, 250
Leander, Marguerite R., 85
Lee, Ruth Webb, 242, 251
Legends of the West, 162
Leslie's Illustrated Monthly, 150
Levy, Lester, 220
Lewis, Meriwether, 160
Library of Congress, 105, 220

Licking County Historical Society, 188
Life and Travels of Josiah Mooso, The, 163
Lightner, Otto C., 260
—— Publishing Corp., 115, 260
Lilly, Josiah Kirby, 213, 215
Limoges, 203, 206
Lincoln, Abraham, 31, 57, 58, 63
——, Mrs. Abraham, 260
Lindsay, J. Seymour, 138
Link Piano Co., 228
Lion pottery, 85
List of Maps of America, in the Library of Congress . . ., 105
Little, Bertram K., 257
Lobster pottery, 85
London Atlas, 105
Long, William A., 70
Lonhuda pottery, 70, 77
Loomis, Herbert D., 22
Lotus pottery, 79
Louwelsa pottery, 70, 73, 77
Low, John G., 85
Luffa pottery, 79
Lumkin, Wilson, 161
Lundborg's, 191
Lyon, A.G., Sr., 31, 53
—— Hobby Mart, 31, 53
——, Dr. I.W., 125

Maestro Co., 228
Magazine of American History, 151
Magazine of Western History, 154
magazines, 51, 148-156
Magnolia pottery, 85
Malaeska, 148
Malkin, Mary Anne O'Brien, 158
——, Sol M., 158
Manchester Art Association, 66
—— Historic Association, 66
Manly, William L., 162
Manners and Customs of the Several Indian Tribes Located West of the Mississippi, 162
mantelpieces, 134
maps, 104-108
Mara pottery, 78
Markham, Kenneth H., 70
Marquette Piano Co., 228
Marshall Field & Co., 191
Marshall, T.R., 59
Mary Gregory, 173
Mary A. Gregory (see Gregory, Mary A.)
Mary Gregory glass, 171-175
Massachusetts Magazine, 154
match boxes, 199
Maust, Don, 189
Mayor, A. Hyatt, 27
McClellan, General, 59
McKenney, Thomas L., 163
McTammany, John, 224
Mebane, John, 251
mechanical musical instruments, 222-231
medals (military), 144, 145
—— (political), 56
Medici, 115
Melodee Music Rolls, 231
Melville Clark Piano Co., 228
Mennen, Gerhard, 125
Metropolitan Museum of Art, 27, 207
Metz, Alice Hulett, 251
Meyer, Franz Sale, 94
Middleborough Antiquarian, 260
Middleborough Historical Museum, 257-260
Midland Pottery Co., 76
military mementoes, 144-147
Miller, Robert W., 173, 174, 175
Mills, Charles, 85
—— Novelty Co., 228
—— Violano-Virtuoso, 228
Ming Tree pottery, 79
Miniature Stuff, 211
miniaturia, 207-212
Miniaturia, the World of Tiny Things, 209
Mission Furniture, 234
Mitchell, Dr. S.A., 106, 108
Modern Quarterly, The, 154

Mokler, Alfred James, 163
Monroe, James, 58, 123
Moore, Colleen, 207
Mooso, Josiah Moore, 163
More Gold in Your Attic, 250
Morgan, J. Pierpont, 159
Morning Glory pottery, 79
Morrison, John L., 112
Morse, Justinian, 224
Mosaic Tile Co., 79
Mostique pottery, 78
Mother-of-Pearl glass, 176
Mott, Frank Luther, 155
Mt. Washington Glass Co., 178
mugs (political), 53, 59, 60
Municipal Lightner Exposition, 66, 190, 196, 233, 237, 260
Munroe Reed Organ Co., 224
museums, 256-266
Museums U.S.A.: A History and Guide, 256
Musicgram, The Journal of Musical History, 221
Musical Instruments (see mechanical musical instruments)
Musical Museum, 222, 223, 226, 228
mustache cups, 139-143
—— guards, 143
Mutlow, William James, 107
My 60 Years on the Plains . . .., 160

Nailsea, 191
Narrative of the Late Massacres in Lancaster County . . .., 160
National Geographic Magazine, 151
National Intelligencer, 156
National Piano Co., 228
—— Sheet Music Society, Inc., 216, 221
Nelson, Wayne M., 50, 51, 52
Nelson-Wiggin Piano Co., 228
New Antiques, The: Knowing and Buying Victorian Furniture, 232, 236
New England Glass Co., 178
New Mirror, 154
New Republic, The, 154
New World, 151
New York Historical Society, 27, 63, 66
New York Magazine, 151
New York Military Magazine, 154
New York Mirror, 154
New York Public Library, 220
New Yorker, 154
nickelodeons, 223, 225
Nineteenth Century Advertising Cards: An Introductory Study, 22
Nineteenth Century Glass . . .., 176, 177, 178
Normandy pottery, 79
North American Indians, 159
North American Miscellany, 154
North American Review, 154
Numsen, William, 123

O'Donnell, Georgene, 209
odor cases, 191
Old Sturbridge Village, 118, 241, 260-261, 262
Old Tavern Signs, an Excursion in Hospitality, 119
Old-Time New England, 27, 62, 66, 257
Old Timers Bulletin, The, 52
Oliver, Judge Peter, 259
On the Overland Stage, 160
On the Plains with Custer, 260
Operators Piano Co., 228
Ormsbee, Thomas H., 234
Others, 156
Otto Young & Co., 87, 200, 201
ovens, tin, 136, 142
Overland Monthly, 156
Owens, J.B., 16
Owens, J.B., Pottery Co., 76
Owl pottery, 85

Palissy, Bernard, 17
paper Americana, 21-37
—— dolls, 150
parian, 63
Parker, Amos A., 163

——, William D., 224
Parkhurst, Jacob, 158
parlor cabinets, 236
Parthenon & Academicians' Magazine, 154
Parvin, Rev. Stuart A., 209
Paterson, James T., 106
Patricia pottery, 71
Pauleo pottery, 78
Pearl pottery, 71
—— Satin Ware (see Mother-of-Pearl glass)
Pearlware (see Mother-of-Pearl glass)
Peerless Player Piano Co., 228
—— Pneumatic Action Co., 228
Peirce, Col. Peter H., 259
Peltier, Alphonse, 178
Pendergast, A.W., 110, 112
Pennsylvania Magazine of History and Biography, 27
Perforated Music Roll Co., 231
perfume bottles, 189-194
perfumizers, 191
Peterson, Charles Jacobs, 148
——, Harold L., 45
Peterson's Magazine, 148, 155
Philadelphia City Hall, 264
Phillips, P. Lee, 105
Philpott, Cecily and Gerry, 166, 167, 168
Phoenix Glass Co., 178
phonographs, coin-operated, 222, 225, 231
photographs (political), 53
Pianino pianos, 225
Pianola, 224, 225
Piano Rolls, 222, 224, 229
Pianos and Their Makers, 224
pianos, player, 222-231
Pictorial History of the Metal Can, A, 128
Pierce, Franklin, 58
Pike, Albert, 163
Pine Cone pottery, 79
Pineapple pattern glass, 183, 185
pins (political), 53, 56, 58, 59
Pinto, Edward H., 38
pitchers (see washbowl and pitcher sets)
Placzek, Bill, 150
Plains and the Rockies . . .., The, 163
plates (political), 53, 59
Player Piano, The, an Historical Scrapbook, 222
Player Piano Treasury, The, 222
player pianos, (see pianos, player)
Plympton & Robertson Pottery Co., 82
Poe, Edgar Allan, 150
Polar Bear pottery, 85
political mementoes, 53-61
Pond Lily pottery, 85
Pony Tracks, 160
pot hooks, 136
posters, 29-37, 53
pots, iron, 136
pottery (see under pattern names and individual companies)
Pottery and Porcelain of the United States, The, 84
Pound, Ezra, 154
Praetorius, M., 214
Prang, Louis, 21, 22
Press Time, 154
Pressed glass (values), 251
Presznick, Rose, M., 251
Price Guide on Carnival Glass, 251
primitives, 240-247
Primrose pottery, 79
prints (Civil War), 150
—— (political), 53
Pritchard, Ruth, 177
Prose Sketches and Poems, Written in the Western Country, 163
Provincial pattern glass, 185, 186
Purdy, Ross C., 76
Pyle, Howard, 150

QRS Co., 231
QST, 52
Quarterly Anti-Slavery Magazine, 154
Quarterly Bulletin (of the New-York Historical Society), 63

Rabbit pottery, 85
Radio Club of America, Inc., 51
radios, 49-52
Raleigh, Sir Walter, 114
Rampaging Herd . . .., The, 161
Reed, Willard, 164
Regel Piano Player Co., 228
Regina Co., 228
Remington, Frederic, 150, 160
Renaissance style, 234
Reproducing Player Piano Owners Society, 228
Republic Player Roll Corp., 231
Revere, Paul, 22
Revi, Albert Christian, 176, 177, 178, 179, 180, 181, 182, 189
Rhythmodik Music Corp., 231
ribbon cases, 44
Richardson, Benjamin, 177, 178
Ridings, Sam. P., 163
Robertson, Alexander W., 82
——, Hugh C., 82, 83, 84, 85
——, James, 82
——, J. Milton, 84
——, William, 84
Rockwell, Robert, 167, 168, 170
Rockwell's Department Store, 170
Roehl, Harvey, 222
Rogers Groups, 62-68
——, John, 62-68
——, Katherine R., 66
Roma pottery ware, 71
Romaine, Lawrence B., 260
Rookwood Pottery, 69, 70, 76
Roosevelt, Franklin D., 56, 57
——, Theodore, 59
Rosaline glass, 168, 170
Rosecraft pottery, 78
Roseville pottery, 76-81
Roskie, Philip M., 250
Ross, Denver, 85
Rozane pottery, 77, 78, 79
Russell, Charles M., 160

Sabin, Edward L., 160
——, Joseph, 160
Salmagundi Club, 63
Sam Houston in Texas, 160
Sanborn, Kate, 115
Sandell, Henry K., 228
Sanders, Arthur H., 222, 224, 228
Sartain's Union Magazine of Literature and Art, 154
satin glass, 176-182
Savona pottery, 79
scent bottles, 191, 193
Schneider, Norris F., 69, 70, 71, 73, 76, 78, 79
Schuster, Mrs. Arthur, 41
Scientific American, 151
scissors (political), 53
Scott, Joseph, 107
screw cases, 44
Scribner's, 112, 154
Scribner's Monthly, 154
Second Value Guide to Old Books, 251
Seeburg, J.P. Piano Co., 225, 227
Shapiro, Elliott, 213
sheet music, 53, 213-221
Shelburne Museum, Inc., 91, 117, 130, 256-257
Shelley, Dr. Donald A., 264
Shirley, Frederick S., 178
Shriver, A.K., 125
Sicardo, Jacques, 70
—— ware, 70, 73, 78
signs and signboards, 109-119
silhouette pottery, 79
Simpson, Ralph, 17
Six Guns and Saddle Leather, 160
skewers, 136
"slices," 136
"Slick, Jonathan," 148
Smith, Mrs. Vernon W., 251
Smithsonian Institution, 74, 80
Snowberry pottery, 79
Snow Tree pottery, 85
Snyder, Dean, 220
soap dishes, 203

Society for the Preservation of New England Antiquities, The, 27, 63, 64, 65, 66, 67, 257
Society of Medalists, 145
Some Magaziner and Magazine Makers, 155
Somers Brothers, 125
song books (political), 53
Southern Bell Telephone & Telegraph Co., 47, 48
Southern Literary Messenger, 156
spice cabinets, 38-44
Spinning Wheel, The, 41, 66, 209
spool cabinets, 40-44
Standard Pneumatic Action Co., 228
Stanton, Edwin M., 63
Steger & Sons, 228
Stephens, Ann S., 148
Stephens Illustrated New Monthly, 154
Sterling, Robert, 61
Steuben glass, 164-170
—— Glass Works, 164
Stevens and Williams, 165, 178
Storer, Mrs. Maria Longworth, 69
Story & Clark Piano Co., 228
Story of Handmade Glass, The, 188
Story of the Shelburne Museum, The, 257
Sunflower pottery, 79
Superman, 150
Svoboda's Nickelodeon Tavern, 229
Swan, Mabel M., 82, 83, 84
—— pottery, 85
Swartchild & Co., 112, 113
Swasey, William F., 163
Sweeney, John A., 263
Sylvan pottery, 79
"S" hooks, 136

Taft, William Howard, 59, 260
Tanner, H.S., 106, 107
Telephone Pioneers of America, 51
telephone pole insulators, 48
telephones, 45-49
Thayer & Chandler, 101
Thomas, Cowperthwait & Co., 106
Thomas Webb & Sons, Ltd., 178, 179, 182
thread cabinets (see spool cabinets)
Thumb, Tom, 258, 259
Thwaites, Reuben Gold, 163
Tibbitts, John C., 189, 251
Tiffany's, 70
tin cans (see cans, tin)
—— primitives, 245
To the Golden Goal and Other Sketches, 162
tobacco cutters, 199
—— jars, 19, 195-202
Toft, Thomas, 17
toilet sets (see washbowl & pitcher sets)

tokens (political), 53, 59
Toney, Mr. and Mrs. Frank K., 210, 212
tools, 242, 264
Toombs, Robert, 33
torch lights
Touraine pattern glass, 185
toy animals (political), 53
Toy Trader, The, 211
trade cards (see advertising cards)
Travels in New Mexico and California . . ., 162
Treasure at Home, 16, 69, 91, 242, 251
Treen or Small Woodenware through the Ages, 38
trinket boxes, 90
Trip from the Sandwich Islands to Lower Oregon . . . A, 162
Trip to the West and Texas . . . A, 163
Tucker, J.C., 162
Turada pottery, 70
Turkey pottery, 85
Turtle pottery, 85
Tuscany pottery, 79
Tuttle, Eunice P., 212
——, J.H., 163
1200 *Bottles Priced,* 189, 251
Twinem, Mrs. Lon, 99
Two Worlds, 154
Tyler, Daniel, 163

umbrellas (political), 53
Underwood, William, 123
Uniforms, Military, 145, 147
Union, The, 154
United States Music Co., 231
University of Michigan, 215
University of Pittsburgh, 215
Used Book Price, Guide, The, 250

Vail, Robert W.G., 160
Value guide books, 250-252
Van Buren, Martin, 56
Velva pottery, 71
Venice, 191
Verre de Soie glass, 165, 170
Victoria, Queen, 232
Victorian furniture, 232-239
—— pottery, 79
Vinar, David, 146
Violano Virtuoso Society, 228
Vocalsytle Music Co., 231
Volpato pottery, 78
Votey, E.S., 224

Wagner, Henry R., 163
Wagon Seat, 243, 245
Wam-dus-ky, 163
Ware, W. Porter, 110, 112, 115
Warman, E.G., 251

washbowl and pitcher sets, 203-206
Washington, George, 31, 54
washstands, 203, 204
Water Lily pottery, 85
Watson, Thomas A., 45
Waverly pattern glass, 185, 187
Way of an Indian, The, 160
Webb, Joseph, 178
——, Mr. and Mrs. J. Watson, 256, 257
——, Thomas & Sons (see Thomas Webb & Sons)
Weber Duo-Art piano
Weekly Visitor, 154
Weller, Samuel A., 69
——, S.A. Company, 69-75, 76, 78
Wells, Albert B., 260
——, J. Cheney, 260
Welte Artistic Player Piano Co., 227
—— Company, 225, 227
——, Edwin, 227
West Statuary Co., 68
Western Americana, Including California and Oregon . . ., 163
Western books (see books, Western)
Western Electric Co., 225
Western Collector, 220
Western Journal, 151
Western Words . . ., 162
whatnots, 235-236
whiskey stills, 242
Whitall-Tatum Works, 190
White Barn, The, 116
White, Billy Joe, 150
Whiz, 150
Wicasset Musical Wonder House, 229
Wilcox and White Co., 224
Wild Men of the Wild West, 160
Wilkes, Charles, 163
Wilkinson, Sir Nevile, 209
Williamsburg pattern glass, 185
Wilson (Woodrow), 59
Winchester, James H., 56
Winterthur Museum (see Henry Francis du Pont Winterthur Museum)
Wolfe, Thomas, 150, 154
Woodland pottery, 78
Wren, Thomas, 163
Wurlitzer Co., 225

Yale University, 220
Young, George F., 76
——, Russell T., 79
Youth's Companion, The, 141, 191

Zanesville Art Pottery, 69, 71, 72, 76, 79
—— —— —— Co., 72
Zephyr Lily pottery, 79
Zinkan, Cecil, 260
Zona pottery, 71